Porn Work

Porn Work

Sex, Labor, and Late Capitalism

Heather Berg

THE UNIVERSITY OF NORTH CAROLINA PRESS

Chapel Hill

© 2021 Heather Berg

All rights reserved

The University of North Carolina Press has been a
member of the Green Press Initiative since 2003.

LIBRARY OF CONGRESS CATALOGING-IN-PUBLICATION DATA
Names: Berg, Heather, author.
Title: Porn work : sex, labor, and late capitalism / Heather Berg.
Description: Chapel Hill : University of North Carolina Press, [2021] |
Includes bibliographical references and index.
Identifiers: LCCN 2020044097 | ISBN 9781469661919 (cloth ; alk. paper) |
ISBN 9781469661926 (paperback ; alk. paper) | ISBN 9781469661933 (ebook)
Subjects: LCSH: Pornography—United States—Employees. |
Pornography—Economic aspects—United States. | Sex workers—
Economic aspects—United States. | Capitalism.
Classification: LCC HQ471 .B467 2021 | DDC 306.77/10973—dc23
LC record available at https://lccn.loc.gov/2020044097

Contents

Table

Porn Work

Introduction

Porn Work against Work

I've worked my entire life, and this is so much better.

Tara Holiday

I've enjoyed it and hated it. . . . It worked for me
in that I was able to survive. It was fun.

Herschel Savage

Fuck overtime! I'd rather be on overtime
humping a hot dude or chick.

Ana Foxxx

Every porn scene is a record of people at work. Sometimes it is also something else. Enjoying it and hating it, the workers I interviewed for this
book situate porn at the intersection of life and work, pleasure and tedium,
entrepreneurial hustles and waged labor. Sometimes, porn work is a way
to refuse other ways of making a living—"fuck overtime!"—and others it
feels much the same. Again and again, porn workers told me that they left
straight (non-sex-work) jobs for porn because they "hated working." But
most also confirm veteran porn publicist Dominic Ace's assessment that
"this is a job, this is a gig."[1] "Are you gonna get used?" he said. "Everybody
gets used in one way or another. Whether you're a secretary, a janitor,

I

whatever. The difference here is it's sex." Porn work is work and work that at once offers ways to subvert the harms of straight jobs and reproduces them.

After we talked about wages, connecting with scene partners, policy, and how porn performance is a lot like working in a bookstore, performer, author, and activist Conner Habib paused to trouble the "work" language I was using. "I don't like the 'worker' part," Habib told me. "I'll use 'porn star,' that's fine. I like being a constellation instead of a laborer."[2] After that interview, I started to ask interviewees if "porn worker" resonated with them. "I absolutely am a porn worker," Ela Darling responded. "I respect it if someone doesn't want to think of it as work, but it is. You can think of it as dancing on the moon—that doesn't change the fact that this is how you pay your bills."[3] *Porn Work* maps porn at the nexus of these realities.

Porn work reveals deep contradictions at the core of (late) capitalism: Workers exit traditional jobs in search of autonomy but often find precarity on the other side. Pleasure makes work livable but also gets us to do more of it. The authenticity we seek in sex and work can be sold off for parts, and it can also be sustaining. Workers organize against the twin forces of state surveillance and neglect. And solidarities break down when workers escape managerial control by becoming managers themselves. If these tensions are familiar to thinkers and doers of straight work, this is because porn work is not exceptional.

Instead, the conditions porn workers have long experienced are exactly those heralded as the most striking developments in this economic moment: intimate life is increasingly brought to the market; individual workers, rather than employers or the state, assume the economic and health risks of doing business; and a hypermobile gig economy is eclipsing more stable ways of working. The difference here is, as Ace suggests, sex, and that difference brings both particular vulnerabilities and resources— intensified state violence and stigma on the one hand and the potential for pleasureful refusal on the other. The "new economy" is not new—porn workers have been living in it for decades. They have found ways to hack and reshape its conditions for as long.

Against the scholarly tendency to treat porn as a text and the wage relation as a given, *Porn Work* centers on workers' creative approaches to class struggle. This is another place in which porn is not quite like straight jobs: Workers here are often craftier than those in straight jobs and have a less romantic analysis of work under capitalism. Their ways of intervening in it are not always transformative—sometimes intervening means ascending hierarchies rather than dismantling them—but they do highlight the contradictions and the stakes. A porn work lens makes for a sharper anti-capitalist feminist critique, not just a more inclusive one.

PORNO DIALECTICS

Habib's position on the "work" question would shift in the years after our first meeting, and he would become more interested in craftily appropriating the language of "sex work" than rejecting it—"as long as we misuse 'work,' we can erode it," he later said.[4] Porn workers are experts at this kind of misuse. Breaking the fundamental rule of waged work, they sometimes take more from the job than it takes from them. Both nimbly responding to current working conditions and inventing new ways of working, they use porn work toward their own ends. This book explores these dynamics through interviews with eighty-one porn performers, managers, and crew members. Interviewees spoke to their experience of working across porn's genres—from big-budget mainstream to low-budget amateur productions and in gay, straight mainstream, and queer and feminist production communities—from the 1970s until the late 2010s.[5] Most were current workers when we interviewed in the 2010s, and this book focuses on their strategies for intervening in present conditions.

Feminist researcher-activists Precarias a la Deriva ground their research on precarious workers in these questions: "What is your precarity? What is your strike?"[6] This book shares these primary concerns. Its political commitments flow from related questions: What changes would mitigate that precarity? What shifts could facilitate that strike? Following Precarias a la Deriva, I am interested in precarity as a "tendency" toward uncertainty—"work and life experiences in permanent construction"— and, crucially, a tendency that should be understood not just as a liability but also as a source of craftiness and alternative vision.[7] "Sex workers are fierce fighters," writes Melinda Chateauvert, "because their jobs demand perspicacity."[8] Conditions that grind can also sharpen our teeth.

Porn Work draws from an expansive archive of struggle. In spite of multiple barriers to organizing—their independent contractor status, the itinerant nature of the work, fierce competition for castings, and the threat of retaliation—porn performers have for decades engaged in collective action.[9] They have formed worker groups modeled on labor unions and ones focused on education and mutual support. Porn workers intervene in more subtle ways, too, manipulating the conditions of porn work to maximize earning potential, resist burnout, and otherwise exert control over their work lives. They develop creative strategies for navigating emotional intimacy. They figure out ways to manage managers, negotiating working conditions in an atmosphere loaded with gendered and racist hierarchy. They learn to perform intense physical labor while minimizing its toll on the body. They make independent contractor status work to their benefit by producing (and hence reaping profits from) their own material. They use paid scenes as advertisements for other income-generating work in porn's satellite industries. And they use porn as a way to avoid more tedious, more extractive, and often less remunerative work elsewhere.

Before porno dialectics as a conceptual tool came my commitment to taking workers seriously when they say that these interventions matter. Dialectical thinking was the best way to make sense of what came next. In my practice, this meant, first, that if workers told me that a form of pushback makes a difference for them, this is enough evidence that it counts. And second, it meant understanding contradiction as a resource rather than a limitation. Dialectical thinking recognizes a range of tactics, misuses, and forms of community that intervene in the wage relation, and it resists ranking these. Building a theoretical core for this book meant putting interviewees in conversation with other thinkers equipped to the task.

I draw from differently situated schools of thought committed to thinking about power as constantly under revision rather than static. Marxists talk about this in terms of "dialectical materialism," the idea that social life is defined by ongoing conflict between workers and those who profit from their labor. A materialist analysis of porn reveals workers as also locked in struggle with the forces that try to make paid sex dangerous or impossible: the state, internet police, and concerned outsiders who want to end demand for sex work in the first place. This, too, is a classed dynamic—as Silvia Federici has long argued, independent sex work is a problem for a capitalist state that hopes to compel waged straight work and free hetero sex.[10] But dialectical thinking reminds us that power dynamics are always in motion.[11] A producer funds a scene in hopes of making money from sex workers' performance labor, but workers may profit more in the long run, having transformed that scene from (only) a site of extraction into (also) an advertising opportunity. Internet censorship tries to isolate sex workers but confronts networks that cross digital borders and workers who find loopholes at every turn.

A focus on ongoing struggle avoids the traps of romanticizing resistance on the one hand and overestimating managerial (or capitalist state) power on the other.[12] Management sets work rules, and workers find ways to flout them. Workers make demands, and managers, when pressed, respond to them. Sometimes, on all sides, this has unintended consequences. Dialectical thinking understands contradiction as the meat of our story rather than as a wrinkle to be smoothed over. Porn work can be better than straight work and also just as extractive. Both things are true, and that is the point.

Survival strategies are often a matter of both/and A source of vulnerability in one context may be a source of power in another or both at the same time, writes resilience theorist Margaret Waller.[13] Porn work provides countless examples of this dynamic: Pleasure at work operates on both registers, sometimes pushing us to work more for less but also materially improving the workday. Demands for emotional labor on set can be straining, but they also prepare performers to craftily manipulate their managers. Framing porn work as an escape from work—one populated by constellations, not workers—at once articulates a critique of work and can romanticize porn's own unexceptional modes of exploitation and extraction. Accessing the means of production helps performers wrest control over their working conditions, but, in making managers out of workers, it can also undermine solidarity.

On a broader scale, precarity brings insecurity, but it also nurtures the nimble creativity workers need in order to navigate uncertainty in life and work.[14] Sometimes, that creativity makes workers more innovative than capital. Porn workers' self-production often follows this pattern. Black, queer, visibly disabled, or fat performers may initially produce their own content because industry gatekeeping limits their access to good work but then come to find that they can make more, under better conditions, without a boss. They may even take market share from the very bosses who had once tried to shut them out. Porn's traditional producer class of white men long relied on rigid ideas about what sells to excuse casting discrimination, but the success of direct-to-consumer scenes, among them the "niche" productions traditional producers assumed lacked mass appeal, suggests that performers have a better sense of the market. In general, writes Shira Tarrant, "niche" genres have been less hard-hit by piracy than mainstream.[15]

Classed struggle shapes the labor market and not always on capital's terms. As the autonomist Marxist tradition makes clear, economic transformation is not simply the result of top-down processes in which capital reorganizes production to extract more from working people.[16] Instead, workers are both agents and victims of economic transformation.[17] Key shifts in the labor market—the growth of the creative sector, automation, and the transition from stable employment to the gig economy—represent capital's (often disorganized) response to what Franco "Bifo" Berardi calls workers' "withdrawal from exploitation."[18] The growing demand for authenticity in porn might be understood not only as a way for capital to tap new commodities but also as part of capital's anxious response to workers' (and consumers') rejection of alienated labor.[19] As with framings of porn as an escape from work, authenticity *can* be an alternative to alienation and it can also create new forms of estrangement for workers.

Again, workers are often one step ahead—this is why I use the language of "struggle" rather than "resistance" (which suggests a certain reactivity). One performer showed me her contract with a major production company, naming each clause the company had added in honor of the performer whose workaround had inspired it. "Every time one of us would find a loophole, [in] the next contract they made sure [to close it]," she said.[20] But the next workers found new ones—this performer circumvented contract rules by building up a reserve of trade scenes (filmed for no pay with colleagues and friends) she would release once her contract ended. The contract said she could not "work" for anyone else but had no authority over unpaid and as yet unreleased footage. Here, as elsewhere, managers do what they can to try to discipline workers, but they do so with limited foresight, reacting to workers' maneuvers and always in partial ways. Taking workers seriously as agents of struggle (and taking everyday acts seriously as evidence of that struggle) is particularly crucial in making sense of porn, a site in which workers exercise significant power and one in which both pitying and disdainful—there is so little distance between the two—outsiders are committed to imaging that they have none.

Subtly flouting managerial power on set or producing one's own content to avoid giving someone else a cut is not the same as organizing a porn union to bargain collectively, but these methods undermine traditional lines of power nonetheless. Experiencing paid sex as more rewarding and more pleasurable than unpaid sex may not be a militant confrontation with patriarchal capitalism, but it does take aim at its foundational assumption that sex should be private and free. These are all part of a broader landscape of struggle. As Marxist feminist theorist Mariarosa Dalla Costa reminds us, "Every opportunity is a good one."[21] And crafty strategies—what anthropologist James Scott famously called "infrapolitics"—are not a poor substitute for more formal ones.[22] Porn workers taught me this. I came to this project looking for formal pushback such as traditional union organizing and political lobbying (and found plenty), but interviewees disabused me of the idea that these are workers' best tools.

John Holloway, writing in the heterodox Marxist tradition, describes anti-capitalist world making using the language of cracks—"moment[s] in which we assert a different type of doing."[23] Holloway cautions against reading these dismissively, lest we prevent the cracks from spreading. Desires to free oneself from the harms of waged work are a kind of crack in its edifice, even if the types of doing they invite—becoming a boss oneself or opening up one's whole life to the market to avoid clocking in—are not all that different, in practice, right now. In the same spirit, seemingly individualized means of struggle are not directly opposed to collective ones. Informal struggle is often collective work, and the creative strategies detailed in this book depend on networks of mutual aid, information sharing, and trade labor.

For the most robust infrapolitical vision, we need Black feminist and queer-of-color critique's commitments to daily acts of refusal and what L. H. Stallings talks about as the radical potential of "imagination."[24] These traditions find cracks in unexpected places and refuse a hierarchy of which ones matter most. Here, cultivating the "pleasure and alrightness" Roderick Ferguson finds where we are told they should not exist and, per Sara Ahmed, not wanting the things we are told to want both count.[25] This is not to make us feel that things are okay even as nothing really changes, and it is not to say that such forms of pushback are radical in any simple way. Instead, it is to appreciate all the ways these strategies chip away at the status quo, even as they sometimes also maintain it. Queer theory's commitment to the both/and is a dialectical one.

Only some of the interlocutors in this book are part of these traditions' core constituencies, and my aim is not to obscure the specificity of their interventions. As the sex work theorist Vanessa Carlisle put it, you do not need to be a sex worker to write about it well, "but you do need to understand a liberation struggle when you see one."[26] I think this is also true of thinkers who do not directly address sexual labor but nonetheless have something to offer our understanding of it. Throughout this book, I engage thinkers who best understand what it looks like to fight with the resources one has.

This perspective is particularly crucial for doers and theorists (often the same people) of racialized, feminized, and otherwise contingent labor, whose marginal status in relation to organized labor and the state has forced them to get creative. Feminist historian Annelise Orleck writes that "we are all fast food workers now" and suggests we pay attention to the nimble strategies precarious workers with a longer historical memory use to organize against "contingent, commodified labor to whom no one owes anything."[27] Here again, lack of access to conventional means of organizing brings not just vulnerability but also sharper vision. Cathy Cohen's now classic Black feminist and queer rejoinder reminds that respectability can hobble the political imagination.[28] This bears out in the ways many workers who once enjoyed a limited compromise with capital and the state (such as mainstream trade unionists) now find themselves with limited tools in the face of its breakdown. It may be better to begin with the perspective, as the sex worker activist collective Hacking// Hustling puts it, that "any system can be hacked, any system can be hustled."[29]

Throughout this book, porn workers' critiques suggest that waged work cannot be recuperated. Even those who do not claim anti-capitalist politics point to irresolvable tensions inherent in waged work as a mode of organizing working life, and most are unconvinced that different bosses or changes to policy will fully resolve these conflicts. "You have to work, you have no choice," Samantha Grace told me, and while she said porn work was better by far than the retail jobs she had done before, she also detailed the ways it reproduced many of the same harms.[30] Not least was the pressure to "make a living" in the first place. Porn work was better than retail because Grace could be her own boss, she said, but that did not resolve the basic problem with the compulsion to work.

This is in line with antiwork Marxism, which maintains that what Kathi Weeks calls "the problem with work" runs deeper than poorly designed policy or the wrong people in charge.[31] Rather than a call for better work, antiwork thinkers advocate a radical departure from work as such. In conversation with workers who "didn't want control; they wanted out," they imagine ways of organizing social and economic life that deconstruct the idea that a living is something we should earn.[32] Tinkering with or sanding off the rough edges of work will not get us there. And precarity, on its own, is not the problem. In any case, there is no going back—the conditions that created limited security for a privileged subset of mostly white, male workers in the mid-twentieth century are gone.[33] Workers wanted more even then, before benefits got slashed and wage stagnation set in. "We must construct an alternative starting point," write Michael Hardt and Antonio Negri.[34] Porn workers do not yearn for a return to the factory or cubicle farm, nor do they look backward to an imagined time when sex and money were neatly disentangled.

If porn workers tend to share antiwork critics' skepticism that reform will be enough, most do not fully embrace the refusal of work that is at the heart of antiwork politics. Instead, most look for apertures for pushback within existing structures, or what I will call "politics for the meantime." They want access to the means of production, legibility (and perhaps even respectability) as workers and sexual subjects, and policy shifts that will make working conditions better *now*. Most would rather be a boss than have one disciplined by collective bargaining or the state. None of these things, on their own, will do much to disrupt porn's (or other waged work's) fundamental dynamics of exploitation and extraction. Some keep these dynamics exactly in place, only with a kinder, gentler face. Performer-producers, for example, can reproduce the same dynamics they seek to avoid.

Small changes, whether in the realm of policy or in individual efforts to be your own boss so that you do not have to work under one, risk strengthening the very systems that harm. And yet, a wholesale rejection of such tweaks risks sacrificing the immediate needs of those most impacted in favor of long-range aims they may never see.[35] When I asked Richie Calhoun about the benefits available to performers, he responded, "We have nothing. We have no medical insurance, we have no union, we have no residuals or royalties."[36] Those things would not resolve all the problems with work—mainstream actors with union representation attest to as much—but they would make a difference in the meantime. Beyond this, even the demands that do strengthen systems that harm rarely do only that. When José Esteban Muñoz tells us "feeling revolutionary is feeling that our current situation is not enough," the point is to understand dissatisfaction as critique.[37] Porn workers' feelings that current conditions are not enough, even if in the immediate this means that most would rather be a boss than have none at all, undermine pieces of the work ethic even if they preserve others. These contradictions do not cancel each other out. A politics for the meantime hopes to hold them in tension.

Porno dialectics are messier than conventional stories of classed struggle because class boundaries are less calcified here. Porn workers are very rarely only *workers*. Instead, they occupy constantly shifting class positions as entrepreneurs, independent contractors, formal employees, contracted and freelance managers, and producers. This shapes and reshapes their perspectives in countless ways. Of the workers I interviewed who were current performers at the time, all but one had also occupied other positions in the industry. This is not a testament to sampling that skewed toward an elite "labor aristocracy." To the contrary, performers with less social and economic capital rely most on creative arrangements such as doing trade shoots and producing their own low-budget scenes.[38] Workers who encounter the poorest treatment when they work under a boss are quickest to try to escape those hierarchies. "A lot of the brothers were quick to start their own companies so that they could have more of a say," explained performer, director, and producer Mr. Marcus of Black performers-cum-managers.[39] "How can we demand [a say] if we're not even represented in the production process?" he asked, adding, "You have to get in there, you can't just be a performer." Most porn workers succeed at this at least some of the time, and this places them in liminal spaces in relationship to the regulatory state and also scholarship and activism: prevailing assumptions about porn (or work in general, for that matter) as a contest between powerful managers and vulnerable workers break down.

In porn as elsewhere, most workers do not want to be *workers*. As thirty-nine-year veteran performer Herschel Savage put it, "Not owning your product, you're in a desperate place. Any time you're depending on people for your livelihood, you're in bad shape, no matter what the industry."[40] This has important implications for this book. It means, first, that most interviewees' perspectives are not coming from a simple place of working-class consciousness. Because workers do not want it, such purity is not something to valorize or try to recuperate. The necessity of beginning with a "different starting point" applies here, too.[41] This represents a significant departure from the majority of Marxist thought, which tends to view class positions as relatively static. The Marxist feminist geographers writing under the name J. K. Gibson-Graham advocate an alternative, "anti-essentialist" class analysis, which takes class seriously without tidying it up.[42] Here, we take part in class processes rather than inhabit fixed class identities. It is not that workers misunderstand their own interests but that those interests are shifting. This is true in the broader history of sex work, where the common transition from worker to madam placed worker-managers in the position of reasserting the dynamics of extraction to which they had once been subject.[43]

If porn makes a mess of class, it still remains true that "every kind of thinking, without exception, is stamped with the brand of a class."[44] Porn work's class formations shape interviewees' perspectives on matters ranging from employment law to fair working conditions. Interviewees acknowledged this, explicitly connecting their analyses to the role(s) they occupy. Performer, director, and producer Joanna Angel put it this way: "Sometimes, I feel like I'm part of the man, so I might not have the same point of view as a lot of other people."[45] When porn's producer-funded trade organization, the Free Speech Coalition, tried to get involved in performer organizing, one performer told me, "They're out of the producer's interest. They shouldn't be meddling."[46] But it is tricky, she added, because so many performers are also managers. "Find me one performer," she said, "who's been in the industry for two years and has never directed for a company, never directed for their own website, and never produced a scene for a Clips4Sale store."

Class positions in porn are slippery, but they matter. Rather than evacuate class of meaning, then, I pay attention to subjects' own sharp analyses of how the class position(s) they inhabit at any given moment shape their perspectives. When I use the terms "worker" and "manager," I mean to signal temporary locations rather than permanent identities. It is possible to speak as a manager and not *be* one. Porn's recent history can be understood as a path toward these uneven and shifting dynamics.

A SHORT HISTORY OF PORN WORK

Rich historical work details porn's history from the perspectives of representational norms, technological and policy change, and porn's central location in the history of the feminist sex wars.[47] Here I offer a short history of changing production practices with an eye for the working conditions they engender and the forms of misuse they open up. It is a history structured by significant change and also points of continuity. First, some constants: Contingent workers creatively navigating varied gigs—rather than stars making a living off porn exclusively—continues to be more the rule than the exception in the world of porn work. Foremost among workers' creative interventions has been taking control over the means of production when they can. From this perspective, the twenty-first century's move toward radically democratized digital production is the most seismic shift in porn's history. Here again, contradiction rules. Wider markets mean more competition for existing producers, directors, and performers but also class mobility for performers and entry points for those who had been previously excluded.

Porn stardom is a recent invention, and it looms larger in most stories about porn than in the day-to-day experience of working. For the bulk of the twentieth century, most porn workers were uncredited and sometimes even faceless in the final cut. Stag films, loops (single scenes, often shown in peep shows), and sexploitation films offered low pay and no chance of stardom to performers.[48] Anticipating the "gig work" scholars would name decades later, a contingent workforce could use this kind of porn work to supplement working-class incomes, often as part of a broader sex work hustle.

The dawn of "porno chic" and the "Golden Age" of the 1970s changed how porn was produced and consumed, though a smaller, quieter market of loops persisted. Big-budget, theatrically released films such as *Deep Throat* and *The Devil in Miss Jones* brought high profits for producers, visibility for *some* performers, and the promise of mainstream respectability. The Golden Age's larger budgets and far greater profits—*Deep Throat* grossed upward of $30 million in ticket sales—did not, however, translate into significantly better pay for performers in the celebrated films of the time.[49] Performers were just figuring out how to leverage their negotiating power, and a centralized (and often mob-backed) network of producers and distributors controlled access to production and distribution.[50] Like others who worked during this period, prolific performer and director Carter Stevens said there was "no money" in porn performance at the time.[51] Here, too, most performers used porn gigs as a supplementary income source and, sometimes, an avenue for creative and sexual expression. The Golden Age's wide-release, plot-driven films drew creatives who felt pushed out of Hollywood and stage acting and found in porn an opportunity to practice their craft. Porn work drew performers who wanted a "chance to make movies" and made space for sexual "outlaws" who wanted to flout social norms, Stevens said.

The hefty costs of theatrical production and distribution made for high barriers to entry for performers who wanted to direct and produce their own material, helping to maintain a rigid class hierarchy. But big-budget films did not fully supplant the low-budget loops producers could sell to peep shows and smaller theaters. If one could access the necessary production equipment and distribution channels, loops made it possible to produce one's own material and short-circuit the social relations of the wage. Then as now, low-budget production could make for better (if less prestigious) work because workers could take control. "There were no real directors; I became a producer to hire myself as a director," Stevens said, gesturing to porn work's most enduring route to class mobility. Then as now, not all performers want to produce their own material.

Self-production requires a different skill set, and some would rather come to set, do the job, get paid, and go home. But the potential for self-production gives workers leverage to the extent that managers face the threat of their own obsolescence.

By the mid-1980s, video would supplant both loops and the theatrically released films associated with the Golden Age. The transition from theaters to video brought a bigger consumer market and cheaper production technology and with it a wave of new producers in search of quick profit. For those producers who could afford to play, shrinking production costs coincided with booming profits.[52] The cost of video-filming equipment was still out of reach for most performers, and distribution remained concentrated among capitalized producers who could access wide distribution networks to video stores around the country.

The transition to video had contradictory effects for porn workers. Some performers were able to parlay video's booming profits into higher earnings, and studios' larger advertising budgets helped make some porn performers *stars*.[53] Elite performers could find job security and higher rates through exclusive contracts, performing a set number of scenes for the same production company. Some performers parlayed their new stardom into self-production through their own production companies.[54] Even those with less star power and start-up capital could strike out on direct-to-consumer side hustles that reduced their financial dependence on managers. Paid fan clubs, for example, let performers charge fans for monthly newsletters, and the porn star strip club circuit exploded at this time. Decades later, such direct fan interaction would come to be the surest route to earnings in an industry racked by piracy.

For others, video meant degraded bargaining power and the diffusion of support networks. The Golden Age's small, tight-knit group of performers had found community with one another, and many veteran performers struggled to gain footing in video's impersonal, sped-up production culture.[55] As Jeffrey Escoffier details in his history of gay porn, the HIV/AIDS epidemic radically reshaped the content and conditions of porn production during this same time.[56] Across genres, bargaining power vis-à-vis management took on new stakes.

The shift away from dialogue-heavy theatrical releases and toward sex scenes strung together with little narrative[57] had broken open the pool of those who might be eligible to take on porn work, since directors no longer had to rely on the relatively small population of performers comfortable with both screen acting and screen sex. Performance labor became less specialized, and with some exceptions among the top stars of the era, individual workers lost the limited bargaining power they had had. Veteran Golden Age performers, writes Peter Alilunas, "were joined by thousands of new, often forgettable faces, rapidly entering and exiting the business."[58] At the same time, widened markets meant expanded opportunities for new performer communities. As porn featuring Black women became a "recognizable subgenre focused on racial difference," writes Mireille Miller-Young, Black actors gained new access to the industry.[59] Porn's history bears this out again and again—bigger, more diffused markets mean more competition for existing workers but also work opportunities for those who had been previously excluded.

The mid-1990s transition to digital shook porn hard, marking a transition from a landscape of small business studios to what Miller-Young describes as a "globalized, corporate behemoth."[60] Profits shifted away from producers and to global distributors.[61] The transition from video to internet porn also made the industry vulnerable to piracy. By the mid-2000s, tube sites had mainstreamed and centralized pirated porn, further slashing profits for the producers who had dominated the video era. Tube sites that got their start in piracy would later consolidate a monopoly by buying up the studios they had bled dry, a story Shira Tarrant details in her mapping of the contemporary industry.[62] In the years that followed, directors would come to do contract work for hire for the same companies that had put their own small production studios out of business. Meanwhile, the performer pool grew larger still, rates got even lower, and long-term performer contracts were almost entirely replaced by a hypermobile gig economy that now even elite workers had to navigate.

Meanwhile, performers and low-wage contract directors still needed work. Many of the workers I interviewed graduated from college around the 2008 financial crisis and described mounting student debt and worsening job prospects in the straight workplace, including in the mainstream creative fields some had initially hoped to enter. In porn they found a better way to get by. Straight work's poor pay and working conditions (not least among them the boredom and inflexibility that characterize straight work even in robust economies) worsened in the years that followed, ensuring a stream of workers who sought an alternative in porn work. This creates a glutted labor market but one that is also open to a range of workers' creative interventions. Millennials are, famously (and much to employers' chagrin), both soured on the unfulfilled promises of waged work and media savvy, two things that help them figure out ways to make porn work for them.[63]

Classed power relations are under constant revision, and many workers found more competition for fewer gigs and reduced negotiating power in the industry during the 2010s. "When I was in the business [in the early to mid-2000s] it was a lot different than it is now," VJ told me. "Now, you're so easily replaced."[64] Current performers agree. "When I hear models negotiate now, I'm just like, 'You're pretty brave,'" Christopher Daniels told me. "If you don't want to do it, they'll find somebody that will."[65] Along with compressed wages, workers also face increasing demands to shoulder the costs of doing business. Larger studios once paid for performers' sexually transmitted infection (STI) tests, a full set wardrobe, and a hair and makeup artist. Now, workers almost always bear these costs.

Managers say that cost-cutting measures are necessary to stay in business as profits shrink. "The traditional business models of 'Big Porn Inc.' are facing severe challenges" from both aggregate piracy sites and direct-to-consumer distribution, write Rebecca Sullivan and Alan McKee.[66] But as privately held companies, studios' books are closed—we do not know how much producers as a whole are making or what their rate of surplus value is. Some company owners did show me their numbers, demonstrating that profits have indeed dropped significantly. While a producer could expect to quadruple their investment in the late 1990s, it might only double today. These are profits nonetheless, and producers calculate rates like business owners under capitalism do. The only question in deciding rates, explained performer, director, and producer Dave Pounder, is "What is the lowest rate I can pay people where I'd still get people to shoot for me?"[67]

Ironically, studios' efforts to exclude performers from porn's profits also isolate waged porn workers from the most immediate effects of piracy. Now as in previous years, performers get no royalties or residuals when they work for a wage—high studio profits have not, on the whole, made for better pay or long-term economic security historically. As Pounder suggests, most porn wages are as low as they can possibly be—everyday performers have never been able to depend on them, and they have had to find other means. And so while established producers are scrambling in the face of profits lost to piracy, most workers have found ways to make money whether or not customers pay for studio-produced scenes. Such scenes are, after all, "just a marketing tool" for many performers.[68] Performers use scenes as advertisements for their self-produced content, personal websites, and services that engage consumers directly (such as webcam performance). Workers contend with a customer base that feels entitled to free sexual labor, but it is also true that a pirated scene advertises these products and services just as well as one that is paid for.

The skills precarious workers cultivate in order to get by can make them more agile than capital. Today, producers' best idea for circumventing piracy is to mimic the strategies performers developed years ago. Recorded scenes are vulnerable to piracy in ways direct consumer engagement is not, write Sullivan and McKee, and struggling producers now seek out "interactivity" as a profit source.[69] But there is not much producers can bring to "interactivity" that performers have not already figured out. Workers know what fans want because they are the people engaging with them. Traditional owners' and managers' efforts to isolate themselves from the daily grind of intimate labor also isolate them from the expertise it brings.

Most journalistic and academic accounts of piracy, like those of managers and owners, do not make an ethical distinction between pirating content owned by studios and pirating content from performers who own their own copyright. Workers say this distinction matters. Both forms of expropriation, the wage relationship is distinct from piracy only by matter of degree. If pirating a studio's scene impacts performers peripherally when it filters down to less content produced over time, pirating scenes from performers' self-managed websites, sites that allow performers to sell digitized clips directly to consumers, and webcam performances all hit workers hard. Performers ask fans to #PayForYourPorn, and the explosion of direct-to-consumer distribution means that consumers can now do so more directly.

If the digital era opened porn up to the risks of piracy, it also democratized production in material ways, lowering the financial and technical threshold for producing a scene and opening porn up to whole new communities of creators, not least sex workers themselves.[70] In place of the video era's higher cost of filming and editing and insular distribution channels, digital brought the possibility of filming and editing on inexpensive equipment and opened up more direct distribution to consumers. Workers still contend with the third-party platforms most use to advertise and distribute material, and, as we will see, are constantly navigating the threats of web censorship, extractive platform fees, and algorithmic management. Even so, porn workers are less dependent on moneyed producers and directors than they have ever been. They use digital technology and the web to produce content more fully on their own terms, find paid work even when established directors fail to see a market for their "niche," and retain ownership of their own product. So, while the transition from video to digital reduced profits for large-scale producers and the workers who depend most on waged scene work, it also made content creation—and ownership—accessible to new people.

Whereas the film and video eras placed the power to determine which bodies and sex acts were visible in porn in the hands of capitalized producers, today anyone can produce porn and distribute it online. This has resulted in a proliferation of pornographic content, particularly in the queer and feminist, fetish, and amateur markets.[71] Antiporn caricatures of who porn represents and the sexual stories it tells always obscured the whole story, and they reveal even less about what porn looks like today. It has been workers, often identifying market niches and ways of monetizing content where studios thought none existed, who broke open these new terrains. When we interviewed in 2014, Ela Darling, a performer, was in the initial stages of developing virtual-reality porn technology. Two years later, she had engineered the technology and become a popular speaker at mainstream tech industry events.[72] Porn has long been at the forefront of technological innovation; now sex workers, rather than capitalized producers and studios, are changing the shape of production. This is not to say that sex workers reliably get the spoils. The non–sex workers who own direct-to-consumer platforms appropriate both sex workers' ideas (and some say even their programming code) and a high percentage of their earnings.

In 2020, the COVID-19 pandemic interrupted production in the global porn industry. Pandemic working conditions are still very much in flux, but in many ways the pandemic meant an acceleration of trends that had long been under way, rather than a novel point of rupture. Performers who had already built fan followings on direct-to-consumer platforms could still maintain an income source through self-produced content and have greater control over safety protocols and partner choice. Once again, established studios' reliance on conventional modes of production made them less nimble. And established studios had less power to force people back to work than straight employers whose workers lacked access to ways of making money on their own.

At the same time, the mass turn to platform-enabled production intensified the dynamics of an already glutted labor market. Performers confronted platforms flooded with sex workers who previously relied on in-person work, newly unemployed straight workers trying their hand at sexual labor, and non–sex worker "tourists" looking to dabble in it. Influencers and straight actors capitalized on the growing popularity of platforms such as OnlyFans while also distancing themselves from sex workers in stigmatizing ways. As in previous eras, crafty hustles were as vulnerable to labor market shifts as waged performance, and increased competition brought reduced bargaining power. Together with stigma and internet censorship, the same atomization that made at-home production both accessible and pandemic-safe also made it hard to build collective power. Workers had limited recourse when platforms' ever-changing terms of service agreements and payment structures threatened their livelihoods. Porn workers use platforms as tools for creative survival. At the same time, those platforms are largely unaccountable to the sex workers on whose labor they are built.

The porn *industry* as it has been traditionally understood does not exist. There is no powerful, centralized body of producers calling the shots. Porn's trade organization has limited power to organize management or set the terms for industry conduct, and porn's annual trade shows have shrunk dramatically. Meanwhile, porn's regional landscape is growing increasingly diffuse, with small-scale productions coming out of private homes around the world and not just the San Fernando Valley. The porn performer community, too, is less cohesive than it once was, and workers have to get creative about constructing networks for information sharing and mutual aid across distance.

When I use the term "industry," then, I am not gesturing to a monolithic or internally consistent body. Instead, I mean to indicate the heterogeneous array of studio executives, agents, producers, directors, technical set and postproduction workers, and performers—and the many people who occupy more than one of these locations—who make porn. This is the closest we will get to a porn industry at the turn of the 2020s. The industry may very well be in crisis, but in the rubble, workers have found countless ways to (sometimes) make that crisis work for them.

AGAINST REIFICATION

The lessons porn work offers about living within and against late capitalism only become available when we take it seriously as work and then read work dialectically. Most scholarship does not do this. Instead, porn scholarship overwhelmingly focuses on issues of representation and consumption. Meanwhile, sexuality studies work on porn and other sex work often turns away from their materiality, a reflection of what Brooke Beloso calls "the feminist erasure of class."[73] Labor scholarship, on the other hand, has strenuously avoided critical engagement with porn and other sex work. "We don't seem to think about capitalism so much when we think about sex," writes Yasmin Nair.[74] For many straight-labor scholars, the reverse is also true—they don't seem to think about sex so much when they think about capitalism. This is in spite of Marxist feminists' persistent reminders that sex—paid and unpaid, on-screen and off—is work.[75] Taken together, these elisions contribute to the reification of porn, turning a work process into a product divorced from the conditions of its production. Reification is, classically, something that helps capital exploit working people. Scholars should not make this easier.

Anti-sex-worker feminists reify porn with a focus on the symbolic damage they say porn texts do.[76] For Catharine MacKinnon, understanding porn's harms "does not require noticing that pornography models are real women to whom something real is being done. . . . The aesthetic of pornography is itself the evidence."[77] Relating to porn workers only through "pictures of their bodies," writes Melissa Gira Grant, antiporn campaigners have more in common with consumers than they would like to imagine.[78] Living, breathing sex workers are, explicitly, not their constituency. They cannot be, we are told, because workers refuse to critique porn "for fear of industry retaliation."[79] But dozens of workers readily critiqued their bosses in our interviews; they also made clear that anti-sex-worker feminism is not for them. "These are people who to my face deny me my humanity," said Nina Ha®tley.[80]

A long history of feminist and queer work critiques the pro-censorship and sexually conservative underpinnings of antiporn feminist thought. For that task I turn readers to thinkers such as Lisa Duggan and Nan Hunter, Laura Kipnis, Jennifer Nash, Gayle Rubin, and Carole Vance, who have decisively won the academic "sex wars," if not policy makers' favor.[81] Here I will just add that, where class matters are concerned, anti-sex-worker feminists reproduce the very conditions they claim to contest. As Alice Echols has famously argued, anti-sex-worker "radical" feminists "abandoned transformative politics for the familiarity of sexual repression."[82] This is as much true in questions of political economy. Per Whitney Strub, where early feminist activism around porn focused on working conditions and control over the means of production, antiporn feminism would come to focus on women performers as "victimized pawns on a male chessboard."[83] This kind of thinking transforms a workplace—a site of struggle—into a dead text and workers—agents of struggle—into bodies passively "used."

Straight workplaces, meanwhile, emerge for anti-sex-worker feminists as nonviolent, respectable alternatives.[84] As Laura Kipnis suggests, antiporn thinkers maintain a strange romance with straight jobs.[85] To the extent that anti-sex-worker feminists have purchase, they help to spackle over the cracks in capitalism's artifice, making it that much harder for such cracks to spread. Anti-sex-worker feminists do this, ironically, while claiming a monopoly on anti-capitalist analysis.[86] It is not possible to destroy a system while pretending that its power is all-encompassing.

Porn studies scholarship offers an important rejoinder to antiporn feminist thought, arguing that porn, like other cultural texts, is produced and consumed in varied ways.[87] "Porn is film. . . . Porn is popular culture," insists media scholar Constance Penley, who calls upon scholars to ask of porn what they do of other cultural forms.[88] What accounts for its popular appeal? How does it both reflect and contest cultural norms? What are our investments in reading it in particular ways?[89] From film scholar Linda Williams's pioneering *Porn Studies* anthology to the newer journal of the same title, porn scholars have taken up these calls artfully.[90] But because much of this work is in the areas of cultural and media studies, and because porn studies as a field often frames itself in response to the limitations of antiporn feminism, here, too, we see a focus on porn as text.[91] Where the field turns to working conditions, it can tend to take for granted that better representational norms make for better work. *Porn Work* argues against the tendency to imagine that different bosses or images make for better working conditions and the celebration of "ethical" (typically feminist and queer) production.[92] Chapter 2 will return to the question of how ethical cultural products get measured. For now, I will just say that good branding does not equal good work.

Writing from an anti-capitalist feminist perspective, Helen Hester notes that porn studies struggles to reconcile its commitments to framing porn as a potentially transgressive medium with an understanding of porn as a commodity.[93] This helps explain why porn studies has had less to say about the everyday conditions of work. *Porn Work* intervenes, and, with a burst of attention to porn labor since I began work on this project, it is in increasingly good company. Here I am in conversation with scholarship focused on the work of performance, questions of regulation, and performers' confrontations with the politics of representation.[94] While its focus is on the day-to-day experience of working, *Porn Work* is also in conversation with macro-level analyses that argue for treating "porn as a normal business," as Georgina Voss puts it in her call for such work.[95]

Once we agree that porn is a "normal business," the question becomes, of course, what one thinks of normal businesses. Porn studies scholars argue that business under capitalism can mean different things, some of them emancipatory. Lynn Comella highlights the importance of context: "Branding anyone associated with the world of pornography as a 'predatory capitalist' fails to recognize that consumer capitalism is not fixed and unchanging. . . . The sexual marketplace, like other realms of consumer culture, can be used for socially progressive purposes."[96] And Eleanor Wilkinson urges against "paranoid readings" of porn that cannot imagine that it might sometimes exist "outside, or at least partially outside, capitalist frames" and finds in "alternative pornographies" such an outside.[97]

For working people, it is not so easy to be outside when there is rent to pay. This is true even when your boss is a friend, yourself, or a feminist. Imagining that we are already outside risks pushing us deeper in still, so *Porn Work* is more interested in the ways workers are struggling *against* extraction rather than comfortably *outside* of it. This is not a story of quiet acquiescence. In understanding sex "as a form of work," *Porn Studies* editors Clarissa Smith and Feona Attwood write that "sex-critical" scholarship "leaves out the possibilities of bodies and pleasure creating sites of resistance."[98] From a dialectical perspective, though, it is precisely through framing porn as work that the potential for resistance (or struggle, as I highlight here) becomes legible. Porn studies' retreat from dialectical materialist thinking makes sense as a response to anti-sex-worker thinkers' claimed monopoly on anti-capitalist analysis—its distorted use leaves a bitter taste. But *Porn Work* urges that we not give up that territory to those who use it cynically against working people.

The irony is, of course, that while I use Marxist labor theory as a tool for intervening in the scholarly conversation around porn, many Marxist thinkers are hobbled by their own commitments to bourgeois morality and sex worker exclusion. Marxists have on the whole been more interested in framing sex work as a debased limit case for capitalism's harms than as a site of struggle. Sex work is, for Nadezhda Krupskaya, the "grave of human relations."[99] It is, to be sure, where many Marxists' dialectical commitments so often go to die.[100] In this, they are joined by anti-sex-worker feminists who identify as anti-capitalist but limit their critique to sex work. Using paid sex as an alibi for all that is broken both reinforces the stigma sex workers say harms them and shields all other industries from critique. Together with workers, Marxist feminists have warned against this for decades. In 1981, Leopoldina Fortunati wrote that Marxism's "moralistic, 'redemptionist' attitude towards prostitution" is "blind, manipulative and violent, as well as being politically non-productive."[101] This book is interested in what anti-capitalist frameworks that refuse such violent moralism can produce. One of those things is a critique of work as such.

Sex worker theorists refuse to let straight work off the hook. "I knew the work was not how anti-sex-work feminists described it," writes Lorelei Lee. "I knew it was as good and as terrible as other, lower-wage work I'd done."[102] Where the porn workers in this book point to the terrible parts, their demand is for better conditions, not pity, rescue, or a return to the same straight jobs they left for porn. Per Melissa Gira Grant, "Sex workers shouldn't have to defend the existence of sex work in order to have the right to do it free from harm."[103] Many of the workers in this book do not defend porn work as it exists right now—some have sharp critiques of it—and I cannot stop anti-sex-worker thinkers from appropriating their or my words in order to shore up systems that harm. I can only offer the reminder that any conditions non-sex-worker readers find troubling here are also a problem closer to home. "Civilians," as sex workers call them, also have bad bosses, boring sex, and workdays that strain. They are, we know, vulnerable to harassment, retaliation, and wage theft, among other forms of workplace violence. Rejecting what Gayle Rubin calls the "fallacy of misplaced scale," porn workers insist that the sex in sex work does not, on its own, make porn's workplace harms more serious.[104]

Throughout this book, I engage with Marxist labor theory and also highlight the fault lines that get revealed when we read it through a porn work lens. The anxiety about the "new" crisis in commodifying the personal, for example, betrays an ignorance of the strategies sex workers have long used to navigate market intimacy. And concerns about the gig economy read only crisis in the downfall of the forty-hour week, when sex workers make very clear that flexibility is a resource as much as it is a source of risk. Knowing that the state is no ally, sex workers have more expertise in mutual aid and community self-defense than many straight workers. And sex workers have more interesting things to say about sexual politics than people wedded to the bourgeois idea that sex should be private and free.

This book is indebted to writing on the political economy of sex work, which uses labor theory to make sense of sexual labor, but also advances critiques of capitalism that get us past the limitations of Marxist orthodoxy. In spite of the enduring narrative that perspectives on sex work tend to uncomplicatedly view sex workers as either hapless victims *or* free market agents, a wealth of sex work research refuses this dichotomy.[105] Sex work scholars have been at the vanguard of theorizing constrained agency, a framework that, per theorist Clare Hemmings, takes "agency seriously precisely in order to understand how power works."[106] *Porn Work* is particularly indebted to research that situates sexual labor within the context of broader trends in global late-capitalist markets,[107] underscores how public policy produces the very vulnerabilities is purports to address,[108] theorizes emotional labor,[109] and investigates workers' organizing histories.[110] Finally, a burgeoning movement in sex work activism and scholarship frames work itself as the problem with sex work and uses sex work as a lens through which to critique the conditions of work under capitalism.[111] Thinkers in this tradition push for recognizing sex work as *work* and improving conditions within it but also, as Kate Hardy puts it, imagining what it might look like to "refuse work itself."[112]

Sex work may be especially well suited for this latter project because sex workers have long pursued sexual labor not just as an economic survival strategy but also as a way to refuse more extractive and less pleasureful ways of working and living. Black feminist histories of sex work in particular highlight this productive tension.[113] In this spirit, L. H. Stallings positions sex workers as resisters of an "antierotic, sex-negative, and work-centric" society and urges against framings that obscure this force.[114] Porn work is not *just* work for all workers all of the time. Sometimes it is a way to refuse at least some of work's harms and imagine worlds otherwise. *Porn Work* takes that seriously while also remembering that porn is how the bills get paid and often in ways that are neither particularly erotic nor a radical departure from the mundane harms of work under capitalism. As the sex worker theorist femi babylon puts it, "Because capitalism is compulsory, it's difficult to engage almost any labor as symbolic of antiwork." And yet, she urges us to ask, "can we move beyond 'sex work is work'? Perhaps to engaging the phrase 'sex work is (anti)work'?"[115] Porn workers navigate the work question in the context of that tension.

In their critique of sex positivity and the "happy hooker" myth, sex worker theorists Juno Mac and Molly Smith write, "Those who do experience sexual gratification at work are likely to be those who already have the most control over their working conditions."[116] This is a position I am sympathetic to and the one I came to this project with, but complicating conversations with porn workers in the intervening years have troubled it for me.[117] This book shares a critique of sex positivity; as sex work writer and activist Audacia Ray puts it, "The sex positive movement is bad for sex workers' rights."[118] This is not least because the sex-positive movement has little energy for questions of class. I am, however, interested in a materialist analysis of how working people wrest pleasure where they can. We know that workers steal everyday pleasures in other working-class jobs: camaraderie, unauthorized breaks, workplace theft—all these things can be pleasureful even when work is compelled and our room to maneuver limited. For the workers who gave their time and insights to this project, moments of pleasure did not line up with social privilege in any simple way. Pleasure can be a way to take control rather than evidence of already having it.

METHODS[119]

Sex worker communities taught me early on that the principle of "nothing about us without us" is crucial. Workers know their own conditions, and any one of the workers I interviewed could write the story of their job without my intervention. My task was to put interviewees in conversation and try to weave their collective knowledge into a narrative and a politic. But it is one thing to say that porn workers' perspectives should be at the center and another to put this into practice when those perspectives do not line up with each other. The performers, managers, and crew members I interviewed for this project do not all share common identities, politics, critiques, or perspectives on what might make porn work better. Solidarities break down, and the "us" gets more and more diffuse. Deep tensions emerge within the space of a single interview, too. The siren song of false consciousness is that it allows outsiders to tidy this up. Dis-consensus can be explained away as evidence of some subjects' lack of understanding, and internal contradiction can get packaged as confusion or self-deceit. This condescendingly assumes, as Stuart Hall famously puts it, that the commentator is armed with "superior wisdom" to which others do not have access.[120] It also neuters contradiction of its value. Dialectical thinking, in contrast, recognizes contradiction as politics. So, rather than abandon "nothing about us without us" because the "us" is messy, we can instead think about what that messiness reveals about late capitalism: class is fluid, autonomy is often paired with vulnerability, and the same forms of struggle can move us forward and also keep us in place.

Approaching interviewees as the experts on their own conditions also required that I surrender the shape of this project to its subjects. I came to this study planning to ask standard questions about porn as a workplace—questions about pay, working conditions, occupational health, conventional labor organizing, and workplace hierarchy. Few studies had approached porn as work, and I thought my intervention would be to do just that. But the questions I did not ask, and the ways interviewees pushed against those absences, turned out to be just as important. Interviewees' answers to unasked questions radically shifted my thinking and, indeed, the directions this project came to take. Workers' stories of the jobs they left for porn are one example of this. I came upon these origin stories by accident. "What's a nice girl like you doing in a place like this?" is tired and, in my own experience in sex worker communities, less important than the immediate task of figuring out how to navigate the conditions of the present. And so I began interviews asking workers *how* they broke into the industry, not why: How did you know if a modeling release's conditions were fair, for instance? How did you learn how to prepare for your first scenes? But workers wanted me to know that they had done other jobs, jobs they wanted out of. They described pursuing porn not because they could not find other work but because they were dissatisfied with the straight jobs they had. This changed the stakes of this project—it would not do to make the case that porn is work like any other, because workers sought it out precisely because they hoped this was not true. For some, this hope delivered.

In other ways, this project's initial commitments to a work lens were crucial to building trust with respondents. Workers and managers alike were willing to engage openly about working conditions so long as they knew I was not there to shoehorn their stories into the same worn narratives. "I can read people very well. That's part of why I'm good at my job," said performer-director Lily Cade when I asked if she had any questions of me before our interview began.[121] She added, "I can tell the difference between your being interested in the realities of this job and trying to trick me into saying I'm exploited." That I came to the project with existing connections to sex worker communities also helped build trust in this way.

As I planned to jump into the interview process, I anticipated that it might be difficult to find managers who were willing to talk about work. With one exception—an employers attorney I met at the Adult Entertainment Expo who, when I told him what I was writing about, replied, "Oh, shit," and scurried away—this did not bear out. Instead, managers were both willing to talk and surprisingly forthcoming, volunteering copies of employment contracts and modeling releases (patently illegal provisions and all), talking about how they get performers to work for less money, and speaking openly about profit as a priority. I suspect that part of what made the idea of a labor study seem less threatening than I had anticipated is that porn debates are so heavily focused on representation and the value of porn as such. When asked, I answered honestly that I am agnostic on porn as a product; this was enough. A popular industry blogger offered to post a call for participants after I interviewed him. It read, "She was very nice and mostly listens. She is not anti porn. She is studying the biz and needs input, it isn't about the psychological aspects or anything and it isn't in any way combative or one sided."[122] What was important for people to know is that I am not "antiporn." Managers did not ask about my class politics; conversations with workers who wanted to know got there quickly enough.

Accustomed to being interviewed, and also misquoted, interviewees were concerned that their words not be appropriated to serve narratives that misrepresented them. Stoya described a "sense of panic when I'm about to say something that could be misquoted."[123] "Make me sound smart!" Raylene joked at the close of our interview, after telling me about a previous experience in which she felt her words had been twisted to undermine her voice.[124] Tara Holiday talked about being reticent to give interviews because she had had so many negative experiences. When I thanked her for taking a chance on me, she replied, "Absolutely, sweetie. I trust you completely."[125] Laughing, she added, "And don't throw me under the bus." Throughout this book, I try to honor those concerns while also advancing the sustained critique to which interviewees, as experts, are entitled.

Feminist and queer thinkers have long argued that those on the margins have a great deal to teach about the center, and porn's location on the margins of respectable work and sex positions workers for critical interventions on both fronts. This is especially true to the extent that the conditions of the margins are being normalized. The mundane uncertainties of working-class life emerge as a crisis, writes Lauren Berlant, only "when they hit the bourgeoisies."[126] This book does not use the term "neoliberalism" because, in the labor context, it so often facilitates such an exceptionalizing move. Where scholars of once secure forms of straight work lament the turn to the gig economy, for instance, they frame as new a way of working that porn workers have long navigated. I am less interested in arguing that such thinkers have left porn workers out than in making clear that they have lost crucial insights in doing so.

Likewise, porn workers have rich experience navigating pressing questions in sexuality studies: How should we talk about consent when there is rent to pay? Should the state regulate intimate life? If "you're like an advert for yourself," as Nina Power puts it, how might we disentangle sexual selves from personal brands?[127] Should we try? Can desire speak for itself? Or is it bound up with histories of racial capitalism that shape what, and who, is valued? And finally, what does it mean to talk about pleasure when everyday people are struggling to survive? The chapters that follow read less like traditional ethnography than an effort to bring interviewees' expertise to bear on porn, sex, and work.

"Porn feels different than it looks," Nina Ha®tley puts it.[128] Against framings of porn performance as exceptionally exciting on the one hand or exceptionally extractive on the other, porn workers describe the work of performance as sometimes fun, sometimes straining, and mostly routine. They highlight the physical and emotional skill required to meet the demands of a scene; point to the grinding toll of everyday workplace racism; and describe porn as tedious, repetitive, and straining in the ways of other jobs. Chapter 1 turns to the set shop floor to explore how workers navigate these conditions. They forge connections with coworkers, resist directors' efforts to get them to do more for less, and carefully calculate the jobs they take according to their demands and rewards. Against the whorephobic discourse of "enthusiastic consent," porn workers insist that motivations for sex need not be pure—consent and desire are not the same.

Anti-sex-worker feminists, consumers, and many porn managers share the belief that money is a bad reason to have sex, and workers face pressure from all sides to make a performance of doing porn for purer reasons. As in many straight jobs, authenticity—loving the job—is a work requirement and one that can serve to extract more from workers, for less. Much left labor theory urges workers to resist that pull, marking distinctions between being oneself and doing a job in order to protect ourselves from extraction. But chapter 2 argues that a dialectical read must take workers seriously when they say that loving the job makes it feel less like work. Porn workers resist the idea that pleasure is a frivolous distraction from the material conditions of work. Instead, pleasure is a working condition.

Like pleasure at work, autonomy cuts two ways. Porn workers use creative hustles to wrest control over their work lives and, sometimes, take more from porn work than it takes from them. Chapter 3 turns to porn workers' strategies for using waged scene work as a marketing tool for scenes and services from which they profit directly. In sex work gig economies, they can seize degrees of class mobility that would be unthinkable in most straight jobs. But circumventing a boss's control in one's own life often means asserting that control over others, and worker-managers become party to the same systems they otherwise critique. Most porn workers are not, and do not want to be, just workers. This demands new ways of talking about class, solidarity, and the politics of gig work.

Performers seek out porn work in part because it offers the potential to make in a few hours what many workers make in a week. Once in porn, many describe workdays almost without end. Chapter 4 explores the porous boundaries between work and life. Most porn work takes place off set and off the clock, and workers spend countless hours getting ready for work, resting after it, self-marketing, and fighting policy that makes the work dangerous or impossible. This places them at the center of a moment in which, for more and more workers, "life [is] put to work."[129] But most porn workers do not wish to recover a way of working that more cleanly separates work and life. A Marxist feminist read instead asks how these categories come to be attached to payment in the first place. How much does porn cost, and how many hours does it take, if we include all the work that makes it possible?

The state does not know what to do with subjects when work and life blend, and porn workers labor at the intersection of state surveillance and state neglect. From racist discrimination to workplace health hazards, the problems of porn work can be traced to bad policy and poor enforcement. Shielded by discourses of privacy and aided by a general breakdown of the regulatory state, managers displace the risks and costs of doing business onto workers with little consequence. But, argues chapter 5, most porn workers do not trust the state to fix these gaps. Preferring a politics of self-organization and mutual aid, they demand privacy from the state and resist the imperative to choose between security and autonomy. The task is to articulate a vision for privacy that capital cannot appropriate in the service of putting workers at risk.

Finally, the book's epilogue returns to workers' framing of porn work as an escape from work. Disidentifying with constructions of porn and other sex work as misery dealing, porn workers rewrite their labor as that which allows them to escape the miseries of straight work. At the same time, they insist that porn work is work. Sitting with that tension, *Porn Work* closes with a meditation on what porno dialectics tell us about the contemporary world of work and what they say about how we might get to something better.

1

Porn Feels Different Than It Looks

Porn Work on Set

At a San Fernando Valley set house, performers waited poolside for filming to begin. We had all been told to arrive at 10 A.M., but filming would not begin until that afternoon. Devlyn Red joked that I should title this book "Hurry Up and Wait."[1] "Most people think behind the set there's big orgies going on," Dick Chibbles said, laughing. "We're all sitting around."[2] One performer reclined with his cell phone. "He's probably messaging with his kid," Chibbles offered. He pointed to two others chatting near the catering table: "They're talking about cars." It was a typical day on set—monotonous, often boring, and with a lot of lag time. In this sense, it was no different from most workdays.

"Porn feels different than it looks," veteran performer Nina Ha®tley told me.[3] The performers I interviewed echoed this—what you see in a finished scene reveals little about what it felt like to shoot it. You do not see the waiting, the retakes, the ankle sprains, the process of building chemistry with a scene partner or the racialized and gendered dynamics that can make that process so fraught. Every porn scene is a record of people at work, and yet the work of porn is invisible.[4] And so, when fans tell Conner Habib they "love [his] work," he thinks, "What do you mean you love my work? You masturbated watching me last night—why don't you say that? Because you don't love that I spent nine hours and balanced myself on a motorcycle with five people shining lights down on me, that's not the part that you like. You don't even think of that part."[5] This chapter focuses on that part, turning to the set to explore the work of porn production.

Porn workers navigate the production process in the context of industry-wide crisis. Paid scenes under a director are few and far between and competition for those castings is intense. Each day on set is both a gig and an audition for future work, and managers are quick to remind performers that if conditions do not suit them, someone else will gladly take their place. Workers negotiate wages, hours, and working conditions while this threat looms. At the same time, the interpersonal skills that make it possible to meet the demands of on-set sex are also tools for navigating (and subverting) power dynamics with managers. Meanwhile, crisis cuts both ways, and workers find power in the dynamics of the gig economy. Porn workers build brands and cultivate performances that make producers money. These same things also give workers leverage. Against the threat of replacement, performers wield name recognition and increased autonomy in an age of democratized production. Managers can be replaced, too, or rather rendered obsolete. This chapter focuses on paid scene work done under a director and producer (we will turn to self-produced scenes in chapter 3), but performers' growing independence from traditional managers shapes the politics of the set even when one is working under a boss. What does this reveal about the dialectics of paid sex?

GENRE AND THE CONDITIONS OF WORK

If porn work feels different than porn looks, it is still true that the look of a finished scene gives clues about its production process. Performers who have the privilege of being able to secure work in various genres—from gonzo to BDSM, features to queer—make calculations about the kind of work that meets their needs. Some seek out productions with directors they respect, industry prestige, or partners and types of sex they personally enjoy. Others prefer not high-status work but the most pay for the shortest possible hours. Genre conventions become less fixed as more and more workers produce their own material and thus set the conditions for their own performances. But in most paid scene work under another's direction, genre gives performers a reliable picture of what they might expect from a workday.

For performers who can afford to pick and choose paid gigs, deciding what genres to work in often means choosing between the more physically intense but less time-consuming work of gonzo (sex-focused scenes) and the endurance challenge of performing in features (multiscene productions that include dialogue).[6] Chanel Preston put it this way when I asked what types of scenes she preferred to shoot:

> I like that I can switch it up. I like acting; I enjoy it. I'm not amazing at it but it's something different, so I enjoy features. I don't enjoy being on set until 4 A.M. But I like that I can go do that, and on another day I can go shoot something really crazy and wild and be out of the office in four hours. But then, I can't shoot that all the time because it's really hard on my body. So some months I am shooting a lot of that and some months I'm shooting a lot of features, and both of them get really tiring. One's physically draining, the other you're up all night.[7]

Performer-director Lily Cade explained, "My favorite sets are those where the people involved care about what they're doing or sets where it's just fast. Either one. If I'm going to be there all day, have it be for a reason. Or get me out in two hours."[8]

Performers are paid by the day, rather than by the hour, incentivizing long days on a feature set. Typically produced by larger companies with bigger budgets, mainstream features pay slightly higher rates. But because they take longer to shoot, average hourly pay often works out to be less than for other gigs. For some performers, features are not worth the effort. Charity Bangs performs mostly in gonzo and said she had no interest in dialogue-driven features "because I've heard how much time and effort is put into [them]."[9] For others, features make for more fun, engaged work. Siri, a "theater geek," said she is accustomed to long hours and enjoys the opportunity to practice her craft.[10] Bad acting in porn is a running joke, and skilled actors are often proud of their talent. Features include parody films, and self-described nerds told me they enjoyed acting out their favorite comic book characters or sci-fi heroines. Because big-budget features are rarer and producers tend to cast the most popular performers, feature credits are also a mark of success. Screenwriter and director Jacky St. James explained, "You can get more attention for a feature than just a sex role. It's grueling work and it's exhausting, but it can put you on the map. If [performers] think strategically, they get it."[11] As a director of romance features, St. James relies on performers making this calculation.

Often producing many scenes on a slim budget, gonzo production tends to prize efficiency—the kind that gets you in and out in two hours. Unlike feature and feminist directors who take on passion projects, directors here are often contracted by production companies to produce content over which they have little creative control. These directors tend to be more aware, then, that performers may want to get done and go home (indeed, they often share these hopes) and more interested in cooperation and efficiency than in workers performing authentic interest in a director's vision. Efficiency can, however, strain in other ways. Directors who prioritize a strict schedule can put an enormous amount of pressure on workers to perform in a regimented way. And while this work requires less in terms of acting, time, and the emotional labor of convincing a director that you are thrilled to be there, it tends to compensate for light story lines with more intense sex scenes (this is why Preston says such scenes are harder on the body).

Preston is one of the top performers in the industry—of all the interviewees featured in this book, she worked most frequently (with eight to twenty paid shoots per month at the time)—which grants her the rare ability to pick and choose projects. Both she and Cade are white, cisgender, and thin and can therefore traverse the industry's genre boundaries more freely. Most performers take the jobs they are offered. Except where performers self-produce, most scenes in the BBW (big beautiful woman) genre and most trans scenes are typically low-budget, gonzo productions, and Black performers are often confined to "urban" and "interracial" scenes (almost exclusively low-budget productions with plot lines organized around racialized themes). Ana Foxxx, one of the few Black women who gets cast in features, was happy to get work that departed from the gigs Black women typically have access to. In addition to the opportunity to do something different—Foxxx starred in the *Ghostbusters* parody, for instance—these films offer higher pay and better working conditions overall. Foxxx explained, "Whenever I'm on set and it's a mixed demographic, they have everything on set: pizza, hair, makeup. And then I go and it's a Black-only title and you're looking around for water. There's a difference."[12] Directors, producers, and non-Black performers often explain these disparities as a budgetary issue. But, as Mireille Miller-Young argues, Black performers encounter poor conditions and low rates even as their performance labor is in high demand among consumers (and thus profitable for producers).[13]

Interviewees overwhelmingly talked about race in terms of this Black/non-Black dichotomy. "There's two different sides: there's the Black side and the white side. . . . They usually only mix when they're doing interracial stuff," explained Raylene, a white performer.[14] "Interracial" means scenes with Black men and non-Black women. The subgenre is, as theorist Ariane Cruz elaborates, grounded in the foundational taboo surrounding sex between Black men and white women.[15] Porn's vision of whiteness can flex to make space for non-Black women of color: a Latina or East Asian performer paired with a Black one still makes up an "interracial" scene, while a white performer with a non-Black person of color does not. Porn's gendered Black/non-Black dichotomy is fixed to such an extent that mainstream's much rarer scenes featuring Black women and non-Black men belong to a separate category labeled, instead, "reverse interracial." This is one area in which the politics of representation indelibly shape the production process. For porn's labor market, this means that industrial segregation impacts Black workers, and Black women in particular, most intensely. This is not limited to mainstream scenes performed under a manager, but it is most intense here. As chapter 3 elaborates, self-produced scenes still exist in a broader racial economy, but performer-producers have more flexibility here to write their own rules.

Non-Black people of color contend with the strains of fetishization, and in some cases (such as Asian men in straight porn) erasure,[16] but no non-Black interviewees reported hiring discrimination or pay inequality at anywhere near the rates Black workers did. Instead, they were careful to acknowledge the specificity of the porn industry's anti-Blackness. Wolf Hudson, a light-skinned Latino performer, was surprised when I asked him whether he experienced racist casting or pay discrimination. "I don't get cast that way. . . . The Latino community and the Asian community, they don't get it as bad as African Americans. When you say 'IR' [interracial] you're not saying those communities, you're saying 'African American.'"[17] This applies to non-Black performers' racialized "preferences" regarding coworkers as much as it does to porn's top-down approach to genre. When non-Black performers refuse "interracial" scenes or charge higher rates for them—both standard practices in mainstream—these moves are explicitly anti-Black. "Girls who say they don't do IR will perform with a Mexican guy," Hudson explained. "You mean you don't do Black." As this book was going to press, worker organizers formed the BIPOC Adult Industry Collective to address such industry racism through mutual aid and advocacy.[18] Central to their efforts is peer education geared toward teaching performers how to produce their own content, a nod to the extent to which class mobility is a tool for escaping workplace racism.

Provisions such as those Foxxx describes are a crucial occupational health measure in a job that can be both physically exhausting (for performers and crew alike) and require fasting. They also give clues to a director's approach to working conditions more broadly—directors who see no need to provide food and water are likely to also skimp on rest breaks and lube supply. As in other jobs, access to safe and respectful working conditions is deeply racialized and classed. Porn's genre boundaries simply name these hierarchies. "Even sometimes working for the same company, just under a different title, I've noticed a difference," Foxxx told me. The pages that follow chronicle a typical porn work flow, and the hierarchies Foxxx describes mark every stage of the process. They do not, however, foreclose opportunities for workers' intervention.

CONSENTING TO WORK

Before the porn workday begins, workers negotiate their terms. They do so armed with a sharp understanding of their location vis-à-vis the power dynamics of waged work. On the one hand, they are keenly aware of their precariousness as de facto independent contractors who can be fired, or quietly not hired again, at will. "If you don't want to do it, they'll find someone who will," workers told me when I asked about negotiating rates, on-set activity, partners, and so on.[19] But workers also say that the reverse is often true—if one director does not want to hire you for the kind of work you want to do, someone else will. Performers may be replaceable, but directors are too, especially as directing has been democratized in the digital era. In porn, you can also hire yourself. It is much safer to say no to a boss if you can be your own. And workers suggest that the algorithmic management characteristic of platform-enabled work, while constraining in its own ways, does not feel "bossed" in the way conventionally waged scenes do. Workers laboring under a single boss risk far more in refusing demands. This is, indeed, a primary reason many sex workers prefer an industry that frees them from a single boss's authority and offers the potential to seize the means of production.

Performers also understand that managers rely on performers' brand names for sales. Directors told me that they rehired performers who were a "pain in the ass" so long as internet algorithms showed their scenes sold well. Performers know full well how much leverage their popularity gives them. In this sense, porn workers have a lot more power than most workers in straight jobs, where workers' lack of name recognition and consumer loyalty makes them more easily replaced. Popular women performers in straight mainstream and men in gay productions have the most leverage in this respect—it is almost exclusively their "brands" that companies use to market product. Men in straight mainstream productions, on the other hand, are keenly aware of their replaceability—"I'm a piece of meat to them," Herschel Savage said when I asked about negotiating.[20] But despite the term "porn star," the industry has fewer stars than it does working actors. Porn workers calibrate the demands they make according to their relative (and always shifting) leverage in the labor market.

More than direct coercion from individual managers, performers highlighted the pressure to remain competitive amid a seemingly endless supply of willing workers. They can say no to any number of things, but in so doing risk damaged reputations, strained relationships, and lost work. This is true across genres. Director Chi Chi LaRue explained that gay performers once chose the sex roles they would play; some preferred "topping," while others chose to "bottom."[21] "Nowadays it's a lot of versatiles. Even the straight guys kind of have to be versatile," he said, referring to performers who perform both insertive and receptive sex roles. "You don't have to be," he added. "No one *has* to do anything."

Likewise, straight mainstream performer-director jessica drake, who has been in the business since 1999, explained why she found outsiders' assumptions about consent in porn frustrating: "I definitely have made all of my own choices in my career—and my life, for that matter. It makes me mad when people imply anything else."[22] She added, "Although, I think talent these days are a bit more malleable than we were back then. There certainly are more people in the industry now, and they do get really competitive. Sometimes I think people tend to lose their voice a little bit. At the end of the day, we have the right to do what we want to do."

Workers and managers echoed this sentiment—performers are free to say no to any scene they are not comfortable with. As in most jobs, someone else will likely take their place. Porn stands above most straight jobs, however, in that individual work tasks are up for negotiation at all. The norm in porn is that performers agree to one set of conditions—this many partners in a scene and this sort of sex—and that any changes must be renegotiated. This is not true, for example, in most office jobs. My aim here is not to make any false equivalences between sex work and straight work—for most workers negotiating sex scenes has rather different stakes than negotiating how many TPS reports one must file—but rather to caution straight working readers not to read their own work dynamics into the porn context.

When I asked about consent practices, one fetish site director offered the checklist he gives to performers before a shoot. The list asks performers to check yes or no next to particular acts but reminds them that "those in blue are required."[23] Performers who want to shoot for the company should be willing to "'help' a male pee" and administer "hand jobs" but can specify what kinds of insertive sex (i.e., vaginal, anal, or group) they are comfortable with. The document is titled "Talent Interview Form & Checklist," gesturing at once to the choices it leaves open and to the reality that, if one wants work, some things must be a yes.

Expectations for written consent vary by director and studio. Alongside queer and feminist productions, kink and BDSM productions tend to have the most performer-friendly policies around on-set boundaries. Workers described a major BDSM company as having the strictest protocols for attaining explicit consent,[24] providing performers extensive checklists that address the sex acts they are comfortable with, those they refuse, any areas of the body they prefer to be touched or avoided, and double-blind indications of whether workers wish to use a condom (so that directors do not have this information when casting a scene).[25] In practice, directors apply these policies unevenly. Some workers described the company as the best place to work precisely because of these safeguards, while others reported consent violations even with such policies in place and suggest that the performers who tend to be rehired for scenes are those who have fewer restrictions. Many productions put a premium on hiring performers who are "authentically" kinky, so having too many boundaries can be disqualifying, signaling to directors and coworkers that a performer is not the right "fit."

Other employers skip written protocols, assuming that if a performer has agreed to do a scene, they are aware of the acts involved and consent to them implicitly. It is not cost effective for directors to mislead workers about this, since they lose money when performers walk off a shoot or are unable to complete a scene. Because each sex act is explicitly monetized in porn's fee structure, agents also lose commission if workers perform acts for which they are not paid. Siri explained the conversation about consent she had with her agent:

> It wasn't explained explicitly like "You have the right to say no to anything," because he's an agent and his best interest is to profit as much as possible from the work he's getting me. The way that he framed the information was kind of like "If they book you for a 'boy-girl' scene at *x* amount of money and you get to set and

they're like, 'Hey, we're going to shoot you for this three-way scene as well,' that's not okay." It wasn't framed like "If you don't feel comfortable, say no." It was like "You're not being paid to do that extra work, so say no."[26]

This is also the norm among performers who work without an agent. In this atmosphere, performers usually come to set with a general sense of the kind of sex they will be having that day (e.g., oral, anal, or group). No interviewees reported being forced to perform scenes they had initially refused. Many directors were repulsed by the idea that anyone be forced to shoot a scene they were not comfortable with, and they resented the perception from outsiders that this is common practice. Antiporn readers may not buy this, but the economics speak for themselves: with so many willing workers, there is little reason to cajole unwilling ones. "A lot of people don't understand," explained director-producer Matt Frackas, "we do not need to seduce or convince or trick girls into this. There's always a supply."[27] Assuming trickery leaves no space for workers' diverse motivations for consenting to sexual labor; it also misunderstands the market.

Beyond confirming consent to a particular kind of scene, it is up to performers to discuss any other boundaries with one another before filming begins. For most, this involves a casual conversation along the lines of, as jessica drake put it, "What do you like, what do you not like, what can we do? What are your dos and don'ts?"[28] With the basic sex acts already established, these dos and don'ts typically concern more subtle issues, such as whether one enjoys hair pulling or finds a particular term triggering. Most performers respect these boundaries. Working with someone who disregards them was the most common reason workers cited for placing other performers on a "no list" of people with whom they are unwilling to work again.

Performers elaborate clear boundaries between sex that looks rough on film but does not feel that way, consensually rough sex, and violence that harms. With a good director and costar(s), a scene that looks exceptionally rough to the viewer need not feel that way for those performing it. Performers agree to film rough scenes knowing that this is usually the case. To revise Nina Ha®tley's earlier quote, porn *should* feel different than it looks unless all the performers involved prefer otherwise. Rope bondage can leave more mobility than the viewer can see, a slap can be delivered more gently than it sounds, and a gagging blow job scene can be deftly simulated. Some workers enjoy rough sex in earnest, and ethically run sets will make space for them to negotiate its terms with their partners.[29] For this reason, some performers who enjoy rough sex or bondage told me they prefer on-set sex. Here, they can be more confident that their partners know best practices (how to paddle someone without risking organ damage, for instance), have the tools to talk about consent, and are comfortable expressing their own needs and boundaries. "Civilians"—that is, non–sex workers—tend to be quite bad at this. "Never in a civilian encounter had I been explicitly asked what I was and wasn't willing to do with my body," writes Lorelei Lee.[30]

In most cases, this is how sex on set proceeds. But sometimes, costars (with directors' implicit or explicit support) push these boundaries and cause harm. Amid a spate of 2015 disclosures of performer James Deen's abusive behavior, Lily LaBeau came forward to describe a scene in which he hit her so hard she "felt an almost crack in [her] ear."[31] During another scene, he spit in her eye, even though this had not been agreed upon and would not be included in the final cut due to policy restrictions on distributing such content. In the spring of 2018, performers Leigh Raven and Riley Nixon disclosed strikingly similar experiences of abuse by Rico Strong on the sets of director Just Dave. Both performers agreed to rough scenes, but what they found on set was violence, not performance. Nixon marked this distinction: "It was a rough shoot. I like rough sex. I love rough sex. It wasn't consensually rough. I mean, yes, I was consenting to it, but it was just way rougher than it needed to be."[32] That these abuses brought performer complaint and wide publicity highlights how sharply they deviate from the norm.

Most workers told me that such on-set boundary violations are rare, at least in the world of professionally produced porn. Performers get consigned to "no lists" quickly when they develop reputations for abusive behavior. While "star" performers and those who direct their own scenes can continue to work even if they have poor reputations (the case in both stories above), men are largely replaceable. For this reason, performers were more likely to experience abusive conditions on sets in which their boss was also their scene partner. The men who get regular casting in straight productions, then, tend to be those who women want to work with. Because they rely on word of mouth, these controls are harder to maintain in amateur productions and small-scale productions outside the major porn-producing communities of LA, Florida, San Francisco, and Las Vegas. As we have seen, the growing diffusion of the porn industry brings greater opportunities for autonomy but can also undermine the safeguards a more cohesive industry makes possible. These dynamics set the scene for the set shop floor.

GETTING READY

Back at the San Fernando set house, Dick Chibbles and Devlyn Red had moved from waiting for their scene to preparing for it. Today the set was the director's sprawling home in the Valley. Directors also film at company-owned locations, hotel rooms, or private spaces rented out for the day. Whatever kind of scene will be shot that day, the first steps usually share a common flow. When studios require a negative sexually transmitted infection (STI) test from performers (most common in straight mainstream), directors typically confirm these results in advance of a shoot with authenticated results from recognized testing facilities or through Performer Availability Screening Services, a service operated by the Free Speech Coalition.[33] A small number of mostly queer, feminist, and BDSM companies leave testing decisions up to performers, allowing a variety of ways to discuss STI status before scenes and providing a range of barrier methods on set. Gay productions are more likely to rely on pre-exposure prophylaxis (PrEP) treatment as prevention (where successful treatment makes an HIV infection nontransmissible), serosorting, or barrier methods.[34] Some performers also ask partners to share their results directly before a scene. Trade and informal shoots (for example, for a performer's OnlyFans site) exist in regulatory limbo, and pre-scene protocols are less standardized here.

Next, performers fill out paperwork—modeling contracts, independent contractor tax forms, and the mandated form proving that they are over eighteen (the "2257," in industry shorthand).[35]

They then move to hair and makeup and prepare the body for scene work with douches, enemas, and the medicines some performers rely on to meet the conditions of a scene. On bigger-budget sets such as the one Chibbles and Red worked on, production companies hire makeup artists.[36] Lower-budget studios have cut professional hair and makeup artists from the payroll to accommodate the digital era's smaller production budgets. Now, many studios expect women to do their own hair and makeup and to own the necessary supplies. It is a prototypical example of the industry's response to lean production and speedup culture: cost cutting means that the workers who remain occupy multiple roles simultaneously.

After preparation, once again, performers wait. A performer's scene rate and a crew member's day rate pay for however long it takes to get the job done. This might be two or twenty hours. Though some directors, production companies, and types of scenes are known to take longer than others, performers generally have little certainty about how long their workday will be before they arrive. With so many moving parts, it is difficult to keep filming to a strict schedule. On sets I visited, filming had to be halted because of audible fire sirens, broken camera equipment, smudged makeup, and lost erections. Unpredictable as LA traffic is, it is not uncommon for workers simply to be late to set.

Long hours on set are just as often attributable to a director's calculation that performers' time is simply less valuable than their own. As profits and production budgets diminish, directors increasingly schedule multiple scenes in one day to save money on locations and extract as much labor as possible from crew members, who are usually paid by the day rather than by the hour. On sets with multiple scenes to be shot in a day, directors may ask that everyone be on set at the same time so that if the first scene's performers are late, they can shoot the second, and so on. Other directors have a reputation for keeping performers on set simply to spend time with them. And so, workers wait.

Waiting can be exhausting, and workers may find themselves already drained by the time they are called to shoot a scene. As Nina Ha®tley put it, "Watch the feature movies for the 2 A.M. scene. It's the one where people are clearly exhausted—they've been there all day. They stagger into the room, fall into the bed, you can tell. . . . One, two, cowgirl, three, four, doggie, five, six, spooning, seven, eight, come on tits, can we go home now, please?"[37]

Crew members, too, talk about monotony as one of porn's greatest strains. One production assistant described his job as mostly handling paperwork, setting up and taking down lights, and "a lot of rubbing baby oil on a girl's ass."[38] "It sounds fun the first couple times, but it gets really annoying, and you're not paid that much," he added. On-set hours are longest for crew members, who arrive first and leave last. They describe exhaustion and fatigue as significant concerns.[39] As in other jobs, boredom is often the most painful aspect of the porn workday.

But time spent waiting is not only a source of strain. Workers also use waiting as an opportunity for community building and side hustling. Performers use downtime on set to upload photos to social media, exchange paid chats with fans, or optimize platform profiles for higher traffic. They also use this time to share information ranging from hair product recommendations to pay scales. On one set, I overheard an experienced performer recommending to a newcomer that she switch talent agents, as the agent she had at the time was known for pressuring performers to take scenes below rate. Another agent, she said, should be avoided because of his habit of charging extortionist "kill fees" to performers who had to cancel shoots due to personal emergencies, keeping them in personal debt to the agency. When the more junior performer explained that she was concerned her contract with her agent made it impossible to leave, the more senior explained that such contracts rarely hold up in court and shared her attorney's contact information. On another set, one performer warned his colleague that the herbal erectile support medicine he was using had been causing adverse reactions in friends. Community building here also facilitates more enduring connections—performers who meet on set might go on to organize together. Waged porn work preserves the break-room camaraderie that is so often a casualty of atomizing gig economies. Managers cannot make performers wait and also keep them from comparing notes.

ON SCENE

Finally, the cameras are rolling. With work agreements signed and bodies readied, the formal part of the workday (at least according to the contract) begins with modeling for promotional stills. "Promo stills" are typically glamour-style solo shots of women performers in straight productions (old-school mainstream directors often call these "pretty girl" shots) and of both performers in gay male productions. Next, performers shoot "sex stills" with their scene partners. Viewers later see these in advertisements and on DVD covers (and their digital thumbnail equivalent). Directors often invite industry journalists to set, and they are free to take still photos as well. The modeling release performers sign for the scene applies here, too, and performers are not paid extra for stills regardless of who takes them or where the photos end up. When I asked why this was, photographer and publicist Dominic Ace explained, "Yes, in theory, the talent could bitch, 'I don't want this dude taking pictures of me for free.' The producer would say, 'don't hire this bitch again. This guy is gonna get me $10k worth of promo for free, you're gonna get me another blonde girl.'"[40] As in other stages of the production process, workers weigh the desire to refuse employer demands against the knowledge of their own replaceability.

Stills require performers to hold sex positions (including insertion) so that camera operators can capture various angles—balancing on a motorcycle, for example. Receptive partners try to stay lubricated and relaxed, and insertive partners struggle to maintain erections while holding a pose. This is hard work and for most performers not the sexiest way to prepare for the hard-core sex that will follow. An exception to this rule is those performers for whom public sex carries an erotic charge. For these workers, the choreographed, hypervisible nature of on-set sex is a benefit rather than a strain, and stills can build sexual tension rather than detract from it.

It need not reinforce the conservative idea of a neat distinction between porn sex and "real" sex to acknowledge that most sex on set is labor intensive in ways off-set sex generally is not.[41] Partner choice, setting, audience, the particular types of sex directors ask for, the need to be constantly aware of the camera, and timing, performers say, make porn sex different from the sex they usually have off set. Performer, director, and producer Prince Yahshua described it this way: "We're not fucking at home; we're playing to the camera. Everything we have to do is open. Some people can get it through the gate, [but for] some it takes a few months."[42] Yahshua explains as much to new performers. "I've actually taught quite a few girls," he said.

> They're like, "Prince, I really need some help here." Okay, you
> can come do a scene for my website. Your training will be a full
> scene, but it's pretty much me positioning you. . . . "No, sweetie,
> hold this, arch your back." This is an art form. When guys ask me
> to help them get into this [I explain], "You're probably King Kong
> behind closed doors. But when you're on the stage, it's lights,
> camera, action, you've got fifteen to twenty people in the room,
> it's a whole different demon. Not for the fifteen minutes or less,
> but five hours you're keeping your dick hard with a million eyes
> on you with a girl that might be into you or is a diva." It's only 20
> percent physical—the rest of it is mental. You see the same sixteen
> guys for a reason. If any heterosexual guy could do this, they'd be
> doing this. The lure is that every day it's a fresh woman, but you
> don't know what mood she's having. If she's saying, "Uh, let's get
> this over with." Anything like that can break a guy mentally. You
> have to go with the blinders on.

Performers develop finely tuned strategies for dealing with these demands.

Performers learn to work in front of an audience of strangers, who may include bored-looking production assistants, journalists absorbed in the spectacle of their first porn set, and, at least on the sets I visited, graduate students nervously trying to stay out of the way. One set I visited was at a rental home notorious for its creepy owner, who found ways to chat up performers as they waited to shoot and would watch from the corner as they filmed, joking about the cleanup crew that would be required later. Directors are often cavalier about whom they allow on set, assuming that performers will work in front of almost any audience. "Visit a porn set" services invite tour groups onto set, in which case the performers' same scene fee includes not only on-film sex but also a live sex show for civilian spectators. Porn work may also require performing in front of people one knows all too well, such as a camera operator one had an unfriendly breakup with last year or a reviewer who panned one's last film. Managing interactions with spectators as well as crew members is one of the many kinds of emotional labor porn demands. To be clear, I mean "emotional labor" not just as effort (as the term sometimes gets taken up) but as value-producing *work*.[43]

The task of managing such interactions is magnified by the distinct but often overlapping responsibilities on-set players have. Each position—performing, directing, camera operating, etc.—carries different demands, and these can clash. "Sometimes during a shoot people forget that they're dealing with human beings," said performer Kay Parker. "The crew get caught up in timing and technical issues."[44] But performers need "time to get back into that space—we're getting ready to be intimate. And there were a couple of times during a scene that I yelled 'cut.' I was at the point where I knew I could take liberties like that. And I said [*pointing to herself*], 'Human being. You guys need to take a moment.' And they listened to me." As Parker suggests, she could intervene in this way because she was at the top of her career. She was also working in the 1980s, when the performer pool was much smaller. Demanding a break midscene would be risky for many performers today.

The sometimes unsexy dynamics of on-set sex persist. Current performer Venus Lux described the assembly-line-like nature of some sets as a source of strain among performers, crews, and directors: "Sometimes it's like 'Come on, just get fucked. Spread those ass cheeks, let's do it.' I'm like, 'Come on, really?' You sometimes feel like you're treated like a piece of meat. Especially when it comes to people who don't know you, they just want to make money off you. And sometimes you encounter photographers—whether it's a bad day or who they are, they just look at you like 'Here's the meat.'"[45]

As in other "intimate labors," to borrow Eileen Boris and Rhacel Parreñas' phrase, porn is rife with these pressure points—moments in which intimacy and the production process run up against each other in tricky ways.[46] Workers representing a range of identities described versions of "here's the meat," and these were most intense for people of color and trans workers such as Lux. Here again, one's ability to make demands is shaped but not totally determined by racialized, gendered, and even algorithmic hierarchies. But workers do not internalize the idea that they are reducible to bodies that work or fetishized identities to be marketed. Instead, they push back against this dynamic both internally and in their engagements on set. Against this backdrop, performers do the emotional work of getting into character, navigating myriad off-set relations, and building chemistry with scene partners.

While popular performers have significant power to determine who their scene partners will be, managers often regard those who have strict parameters as inflexible. Performers are not forced to shoot a scene with partners they wish not to work with, though some agents put a great deal of pressure on workers to take whatever scenes are offered. The dynamics of partner choice have also changed significantly over time. With a performer pool that has grown dramatically in the past forty years, performers have come to expect that they may arrive on set slated to work with someone they have never met. Parker, who performed from 1976 to 1985, explained that during that time "it was a fairly small group of people. There were about six men who were mostly cast. We all knew each other, and we were fairly comfortable. These were not necessarily people I would have taken as sex partners in my private life, but I felt comfortable with them. Some I even went as far as to call friends."

In contrast, Raylene—who worked as a contract star in the late 1990s, retired, and returned to performing as an unsigned performer in 2009—noted, "When I was under contract, I had a yes and a no list. This time around, you work with people you've never met and you'll never see again, which I find dangerous."[47] The performer pool has only gotten larger in the years since. Some described partner variety as exciting, affording the opportunity to be with a "fresh" partner, as Yahshua put it. But most performers said they prefer to know who their screen partner will be or, better yet, to have a say in who that person is. More often than not, this is not because they want to be sure they are attracted to their screen partner but because having a good partner makes it easier to negotiate safety practices and on-set boundaries. It also makes the work more fun. Parker's analysis resonated with many of the workers I interviewed—most value screen partners with whom they share collegiality or even friendship rather than those with whom they would choose unpaid sex off set.

Workers' complaints about porn sex centered on work practices, not on whether on-set sex was the best they ever had (some even said it was). Performer-director Lily Cade put it plainly: "We're making a product. I'm not attracted to all my costars. They don't know and they shouldn't know that. If you're a good performer, they shouldn't know. Once you show up, even if you're not attracted to them, find something you are attracted to and get over yourself."[48] Few performers said they only perform with partners they are attracted to, and many described the ability to shoot a convincing scene regardless of sexual chemistry as a key element of their professionalism. Likewise, managers expect these skills of performers.

For many, though, "finding something you're attracted to" is more complicated than the process Cade describes. Christopher Daniels described it this way: "When you're not attracted to your scene partner . . . just grin and bear it. Just get through the day. The scene needs to be finished and you need to get your paycheck and you need to catch a flight. . . . Remove yourself mentally, really zero in on one thing you like, or zero in on your laundry, your to-do list, whatever. Remove yourself from the situation."[49] Manufacturing feeling—both as it can be read by the viewer and as it impacts relationships with managers and coworkers—is a primary task of porn work. For some performers and on some workdays, the grinning and bearing it Daniels describes works. For others, a good scene requires intense physical and emotional chemistry. Manufactured feeling across this spectrum requires careful emotional labor.

When asked what they looked for in a performer, managers cited "professionalism" as a key trait, but when I asked them to explain, they described not duty-bound order following but personal investment in the work. Chapter 2 takes more time to trace this demand. Workers are adept at performing this sort of professionalism—some describe "wanting to be there" as a sort of work ethic—and they hope that on-screen partners will bring this ethic to scenes as well. More precisely, performers hope for a delicate balance of wanting to be there and detached professionalism in their on-screen partners. Ela Darling described the frustration of working with women who don't actually enjoy having sex with women but added, "As far as I'm concerned, as long as you can convince me that you're attracted to me right now, I don't care what your sexual identity is."[50] Willingness to do this relational work is part of what it means to have a sex-work ethic.

This is not a radical departure from the kind of "work ethic around sex" Feona Attwood describes in unpaid sex.[51] Performers may come to the industry already armed with the skills required to bring their "feelings more into line with how they suspect sex 'ought to be' experienced," a capacity women in particular cultivate long before direct payment is at stake.[52] "A lot of women's heterosexual sex is or has been characterized by negotiating their own lack of 'enthusiastic consent,'" writes Charlotte Shane, pointing out that sex work was not her first occasion for navigating complex motivations for sex.[53] Marxist feminists have long argued that unpaid heterosexual sex is labored—a respectable but sometimes more extractive kind of sexed work—and so much gender socialization centers on teaching sexual subjects how to perform in ways that produce value.[54] Workers involved in paid sex can find these labors less straining, since the terms of the exchange are more straightforward and more open to negotiation. But unpaid sexual subjects usually bring feelings "into line" only with their intimate partner(s), at least at the point of sexual contact, while porn work requires emotional labor on multiple registers.

Not all kinds of arousal can be seamlessly brought to the market. Too much can slow things down, frustrating coworkers who would like to get done and go home and adding expense for producers, who pay hourly rates for locations and some crew salaries. On one set I visited, a first-time performer showed far too much interest in his more experienced partner, pestering her during downtimes and wanting to cuddle and kiss after the cameras had stopped rolling. She "just want[ed] to go home," as she told me later. It was not that the sex had been bad; it was just that her rescue dog did not like being home alone, she told me. On another set, a director admonished a performer for having an orgasm during her scene. With the performer too flushed and sweaty for a good shot, production had to be halted midscene so that makeup artists could "fix" the situation. Interviewees described having to minimize a sense of connection with on-screen partners in order to avoid "finishing" (ejaculating) too quickly or forgetting to "open up for the camera." Performers must at once seem to want to work "not just for the check" and keep production budgets in mind at all times. The work of simultaneous connecting and distancing is demanding, a reality with which workers across intimate labors are familiar.[55] In contrast to these labors, porn's boundary work of connecting just enough

Porn Work on Set

is intensified by the presence of the camera—workers perform to manage their own emotional process and relationships not only with coworkers but also for the viewer.

Some porn workers describe cultivated detachment as important for staving off the emotional fatigue work can engender. Christopher Daniels described filmed sex as a "physical act that affects you emotionally."[56] "It can wear on you a bit," he added. Raylene spoke of an "emotional hangover" after scenes, but she learned how to "compartmentalize and walk away and forget that I even had the day. Like, 'well, that was fun,' and then I don't remember who I worked with."[57] Detaching just enough—a calculation unique to each worker—can help mitigate work's emotional strain. Most performers do not describe this as a dissociative response to trauma, as psychologizing outsiders often assume. Instead, cultivated detachment is a mindful process and one workers across a range of labors use to ensure that not every part of themselves is put to work.

At the same time, workers forge meaningful connections on set. As we have seen, such connections are less often characterized by intense sexual passion than by collegiality, friendship, and community. By way of illustrating camaraderie among colleagues, Ela Darling described an outpouring of support when she came down with the flu on set. After the director tied her up—a time-consuming process—in preparation for an elaborate rope-bondage BDSM scene, Darling became nauseous and told the director. The director patiently untied Darling as her costar, rubbing her back, ensured, "It's okay girl, we've all been there."[58] They all went home for the day. Back at set the following day, Darling found herself fatigued. The director and Darling's costar agreed that they would change the scene so that Darling could lie down and her partner would take on the more physically demanding role. "And through it all," Darling told me, "nobody complained. Everyone was totally supportive, kind, caring, and loving. That's the industry I'm working in. People think I'm victimized about my work, but there's no other job where I could get sick or have to flake for all of the reasons I was unable to perform my job that day and still have nothing but support." Darling knows—she worked as a librarian before porn. Others echoed this sense that porn sets are unique in the mutual understanding and support workers can expect. "I just love being on set because you're friends with everyone for the most part. It's like a really weird family," Chanel Preston told me.[59]

Not every set is a space of mutual support. Preston added that at other times, "shoots are really difficult, [with] a lot of negativity or stress on the set for some reason." Serious conflicts around working conditions and consent practices, together with more quotidian social tensions, also shape on-set relationships. Darling's experience was noteworthy because it is common for directors to send performers home with no pay when they or their costar cannot perform. As in most jobs, the experience of being on set changes from gig to gig.

The demands of emotional labor intensify when performers take on multiple roles in a production. As budgets decrease and barriers to entry lower, more and more directors perform in their own scenes. Performer-directors take on distinct and sometimes conflicting roles simultaneously. Tanya Tate, who began as a performer and now directs as well, explained, "You're a one-man band."[60] After coordinating crews, dealing with any no-shows, making sure paperwork is done, and checking lighting and sound, performer-directors must then "jump [in front of] the camera, be on set, *enjoy everything*. At the same time, you're directing the way it's going. . . . In the back of your mind, there's still a part that's like, 'Is this going well?'" Likewise, Alex Linko described the "balancing act between thinking technically and thinking sexually" that informs his work as a performer-director.[61] Such dual roles are not limited to performers who take on directing positions in an official capacity. Tate explained that by the time of her first directing gig, she already had years of experience "leading" scenes in which she performed. Experienced performers take on such roles all the time. In this way, they wrest creative control, support coworkers, enhance their own brands with well-done scenes, develop directing skill, and model a porn work ethic.

Directors who do not perform describe a different sort of emotional labor. As veteran director Chi Chi LaRue put it, "When you're a director of pornography, you're a cheerleader, you're a counselor, you're a father, you're a mother, you're a boyfriend, you're a girlfriend, you're Dr. Phil for God's sake!"[62] I did not observe this sort of management on any of the sets I visited, and performers did not describe it as a major part of their work experience. Of course, one does not always know they are being emotionally managed. But when I asked directors what tasks made up their work, this kind of emotional management emerged as equally if not more important than staging a scene, directing performances, coordinating lighting and sound, and keeping budgets in check. This often had a distinctly paternal character—I heard the phrase "herding cats" more times than I care to count.

When I asked performers what made a good director, they described someone who makes them look good on-camera, pays well, asks what they are comfortable with rather than simply making demands, keeps to a schedule, and has a well-provisioned set with water, food, lubricant, and condoms for those performers who wish to use them. Directors, on the other hand, often responded to this question by listing the ways in which they "took care" of performers (whom directors in straight porn almost exclusively framed as young women) by dissuading from working in porn those they thought were too young or wanted to work "out of desperation." Directors struggle to reconcile this investment in paternalism with their primary task: managing the performance of hard-core sex in order to make a saleable product. From the perspective of their own bosses (many directors have them), a good director is one who gets the shot.

A good shot is the product of careful collaboration. Directing and filming here martials some of the same skills as mainstream production, but capturing hard-core sex well requires its own deft maneuvering. So, too, does performing it. Directors ask a performer to "open up" for the camera, manipulating one's body such that the camera can capture a range of angles (including insertion). The positions most conducive to open shots can be different, and more physically demanding, than those that performers find most comfortable or pleasurable. Performers are free to decline to shoot a certain position, but as with partner choice, they are keenly aware of the costs of being seen as recalcitrant.

While waiting on set with Dick Chibbles, Devlyn Red, a BBW performer, explained the physical labors of porn:

> Reverse cowgirl is the most common [position] requested, but it's the hardest and most painful.[63] [That is,] porn reverse cowgirl, not where you're bent over. You're using your thigh muscles to lift your body, and then you have really big boobs that are levitating and then dropping with nothing to cushion them. It hurts like a bitch. And they want it for an extended period of time because it's the best overall visual of your entire body. . . . It's ideal for a movie, not ideal for the performer. And the guys are always helpful, they put their arms up to balance you.[64]

Chibbles, her screen partner, interjected: "We do what we can."[65]

"You can balance your hands on their chest," Red responded.

"Not directly on the sternum," Chibbles said, "'cause it's like CPR."

"And if you move and you're wearing nails or anything, you jab them or slice them," Red added. Chibbles went on: "Or if the girl's moving to phantom-length zone, where they come completely off [their partner's penis]. . . . It's one of the reasons I don't like to do girl on top unless I'm controlling your depth. I usually just say, 'It's gonna be the easiest day for you, if we do any girl on top, just hover above me, I'm gonna [thrust] from underneath.'"[66]

The conversation offered a rich view into the efforts performers make to facilitate for each other. Not all performers engage in this way, but the collaborative spirit Chibbles and Red model is common among experienced performers. Performers find creative ways of ensuring safety, comfort, and sometimes pleasure for themselves and their scene partners, all without disrupting the shot. With a subtle tap on the thigh, for instance, receptive partners signal to insertive partners that they should slow down or adjust to a shallower thrust. The camera needs energetic sex, but not a bruised cervix, and skilled performers get the job done while also practicing mutual care in ways the camera cannot see. Porn feels different than it looks not only in the sense that it can be more tedious; it is also often gentler.

In addition to illustrating the work of collaboration, Chibbles and Red's conversation shows that the physical strain and potential risks of porn work are not limited to STI exposure. Repetitive stress injury, pulled muscles, fungal infections such as ringworm, sprained ankles, sunburn, pinched nerves, and even cuts from too-sharp acrylic nails are often more present concerns for porn workers. Chibbles went on to describe a scene in a *Star Wars* parody in which he played Chewbacca and had to wear a costume consisting of "thirty pounds of fur." "It was about 135 degrees inside that outfit," he explained, and after each five minutes of filming, he had to halt production and cool down. The scene took five hours to shoot. In this case his screen partner, crew, and director were solicitous. Chibbles is white, and this was a big-budget mainstream set. Performers working at the intersections of racism and/or transphobia, and on lower-budget sped-up sets, do not always experience this level of care; broader hierarchies shape exposure to risk.

Long scenes, especially with insertive partners who have larger-than-average penises, can pose the risk of friction burn and torn tissue for receptive partners. That performers are often not physically attracted to their screen partners or are simply too busy paying attention to the many aspects of filmed performance for their bodies to be aroused compounds this risk. Muscle relaxers can facilitate the process but can also disguise injury, encouraging performers to continue filming past the body's limits. Lubricant helps, but it can be difficult to stop a scene to reapply, and only the most conscientious directors stock a variety of lubricants from which performers can choose. Employers have little incentive to provide such safeguards because they do not pay the costs associated with workplace injury.

A minority of employers in straight mainstream production allow condom use on set. Condom use was once standard on gay sets but is increasingly uneven. Performers have varied perspectives about on-set condom use, and these should not be confused with their perspectives on the appropriateness of mandatory condom legislation. Interviewees were, by and large, confident in industry norms' ability to reduce the risks of HIV, hepatitis C, and syphilis, the STI risks that most concerned them. Many regard chlamydia, gonorrhea, herpes, and the human papilloma virus as risks that are not inevitable but that they might reasonably expect at some point in their careers (indeed, these STIs are common among sexually active adults, paid or otherwise). I did not ask performers to disclose their STI status. Some volunteered that they had contracted infections but did not know whether they were exposed at work or in their private lives; others identified that they were exposed at work; and still others told me they had worked for years in the industry without incident. The latter case was more common among workers who work on condom-only shoots, those who work only in "girl-girl" scenes, and those who shoot BDSM and queer porn, in which insertive sex is less common and fluid exchange is often minimized.

Physical labor is not the whole story of porn work, nor is the physical labor of porn reducible to its potential risks. As we have seen, porn's emotional and physical labors cannot be easily parsed out. Porn is, as Christopher Daniels told us, a "physical act that affects you emotionally."[67] But workers are not passively affected; they also act on porn work's conditions in countless ways—from calibrating emotional connection to executing reverse cowgirl just so. Then the scene wraps, and workers go home. But first, they get paid.

Now we return to the set I described earlier, where the more seasoned performer was perturbed by her newbie partner's interest in cuddling after the scene. She was, you might recall, anxious to get done. She had other things to do, not least hang out with her dog. We waited for the director to distribute checks, but he was busy chatting and setting up for the next scene. The checks arrived an hour later, but this performer's check was $200 less than her agent had told her to expect. Not wanting to alienate the director, she was in the uncomfortable position of having to call her agent to clear things up. The agent then called the director, who grumpily paid the performer the agreed-upon amount, later telling me that her performance was not worth the rate. I do not know whether the miscalculation was deliberate, but performers did talk about such discrepancies as an ongoing problem. A key reason they maintain agents' services is so that they can rely on someone else to resolve rate disputes.

Ela Darling explained, "When you're on set, you're fucking, so anything that takes you out of the sexy mind-set, when you have to be angry business girl, [means] I don't have the same chemistry. It's hard to go from that mind-set to a scene."[68] Performers who find that this character shift makes their jobs harder often prefer to work with agents, who can, as Darling put it, "be the asshole for you." Such interactions are gendered on multiple levels. Women are called upon to perform normative femininity not only in front of the camera but also behind the scenes in their interactions with management. Darling explained that having an agent—the vast majority of whom are men—say no for you can make it easier to sustain that performance.

When performers work with agents, agents also handle rate negotiation during the casting process. Performers who work independently do their own negotiating and enforcing of the agreed-upon terms. They must proceed delicately, but seasoned performers often find ways to get their rate without compromising their rapport with management. In both cases, production studios set the terms for how performers are paid. Some pay same day, while others mail checks to agents or directly to performers who work independently. Performers prefer same-day pay because crooked agents sometimes withhold pay or use it to pay down inflated debts. And studios may delay sending checks or, in some cases, not pay at all. Performers can sue for unpaid wages but must take on the associated legal costs, risks to privacy, and potential damage to their reputation.

As in other jobs, most porn managers hope to extract as much labor from workers for the lowest possible pay. "We do try to lowball [performers], but I think everybody does," one celebrated director told me.[69] She was not a particularly bad boss—performers actually said they liked working for her—but this is just how business works. If porn employers pay the lowest possible rates, the social world in which porn is produced shapes which workers can be most effectively "lowballed." Porn is one of any number of industries in which "surplus value depends on cultural value," as theorist Rosemary Hennessy puts it in a broader context.[70]

As is always the case with matters attributed to the free market, decisions about whose labor is worth how much are deeply political. Porn's standard pay rates are structured by normative ideas about sexuality. At the most basic level, rates are organized around the idea that non-Black cis women need cajoling to agree to sex, whereas Black cis women and cis men in general are always already available for it. This is the explicit rationale workers and managers presented when I asked why most cis women are paid more than cis men in the straight mainstream industry. Performer-director Dave Pounder explained gendered rate differentials this way:

> Most guys want to do porn. Most girls don't want to do porn. If you find someone who's willing, the only reason they want to do it is because they're getting paid. If you pay the guys half of what you pay the girls, they're still gonna want to do it. . . . In order to have a working male talent pool, you have to pay enough for them to make an exclusive living out of it. And I don't want to lowball guys. If I get a crappy guy who can't perform—I paid the location, I paid for the girl, if he climaxes in two minutes, I have to shoot all over again. If I tell a girl it's twenty dollars for a shoot, nobody will shoot for me. If I tell a guy its twenty dollars for a shoot, he'll do it but he'll fail.[71]

Managers use these ideas to push rates down. As Mr. Marcus explained, "Everyone has this little thing they like to poke you with. Like 'I know guys who will do it for free, I know guys who will do it for cheaper.' Girls won't do it for free, but they might do it for less."[72] Several lower-end director-producers said they did not need to pay male performers at all—amateur men would perform for free for the opportunity to have sex with a "porn star." Sex work tourism can be a kind of scabbing.

Entrenched codes in the broader sexual economy that mark Black workers as "hypersexual," available, and cheap rationalize racialized pay inequality.[73] In straight porn, racist pay disparity is most pronounced among women. Men's rates in straight productions are so low in general that producers have less room to enforce racial disparity. A scene rate would barely cover gas money if Black men's wages were cut in proportion to Black women's. Black women's average wages fall $200–$400 below those of their white counterparts. The Black men I interviewed happened to be among the top paid in the industry, due to their long tenures in the industry, strong fan bases, and, perhaps most important for rate determination, status as one of few Black performers white women agree to work with. Mr. Marcus worked with "a lot of girls who wouldn't normally have sex with a Black guy, but for some reason, I'd get picked," he said.[74] Interviewees acknowledged they were among the token few and that this afforded them casting opportunities in mainstream "interracial" productions, which pay significantly more. They were also more likely than other performers to start their own production companies, affording more control over their own rates as well as (sometimes) the rates they pay performers who work for them.

Porn managers leverage racial and sexual hierarchies to get as much from workers for as little as possible. They insisted that paying Black performers less was not a reflection of their own racism—it was profit motive, not prejudice, that drove these hierarchies. This was true even for Lexington Steele, a Black performer, producer, and director who was sharply critical of racism in the industry. "At the executive level," he said, "there's one predominant color. It ain't white, it ain't Black—it's green."[75] But markets are always already racialized. Racism is not an external system managers use to get more for less. Instead, as theorist Cedric Robinson elaborates in his theory of "racial capitalism," racism and capital accumulation have been bound up from the start.[76] Racial capitalism shapes workers' uneven experiences of waged work at every turn.

Alongside gendered and racialized pay differentials, the presence or absence of penile penetration is the central measure by which pay rates are determined. Pay, Kink.com CEO Peter Ackworth explained, is "determined by how many cocks are involved. There's a base and then an extra $200 for each extra man."[77] "Girl-girl" scenes pay less (even when they involve penetration by hands or sex toys) because, as Ana Foxxx put it, "they don't have a penis."[78] Here, the industry mirrors wider cultural perceptions about sexuality, including the idea that the presence of a penis is what makes sex *sex*. It is standard to add between $100 and $200 to a receptive partner's scene rate for each additional partner with a penis in group sex scenes and an additional fee for "double penetration" scenes involving two partners with a penis at once. Cis men and trans women working as insertive partners ("tops") do not typically receive an additional fee for such scenes, even though such scenes mean additional work—longer wait times on set, more bodies and personalities to contend with, and more potential STI risk.

Finally, women can charge additional fees for their first scene of a certain type as they move up the hierarchy of penile penetration. A first straight (for performers who have only shot "girl-girl"), anal, or group sex scene could garner fees upward of two times the standard rate. It is standard for non-Black women to wait to film scenes with Black men so that they can charge a premium for their first "interracial" scene. Others refuse such scenes entirely. Some non-Black performers who refuse to shoot with Black partners say their agents are responsible, and indeed some agents told me they disallow "interracial" work in order to maintain what they see is a valuable fan market of racist consumers. But many non-Black performers believe that "interracial" work will undermine their market value, and they adopt discriminatory practices on their own terms. There is no data to suggest "interracial" work has this effect—like many ideas about porn's markets, it is received knowledge purveyors cannot easily trace. Porn's racist hierarchies are not fixed but rather remade, often by workers themselves, every day. Here, non-Black workers' strategies for maintaining autonomy and commanding the highest pay directly undermine Black coworkers' claims for income and career mobility. In this, porn work fits within a long history in which white workers (and those included in whiteness's unevenly expanded boundaries) have sought class power on explicitly racist terms.[79]

But porn work is also sex, so questions about racist discrimination among performers cannot be so easily reduced to an analogy of factory workers' hate strikes against integration. Some non-Black performers who refuse "interracial" work told me they do so because they are simply "not attracted" to Black partners. Also at stake, then, is how we talk about consent when desire is constructed by histories of racial capitalism. Philosopher Amia Srinivasan parses this tension in the broader context and argues against a liberal feminist "naturalisation of sexual preference."[80] The point is to suggest not that one should have sex they do not desire, she says, but rather that we have to do more to ask how desire gets formed in the first place. Asking these questions in the porn work context means holding together matters of erotic preference and material self-interest and acknowledging that both are products of racial capitalism.

Wide disparities in porn pay are maintained because capital benefits from hierarchy among workers, and workers who stand to gain from their relatively higher position hope to preserve that privilege. Indeed, when higher-paid non-Black, thin, cis women performers talked about rates, they described higher pay in terms of hard-won star power and negotiation skills, not relative social privilege. This is also true of size-based hierarchies. April Flores, who performs in BBW, queer, and feminist productions, talked about getting paid lower rates as a BBW performer (she did not describe racialized pay disparity as a non-Black Latina). I asked whether standardizing rates could help address wage inequality. She said, "That's a really good idea, yeah . . . but people wouldn't be comfortable with that. Someone who's super well known would say, 'Well, why is this person who doesn't deserve my rate getting that?'"[81] Here again, vexed solidarities trouble the task of coming together to improve conditions.

Porn's location in the creative sector further complicates a call for standardization. Porn is art, Flores reminded me, and the art market resists standardization. "I know a lot of people don't see porn as art, but it is," she said. "In the creative world, price is always fluctuating. There's not a standard payment. . . . When you're creating something like a painting or a sculpture or a film with sex . . . the value is determined by whatever someone will pay. Standardizing in theory sounds great, but I don't think it will work." The distinction between these cases for me is that the painter or sculptor owns the final product—if a sculpture explodes on the market, the creator wins the spoils. This is not true when porn performers work for a wage, but Flores is not alone in likening porn performance to creative labors in which ownership rules differ. Performers who view porn as simply a job are more likely to support the idea of rate standardization. But for those for whom performance is art and expression, the vicissitudes of art markets, and hence porn pay, are part of the bargain. And as we learned, part of porn's appeal is exactly its distance from feeling like just a job.

Of the various topics we discussed, wages were the only thing interviewees were consistently unwilling to go on record about. Surprised when Conner Habib readily volunteered information about his rates, I mentioned this to him: "I suppose it's rude to ask someone you have just met what they make, but rates seem even more secretive in porn." "I don't think it's rude. I wish it weren't rude," Habib responded.[82] It is funny, he said, that "people who got over the sex thing still won't talk about money." Indeed, there is a striking gap between the ease with which porn workers discuss issues most outsiders would think of as far more sensitive and many workers' refusal to discuss money at all.

This silence applies not only to on-record interviews with those outside the community but also to conversations among workers. There are exceptions of course: performers who are close friends may discuss rates with each other, and it is not uncommon for more experienced performers to tell newcomers that they are working for too little. Everyone has a stake in this, as established performers are concerned about newcomers undercutting them. But standard practice is that workers simply do not discuss pay rates and directors actively conceal them on set. Across industries, secrecy around pay rates serves as a ballast for wage inequality. Employers know this and prohibit workers from sharing information about wages.[83] Some porn employers include nondisclosure agreements in modeling releases and threaten performers with retaliation should they discuss rates, but more commonly, a culture of nondisclosure simply discourages these conversations. Such codes did not, however, stop workers from sharing information about pay rates with me so long as I anonymized what they shared.

Performers are aware of pay disparity in spite of employers' efforts to obscure it. More to the point, performers who are paid lower-than-standard rates due to race, size, age, and appearance are keenly aware of that fact, while performers who make top rates in their gender and genre categories often assume that wages are generally equal. To my question about wage disparity, one white woman responded, "I don't know, I'm not Black."[84] Black performers may come to work an "interracial" set, then, knowing that they are being paid less for the same job, even in comparison to the performers they will be working with that day. As Ana Foxxx put it, "We're doing the same thing. We're both gonna suck a dick."[85] Black men described the additional emotional work required to perform with white women they knew were charging higher rates for scenes with Black partners. Upon seeing his white screen partner's inflated "interracial" rate, Prince Yahshua remembered thinking, "Do you know how many scenes a Black girl would have to do to get this one check?"[86]

Some Black performers described getting paid less when working for big-budget mainstream (read: overwhelmingly white) companies. Some agents' refusals to represent Black workers (or to do so only very selectively) contribute to this problem, since agency workers tend to secure higher rates. But more common than Black workers receiving lower pay from big-budget companies is that this kind of work is simply not available to them. Instead, work is mainly available with smaller companies that specialize in "urban" or "interracial" content. Sinnamon Love described a significant pay cut when working for such productions: "Lower-budget, ethnically themed movies would only pay $400 or $500 for 'boy-girl' scenes, and at the same time, I'd go work for another company and they'd pay my standard rate of $1,000. . . . It's a budget issue."[87] Describing this differential, Foxxx said, "It'll be like a $400 decrease for the same exact thing, for the same act."[88] One of the few Black women to be cast in big-budget feature films, she talked about their overwhelming whiteness: "Every time I've been on a cool set like that," she said, "I've been the only one." When better-paying companies hire Black performers much less frequently, hiring discrimination is directly responsible for porn's racial pay gap.

Performer name recognition, saleable appearance, and reputation among managers and other performers also help determine where a performer falls in rate ranges. More and more, directors hire according to name search and download algorithms, and a performer whose fans tend to pay can bargain up her rates. Performers also make tactical decisions about rates according to their own analysis of the market. "If you're working too much, raise your rate. If you're not getting enough work, lower your rate," explained Charity Bangs.[89] But again, entrenched hierarchies often prevail, and even very popular Black performers are at a disadvantage in rate negotiations. This gives lie to managers' line that they pay according to expected revenues—"interracial" scenes' consistent popularity does not translate into better pay for workers.

The highest-paid cis woman I interviewed—a white woman in her late twenties—charges $1,500 for a standard "boy-girl" scene, in contrast to the $500 the lowest-paid cis women—a Black woman in her midforties—reported. Top cis men performers of all races and ages reported rates of $1,600 per straight scene, while others (mostly older white men) work without pay simply for the opportunity to have sex with a porn star. The highest paid man in gay productions can command $5,000 per scene, while others make only $600. Increasingly rare contract performers have the highest standard scene rates, though their salary also includes a host of mandatory unpaid activities, such as guest appearances and public signings. One woman on contract in straight mainstream porn made $3,000 per scene, while a gay production company's contract guaranteed $2,500–$5,000 depending on the scene.

Standard rates outside mainstream vary but are generally lower. Queer and feminist productions pay flat rates—equal among all performers and

Table 1. Average pay rate range in mainstream porn production

PERFORMER DEMOGRAPHIC	SCENE TYPE	RATE
Women (cis and trans)	Penile-vaginal intercourse (receptive partner)	$800–$1,000
	Penile-anal intercourse (insertive partner)	$800–$1,000
	Penile-anal intercourse (receptive partner)	$1,000–$1,200
	Sex with another cis woman ("girl-girl")	$600–$800
	Blow job	$250–$500
	Solo masturbation	$300–$500
	Additional partner	Add $100–$200 to above rates
Cis men*	Penile-vaginal or penile-anal intercourse, straight production	$300–$600
	Penile-anal intercourse (receptive or insertive), gay production	$800–$1 200
	Blow job	$200–$400

Performers who are out as trans men and genderqueer people typically work only in feminist and queer porn, which share a flat rate structure.

independent of the sex acts in which performers engage—of $200–$600 per scene. Directors in queer and feminist porn voiced hopes that flat rates help combat mainstream's pay hierarchies and establish more meaningful consent practices, as performers would not be compelled to have a kind of sex with which they are not comfortable simply for the money. But some workers prefer higher pay to bosses making this choice on their behalf, especially since the cost of equalizing pay is lowering everyone's rate.

Flat rates may be more attractive to new performers and those who are unlikely to be cast in mainstream productions, but they can mean a significant pay cut for workers accustomed to making much more for similar labors elsewhere. As Maxine Holloway, who performs in BDSM as well as queer, feminist, and mainstream productions, suggests, the idea that flat rates promote meaningful consent and equality among performers is a "nice theory, but it's not as if it's coming from a place of their being able to offer that extra money anyway. It probably means I'm just not going to do anal, because that's not my valuation. . . . So the flat rate is I think more derived from budgetary needs than equalization."[90] Such productions are ultimately for-profit enterprises—how *much* profit we do not know because, as in mainstream production, producers and directors in queer and feminist productions are not forthcoming about their profits.

Amateur-scene distribution companies typically pay for filmed scenes rather than particular performances. "Submitters," as distribution companies term them, are paid $200–$700 for an entire scene to be distributed among the submitters as they choose. Submitters do not necessarily think of themselves as workers, and some strategically distance themselves from anti-sex-work stigma. Self-identified amateur performers Fifi and Edwin, an off-screen couple as well, explicitly disavowed the idea that they were working. "What we try to do is get paid for living our life," Edwin explained.[91] These labors are still of interest to a study of porn work, though, because distributors extract profits from them. And Fifi and Edwin saw their efforts as work-like enough to respond to a call for participants in this study. In amateur, queer, and feminist porn (and, to a lesser extent, mainstream), the expectation that good performers do paid sex for reasons other than pay can complicate rate negotiations. Workers negotiate in the context of broader ideas about what forms of consent count.

SEX AND MONEY

Porn workers' critiques reveal the limits of the discourse of enthusiastic consent, the liberal feminist idea that the only good sex is "enthusiastic, deliberative, hotly desired, and/or engaged in *for its own sake*."[92] The idea that sex must be "for its own sake" sets up paid sex (and the various other encounters in which people say yes for a range of reasons) as the wrong kind of sex and thus sets up sex workers as the wrong kind of sexual subjects. Sex can be instrumental, tedious, and even physically uncomfortable and still consensual. And workers find countless ways to mitigate the strains of instrumental, tedious, or uncomfortable sex. Pretending that this is not so makes it harder for workers to claim the boundary most say does matter—not between "hotly desired" and instrumental sex but between negotiated encounters that meet their needs and those that cause harm.[93] It also ignores that all parties in paid sex (and indeed in most sexual encounters) wield some forms of power—the wage runs up against star power; the threat of replacement confronts the possibility that performers could walk at any time, leaving producers with a lost day's production costs.

Over the course of our interviews, porn workers were careful to mark the distinction between desire and consent. "There's what performers themselves want to do and don't want to do, and there's no question there, among performers at least," explained Richie Calhoun.[94] As we have seen, this is usually true. "But then," he went on, "there's always some limitation, whether it's that you have to be slow or that you have to keep this angle or that you have to do these four positions or that you have to not do anything wild." This last piece is significant—sometimes porn sex leaves less space for enthusiastic desire not because it is too rough, as outsiders often assume, but because it is too tame. Thus, performer Siouxsie Q writes about wanting rough sex on a feminist porn set. The director discouraged it in order to appeal to an imagined feminist audience. This was fine with her. "Performing in porn is a job," she wrote, "and I certainly don't need every scene to be the hottest event of my life."[95] There are products to be made, and performers are working. This is not sex "for its own sake," and most workers say they are okay with that. "Enthusiastic consent" cannot accommodate this reality, and so it establishes new forms of erasure even as it does important work in breaking down others.

When sex workers appropriate dichotomous ways of talking about consent in order to counter outsiders' claims that all sex work is non-consensual, they risk hardening a binary that was not written by or for working people in the first place. Class-and-race-privileged sex workers' efforts to draw a hard line between their consensual work and others' non-consensual work, writes sex worker theorist femi babylon "might protect sex workers who are actually sex workers by choice, it does not protect the rest of us who fall into that murky gray area in between."[96] A dialectical account of workplace consent is most interested in that murky gray area.

Porn workers intervene in a broader conversation about what it means to consent to do any kind of work. Maxine Holloway put it this way: "Consent is the most explicit with lists and everything like that in BDSM porn. . . . But I think a lot of responsibility is put on the performer to know their safe word, know their boundaries, to be in control. Which is important. But understanding the position of power that the director and the company have is important too; you're the one with the money, you have the ability to rehire, give this person a good referral, or not."[97] The dynamics of the wage relation shape what consent means in practice. This is not, of course, unique to porn or other sexual labor. If, as jessica drake suggests, "talent these days are a bit more malleable than we were back then," this is true of all workers facing the pressures of a precarious labor market. The "silent compulsion of economic relations" constrains consent across all sorts of work (including unpaid sexual work).[98] Abstracted visions of consent ignore this at their peril and ours, underestimating sex workers' autonomy at the same time as they overestimate autonomous consent in other areas of (non-sex) work and (unpaid) sex.

And yet, an analysis that suggests that money is the only, or even primary, force shaping porn's politics of consent would also be missing something. Workers make calculations about what they are willing to do based not only on material concerns but also on their own sexual desires and wants to "do a good job" and "be a team player." Work ethics are also informed by sex ethics, such that being up for most anything and genuinely aroused during scenes means not only that one is a good worker but also that one is a good sexual subject—open-minded, adventurous, enthusiastic. These factors bleed into one another—there are no neat distinctions to be made between what one desires and the origins of that desire. Most sexual encounters (paid or otherwise) are not purely "for their own sake," and so a model of consent that sets this up as the gold standard will obscure more than it reveals.

Again, such a model is also out of step with workers' priorities. Thus, sex worker activist Jolene Parton makes clear that "as long as a sex worker is getting paid fairly for their non-coerced work, I don't care about enjoyment."[99] And sex work scholar Chi Adanna Mgbako reminds us that the question of whether sex workers enjoy sex at work reflects non–sex workers' assumptions, "not sex workers' economic priorities. It is also a question we seldom ask regarding the labor of other workers."[100] It is a question we should ask of other workers. The answer would reveal much about the incompatibility of enthusiasm with most work. And yet, we labor at a moment in which workers are expected to demonstrate enthusiasm in the face of diminishing returns. This is as true outside porn as it is on the set shop floor.

In key ways, the process of doing porn work—the tedium, the moments of solidarity and connection with coworkers, the tired bodies—is not all that different from that of doing other labors. The story behind a signed porn contract is, however, quite unlike the story of saying yes to most straight jobs. When I was working as an adjunct, I told a performer friend that my class sizes had gone up 50 percent with no discussion and no change in pay. She told me to refuse and responded pityingly when I explained that this would get me fired. There are more contingent academics than there are people who can successfully carry out a double anal scene, and I could not strike out on my own direct-to-consumer hustle, I said. Then, she joked about the mutiny that would ensue if a director added so much as an extra partner to a scene without renegotiation. Porno dialectics highlight these relations and reveal the set as a space of contest.

2

I Was in Love!
And Then It Was Over

Authenticity Work

Fans asked her again and again whether what they see in porn is real, so Sovereign Syre recorded a video with her answer. In "The Porn Performer as Quantum Mechanic" she explains, "Everything about [porn] is false—the scripts, the performers, the setting. And yet, you're expected to sort of generate an authentic experience."[1] "The demand on the performer is very real," she says, "to give a very personal part of themselves." Here, the usual rules of acting are inverted: "A bad performer is actually a good performer, in the sense that they're actually able to simulate these experiences very well." Occupying two realities in this way is a kind of quantum mechanics, says Syre.

Porn workers confront managers' and fans' desires for authentically invested workers and scenes that look real. The call for workers to "give a very personal part of themselves," as Syre puts it, also positions porn work at the center of a moment in late capitalism in which all sorts of workers are called to "do what you love."[2] Porn workers' encounters with this demand are intensified because the specter of sex work gives "do what you love" discourse its teeth—working instrumentally is "prostituting oneself." Meanwhile, actual sex workers are exposed to the combined forces of stigma and outsiders' rescue fantasies. Porn workers labor at the tangled nexus of these realities, and their approaches to the question of authenticity reflect this. Is work in which we can—or are urged to be—authentically ourselves better work?

Labor scholars warn that workers' desire for work that feels less like work is intensely vulnerable to co-optation. In creative labor especially, capital cynically appropriates workers' "sincere (even, perhaps, romantic) attempts to make a life at some distance from the demands of work" and in so doing compels "an ever more frantic psychic investment" from workers, write Nicholas Ridout and Rebecca Schneider.[3] In porn work this manifests as attempts to create filmed sex at some distance from routinized performance. Authentic pleasure creates that distance from straight work, which performers overwhelmingly frame as pleasureless. Managers do use this dynamic to extract more work for less; they frame authentic pleasure as a substitute for good pay and compel additional emotional labor of performers, who must demonstrate their personal investment in the work. But porn workers' demands for authenticity in their own work cannot be dismissed as romantic, manipulatable attachments. Employers want authenticity from workers, and workers demand authenticity in ways that both meet this expectation and resist its terms.

This chapter traces where authenticity demands come from, how they shape the porn work process, and how workers navigate them. I focus on authenticity as a performance of "wanting to be there" emphatically, not "just for the money." I do not guess at whether pornographic representations or performances are indeed authentic, nor am I in search of a true authenticity against which other forms can be understood as copies. Sarah Banet-Weiser's pioneering work on the mainstream market for authenticity makes clear that efforts to search for a real beneath the artifice tend to feed right back into the market.[4] Authenticity is a social construct, and as Richard Peterson concludes in the context of music labor, it takes "authenticity work" to maintain.[5] Authenticity work is, as Brooke Erin Duffy's research on blog labor makes clear, intensely relational—self-expression and branding cannot be neatly parsed.[6] Authenticity pays, and workers in a range of jobs learn to navigate its demands. Cultural attachments to authentic sex are, however, more burdened than those to authentic sound and fashion blogging.

THE MARKET FOR AUTHENTICITY

Fans ask Syre if her porn is real because many seek realness in the scenes they consume. Indeed, the promise of realness is foundational to the pornographic medium. What sets hard-core apart from soft-core is that "hardcore porn insists on its status as presentation—that the acts shown are also done 'for real,'" writes Susanna Paasonen.[7] At the same time, porn's reputation for artificiality is in some ways well earned, and the medium maintains an "awkward balance between the hyperbolic and the documentary."[8] Negotiating that balance takes work, and it shows up on-screen.

Porn scholars have written extensively about how what Helen Hester calls the "appetite for authenticity" shapes porn's final product.[9] Per Linda Williams, we see this most basically in the expectation of an ejaculation shot and close-ups that show insertive sex is really happening.[10] Porn workers across genres talked about their encounters with authenticity demands, but the precise balance between hyperbole and documentary shifts according to genre. In mainstream, the aesthetics of authenticity shifted as amateur porn became increasingly popular in the late 1980s and professional producers came to mimic its visual cues.[11] Amateur porn's nonprofessional status is key to its look and marketing, and mainstream viewers would increasingly find rougher sound and image editing, a move away from heavily scripted scenes, and camera angles that position the viewer as a passive participant rather than a distant spectator. Feminist/queer porn might mark authenticity with visual cues that suggest bodies unvarnished (e.g., body hair or a wider variety of physical types) and sexualities unscripted (e.g., a range of gender expressions and a focus away from insertive sex). Across these genres, "real" porn's aesthetics are, writes Paasonen, "coded as truthful, authentic, and somehow less manufactured."[12]

Beyond its aesthetics, authenticity informs workplace relations the camera cannot capture. "Less manufactured" means less labored. Professional scriptwriters, camera crews, and film editors become unessential for the production of scenes that are amateurish by design. Veteran performers become more replaceable than ever when less seasoned performers will work for lower wages and present the added benefit of a fresh face (one who more plausibly can be seen to perform not as a career but perhaps on a lark). Veteran performers who had traded in their acting ability before the turn to amateur aesthetics said they were by the late 1980s confronted with a glut of competitors whose lack of acuity here no longer mattered. As feature-length films fell out of favor in the late 2000s, script-readiness would be further devalued. The preference among some producers for actual amateurs intensifies this dynamic—amateur performers in Kink. com's upper-floor parties, Melissa Gira Grant explains, "may be acting out

S&M sex they also enjoy at home, but on set, they are performing work that once commanded a fee."[13] We see similar trends in the mainstream new media sector's move to "shed regular jobs" in favor of volunteer labor and in journalism's growing preference for first-person narrative over traditional investigative reporting.[14] These shifts are profitable for employers not only because they answer to some consumers' aesthetic preferences but also because they can compel workers to do more for less.

Throughout the production process, those who retain their jobs must do the additional labor of performing authenticity—"wanting to be there" and not just for the money; being oneself; and engaging with coworkers in ways that are not straightforwardly performed. As Syre suggested at the opening of this chapter, a bad performer is in this sense a good worker. Managers make this clear—good performers are those who are not "working" in the traditional sense. A straight gonzo director-producer laid out recommendations for casting on a panel at the 2015 Adult Entertainment Expo: "It's great now . . . because you have social media, [so] you get an idea of the girls' personalities a little bit. Before you cast someone, you can tell a little bit about their psychological state. . . . How eager they are to do it. How motivated by money they are to do it as opposed to the fun aspect."[15]

In response, an audience member probed: "Is it better to hire people who are there for money or fun?" He replied: With a money-motivated performer, "you have someone who might not put in the best performance. They might not have a great attitude. They might be a little distant to the other talent. It might not work out as well as someone who's really eager to be there for the experience as opposed to the paycheck." On the same panel, a director-producer regarded for her work in "alt" porn concurred.[16] She added, "[In casting] when you do contact them, if the first thing they say is 'How much do I get paid?' we usually stop talking to them after that, because we've had experiences in the past. We know that [with] that kind of girl, there's going to be a problem somewhere down the line."[17] Performers who are focused on pay rather than "the experience" might not be so willing to adapt to unpredictable hours, the changing demands of a scene, and any number of other contingencies. Having a "good attitude" in this context means being happy to work how and for as long as management says it takes.

In this, porn managers align with corporate human resources experts. A 2012 human resources management study tracking 20,000 new corporate hires found that of the 46 percent who failed within a year and a half, 89 percent did so due to "attitudinal" reasons such as low levels of "coachability," "emotional intelligence," and "motivation" and poor "temperament," rather than lack of concrete skills.[18] These findings, taken from companies such as IBM, General Motors, and MasterCard, resonate with what porn directors told me they look for in a performer. More than the most conventionally attractive or gifted performer, they seek someone with a "good attitude" who, on- and off-camera, seems not to be there only for the check. In interviews with managers, I encountered much grousing about "divas," but no one complained that an actress lacked the agility to perform a certain sex position. Authenticity demands manage workers.

They also manage stigma. Sex work stigma and related anxieties around paying for sex—both traceable to anti-sex-worker feminist thought—give pure, noneconomic motivation its affective force. This is most obvious in feminist producers' narratives about production ethics. Feminist/queer productions frame authenticity as *the* feature that makes them an ethical alternative to porn's more artificial varieties.[19] In her *Feminist Porn Book* piece, "porn star, writer, social worker, performance artist, and self-professed gender and sexuality geek" Dylan Ryan describes authenticity's central role in feminist porn. As she and director Shine Louise Houston envisioned what would become the first film in the *Crash Pad Series*, "authenticity took on a somewhat mythological quality and became the Holy Grail in our vision of pornographic filmmaking: if we could achieve it, we truly would have transcended the existing constraints of the known porn world."[20] But feminist and mainstream porn integrate authenticity as a labor management and marketing strategy in strikingly similar ways, even as the language and aesthetics of authenticity manifest differently.

Anti-sex-worker feminist thought defines how these constraints are understood, and "ethical" porn sets itself up in direct response to this critique. Thus, Gail Dines describes porn as a "Multibillion-dollar Industry That Renders All Authentic Desire Plastic," and we see echoes of response in feminist pornographers' own narratives.[21] Dines points to a central tenet of anti-sex-worker feminism: authentic sexuality is antithetical to market-based sexuality, and the latter is a poor, "plastic" facsimile. Here, authentic sexuality is static and natural but, counterintuitively, also in need of careful guarding—if the right kinds of sex come so naturally to us, we would not need to be constantly reminded to perform them. Likewise, anti-sex-worker feminists argue that financial exchange negates consent—"money is a means of coercion in prostitution"—even when workers say otherwise.[22] Anti-sex-worker feminists have so successfully set the terms of debate that their assumptions about the value of authenticity—and the dangers of pay—populate the narratives of those who make porn. Though they disagree on what those constraints are, anti-sex-worker feminists agree with many porn managers (and some workers) that authentic sexuality can transcend the constraints of the "known porn world."

Feminist directors say that authenticity is what sets them apart from the mainstream. Feminist director-producer Madison Young, for instance, wants no part of mainstream porn in which, she says, "young women with crisp fake tans, long platinum blonde hair extensions, silicone breasts, and acrylic nails are fucking cocks that are artificially erect. They vocalize a performative sense of pleasure. . . . This assemblage of 'fast food' pornographic sex continues until the female performer is instructed to 'fake' an orgasm."[23] In stark contrast, she describes feminist porn as "creating space for the expression of authentic self in relation to our sexual desires [that] has the ability to radically change pornography." Framings such as this inform marketing—feminist directors advertise their scenes as ethical, and articles advise conscious consumers where they can watch porn they can feel good about.

This setup—feminist porn is authentic and therefore ethical, while mainstream is artificial and unethical—is striking for a few reasons. First, it accepts the antiporn premise that mainstream productions are abusive; in antiporn and ethical-porn arguments alike, mainstream performers become symbols in service of an argument rather than workers struggling (and sometimes winning) on their own terms. Performer and author Mikey Way put it this way: "For porn to have a feminist counterpart, that would imply something about it was inherently anti-feminist in the first place."[24] As media scholar Julie Levin Russo points out, the idea that there is such a thing as nonperformative sexuality also runs counter to the insights of queer and feminist critique from which ethical porn claims to draw its language and politics.[25] The premium on authenticity, writes performer and author Vex Ashley, "demonstrates a wider misconception that 'real sex' is not and cannot be performative."[26] Ashley poses another—queerer—approach: "Instead of rejecting fantasy and performance, it can be expanded; more voices, more ideas."[27] This has implications for porn texts but also for the work of making them.

Efforts to distance ethical from mainstream porn are also loaded with the politics of class. Way describes a feminist porn studio asking her to sign a form promising "that filming for them was just a hobby, not my job."[28] This is, literally, sex-worker-exclusionary feminism, and it explicitly targets poor and working-class performers. Alongside money-motivated performances, class-coded "fast-food" production and garish markers of feminine sexuality emerge as the most offensive features of mainstream production, and feminist porn becomes a respectable upmarket alternative.[29] As Constance Penley details, working-class aesthetics have long been a key feature of mainstream porn—indeed, they are part of what so irks its critics.[30] There is an echo of antiporn in feminist porn's efforts to distance itself from the trashy mainstream. And yet, mainstream directors share commitments to authenticity, even if they are sometimes more welcoming of a fake tan.

Mike South, a mainstream gonzo director, was proud to tell me about his selective casting process:

> I don't shoot anybody that I believe is doing it out of desperation, whether it's for drugs [or] a quick fix of a financial problem that's only going to be back in thirty or sixty days. . . . And then on the flip side, I had one girl who was from a very wealthy family here in Atlanta. She went to country clubs, she had a great job, and when I asked her why she wanted to do it, she said, "Because I'm a freak." That's more along the lines of the answer I'm looking for. I don't care if you're doing it for the money—that's part of it. That's understood. But what I'm looking to weed out is that whole desperation factor.[31]

South went on to explain what he does when an applicant does seem to want to get into porn out of economic desperation. "I'll look for other ways that I can help her. Maybe get her a job at the local video store or the local magazine. Whoever I know that might need a Girl Friday." South's concrete efforts to find alternatives were uncommon, but managers in a range of porn genres echoed his aversion to hiring women (men's and gender-nonconforming people's sexuality rarely needs guarding in these narratives) who need the work. Like anti-sex-worker feminists, many porn managers maintained the idea that economic motivation negates consent to do sex work. For some, this translated into the conviction that they—management—should arbitrate the correct reasons to do sex work. Zahra Stardust found a similar dynamic in her study of porn labor in the Australian context. Here, too, producers "gatekeep who can make the decision to use their body for work."[32]

If the premium on authentic sex is borrowed from anti-sex-worker feminist thought, so, too, is this eagerness to guess at working-class women's motivations for doing sex work and offer unsolicited alternatives. For anti-sex-worker feminists, these commitments have historically meant barring women's entry into sex work and offering in its place respectable work in factories or as domestics. Like retail work at a video store, the alternatives offered almost always require longer hours with lower pay. Often, they are the very same jobs workers left in favor of sex work; trafficking scholar Laura Agustín critiques the paternalism of this "helping" approach.[33] These same tendencies shape managers' efforts to help women by refusing them work. Among both sex workers' managers and their feminist helpers, an investment in non-market-driven sexuality informs the market for authenticity.

Consumers, too, might find authenticity a balm against the stigma associated with commercial sex. In the context of messages that sex workers are forced into their work at the hands of monstrous managers and consumers, there is an air of ethical consumption in seeking out authentic porn. The stigma of selling and buying sex is not quite as heavy when performers appear to be there "not just for the money" and viewers can imagine themselves as there not just for base titillation. Thus, if the market for authenticity reflects consumers' increased interest in "the interiority, multifacetedness, and behind-the-scenes lives of porn performers," as Feona Attwood puts it, I think we can understand this at least in part as a manifestation of consumers' discomfort with commercial sexuality.[34] This bears out in studies of porn consumption, where women in particular say their enjoyment is tied to their perceptions of a scene's authenticity.[35] But like anti-sex-worker "end demand" campaigns more broadly,[36] ending demand for professionally produced porn can degrade working conditions, require additional (and unpaid) labor of workers, and ensure management increased power and profit. Well-intentioned desires for porn products that evidence performers' real pleasure place heightened demands on the very workers they hope to "help." As Elizabeth Bernstein notes in the context of escort clients' interest in the "girlfriend experience," this is not unique to sex work—service work in general demands that the "market basis of the exchange" be "temporarily subordinated to the client's fantasy of authentic interpersonal connection."[37] What strikes me as particular to the porn work context is that clients, managers, and feminist commentators are convinced that they are doing workers a favor in demanding that subordination.

The ease with which porn managers integrate anti-sex-worker narratives into their labor management strategies underscores this point. Sometimes, helping sex workers even means paying them less. Adopting the narrative that sex for money is a problem, some porn managers posited less money as a solution. Farrell Timlake, owner of amateur-porn distributor Homegrown Video, explained:

> Our pay is a little lower than the typical producers are paying.
> . . . So, part of the intention of that is to really get the people that
> want to be doing it for the exhibitionist thrill. We definitely stay
> away from people that seem desperate about the money. . . . Part
> of our whole pitch is that it's got to be about the fun. That's really
> what we're looking for; it's got to be real emotion. Keeping that
> authenticity is all about getting that emotional connection of
> people that are really there for the *right reasons*.[38]

Likewise, feminist porn performer, director, and producer Courtney Trouble noted that, because feminist porn pays so much less than mainstream—$200–$400 in contrast to $800–$1,000 per scene—performers come to it for the right reasons: "People only apply to work for me if they really want to, which is kind of nice. I'm never concerned that somebody doesn't want to do porn but they're coming to me because they're desperate for $2,000. Even then, it's sex work, so that's what you do for $2,000, but there's a certain amount of ethics from the people creating the pornography, too, of taking advantage of sex workers."[39] For both Trouble and Timlake, lower-than-average pay helps allay concerns about consent and authenticity in commercial sex. It also saves companies money.

Porn is just one of the many late-capitalist workplaces in which the exhortation "Just be yourself!" functions as a managerial tool.[40] The dictate to be oneself at work is, as Kathi Weeks details, a cornerstone of the late-capitalist work ethic. Here, calls for committed self-identification with work take the place of duty-bound acquiescence to the fact of working to live.[41] Loving and identifying with what you do is in some ways a welcome reprieve from the alienation and boredom that characterize work's other affective regimes, but management's commitments to authenticity are inextricably tied up with the profit motive. "The emphasis on 'pleasure in work,'" as Angela McRobbie suggests, "can be a profoundly effective form of new disciplinarity."[42] In porn, discomfort with market-based sexuality merges with these late-capitalist management strategies to make porn a laboratory for the dictate to "do what you love."[43] Feminism's own limitations around class—what Brooke Beloso calls its "declassification"—help create feminist visions of authenticity that are easily absorbable by capital.[44]

At the same time, workers have their own reasons for desiring authenticity. Performers' hoped-for outcome from an individual gig extends beyond a day's pay and the promise of being hired again. A scene is also advertisement for the range of income-producing activities workers undertake. One may wish to withhold one's full effort from that day's employer, but a lackluster scene could be as damaging to the performer trying to draw customers to her various side hustles as it is to her boss. Self-entrepreneurship is a material reality here, rather than a disciplinary ruse.

Beyond this, real pleasure can be sustaining. In sex work as elsewhere, it makes work feel less like work. And authenticity claims can be a means of refusing anti-sex-worker stigma. In her study of webcamming, for instance, Angela Jones finds that models "claim sexual agency and reject emotional labor by emphasizing that their orgasms are authentic."[45] Here, too, Jones finds that authenticity claims can be a way of taking aim at alienation under capitalism. At the same time, claims of authenticity can also bolster status in the whorearchy—a phrase sex worker activists use to describe the "class system among sex workers"—by distinguishing oneself from sex workers who do sex work because they have bills to pay.[46] Porn workers navigate the politics of authenticity at the intersection of these forces. I did not ask interviewees whether they did porn because they needed money—it seemed obvious that most workers go to work because they have bills to pay—but they wanted me to know.

For many, it was important to make clear that they were not there just for the money. Stoya warned that too much focus on porn as a job like any other can obscure that "I only do my job when I love my job."[47] Having been involved with feminist and queer organizing during her undergraduate career, Siri said she entered the industry committed to combating the "hatred of women's sexuality."[48] "Having a job where I can be openly sexual is so freeing," she explained, "and then the fact that I'm getting paid to do it is just the cherry on top."[49] Nina Ha®tley described herself as a "sexual missionary" and, like many others, said that she was proud of porn's role in a movement for sex positivity.[50] Richie Calhoun talked about his decision to enter porn as a way to "get into that conversation" about sexual shame and push "that spot in our psychology."[51] And Raylene talked about the social value of porn, joking that sperm banks would be at a loss without it. "I do think that it really does help some people," she said more seriously.[52]

Performers who work in feminist porn were even more likely to point to such motivations. Chelsea Poe explained that, in contrast to the mainly financial motivations she ascribed to mainstream performers, queer performers are driven by a DIY "queer, punk ethic." "I think we do care about paying our bills and stuff, but it's such a punk ethic that's so much about our political beliefs. . . . Porn has no interest to me if I'm just sitting there contributing to something that I'm against. It's what makes it different than working at Starbucks. You're just paying someone else's bills and getting a cut."[53] In line with this perspective, Poe has been a vocal opponent of transmisogyny in porn, and she generally works for productions whose politics are in line with hers. The lines between DIY and mainstream blur, though, when DIY aesthetics come to be attached to the usual profit motive. Then, DIY porn *is* like working at Starbucks insofar as you are "paying someone else's bills and getting a cut." Stardust puts it this way: "When DIY porn becomes about profit-making . . . [it] no longer is anticapitalist; it becomes integral to capitalism."[54] This is the double bind of authenticity—a rejection of working just to pay someone else's bills can be put to the service of doing just that.

AUTHENTICITY AT AND AS WORK

The independence and "DIY" spirit that characterize feminist and amateur porn provide ample opportunity for workers to control the terms of their labor. In her *Feminist Porn Book* essay on the practice of directing and producing feminist pornography, Tristan Taormino notes, "The production must be a fair and ethical process and a positive working environment for everyone."[55] In the service of this goal, Taormino seeks to "empower the performers to show us what they want to do, to share a part of their sexuality with the camera," and she hopes that this will allow her to "capture some level of authenticity, a connection between partners, and sense that everyone's having a good time."[56] We can think of films produced with these priorities in mind as "organic, fair trade porn."[57] "Ethical" porn's focus on worker-driven production is an important intervention in mainstream's rigid gender, race, and sexual codes. True worker control also crucially resists the conditions in which workers are asked to perform in ways that bring physical or psychological distress. At the same time, it can function to ask workers to do more for less. "Sharing" one's sexuality can be more labor intensive than simply playing a part.

Labor scholars have long praised worker control over production processes as a means of improving both working conditions and workers' sense of autonomy.[58] This bears out in the porn context, but the particular demands of performing authenticity can also make it harder to negotiate pay, working conditions, and boundaries around working tasks and hours. Authentic investment is both a form of work in itself—the performance of "wanting to be there" is part of the job when managers want workers to come to set for the "fun aspect"—and can make it harder to negotiate other work terms. Performing authentic investment can also make for a longer day. Performer, producer, and director Joanna Angel explained how her sets are different from big-budget mainstream productions:

> My sets are kind of family-like. . . . *It's not just another day at*
> *work.* . . . I always say to people, "Hey, come at one o'clock, but
> you're probably going to be sitting around till four." We're not the
> most punctual of sets, because we tend to take a long time to shoot
> things because we're all joking around and hanging out. I try to
> make it feel like a summer camp. . . . I really do want the energy to
> be good and I want everyone to have fun. I used to have a camera
> guy that worked for me, and he was so militant about everything
> running a certain way and the quality being held at a certain
> standard. That didn't work out on our set because I want everyone
> to have fun.[59]

Here again, having fun at work is a job requirement, with joking around and hanging out as part of the relational work of porn. Like other manifestations of the "Have fun!" management approach, this can both improve the experience of working—who would prefer bad energy, after all?—and demand more of workers.

This is as true in the work of production as it is behind the scenes. When we spoke in 2014, Bella Vendetta was a thirteen-year veteran performer and director in the alt and BDSM genres. While she's an outspoken critic of low pay rates in feminist porn, Vendetta maintains that "there's a special magic to 'You guys do whatever you want and we'll film it.'"[60] She told me she does not usually take performing gigs in feminist porn because the rates are so low but signed on to shoot with a well-known feminist director because she felt passionate about the project. After paying her own travel expenses to get to the filming location and covering her own sexually transmitted infection testing costs, Vendetta arrived on a set that had autonomy in abundance: "I'm like, 'Oh, so you're not just hiring me for $400 to be a performer. I'm also styling, doing my own hair and makeup, and coming up with the content for the scene. Okay, I get it, so I'm really doing, like, four jobs. That's cool, but be up front about that.'" Offering another critique of producers who extract added labor under the guise of feminist authenticity, Mikey Way writes, "Fuck your feminist porn."[61] Describing a workday with a feminist porn company, Way writes, "This company gets everyone so worked up about them supposedly being an ethical alternative to mainstream porn that nobody notices that they're an international corporation paying next to nothing for people to style, shoot, produce, edit, and perform in their own work."[62] It is not so much that authentic scenes are less produced but that the labor of their production is both concealed and concentrated with performers.

This is also true for mainstream productions that prize authenticity. Alex Linko performs in, directs, and operates the camera—all at once—for gonzo scenes. He explained his understanding of management's rationale behind creating jobs like his: "If the cameraman and the male talent could be the same guy, that saves someone's salary. No sound guy anymore. All the sudden, these big crews that people were used to turned into two people, then one person."[63] Champions of corporate downsizing and lean production would no doubt recognize this strategy.

Not only do performers in feminist porn often do multiple jobs for the price of one, but, with the rare exception of the few directors who work for mainstream, big-budget production companies, that price is a fraction of what performers in other genres can expect. These productions, producers say, are far less lucrative than mainstream ones. But low profits are an excuse for low pay only if we subscribe to the romance of DIY entrepreneurship. The lessons from other culture industries suggest we should avoid this: Kit Smemo describes a "petit-bourgeois entrepreneurship" that covers up classed relations in hard-core punk music production.[64] The DIY entrepreneur is, he reminds us, still a boss. As Lynn Comella's history of the feminist sex-toy store movement reveals, self-styled ethical bosses are themselves deeply conflicted about how to reconcile transformative politics with the profit motive.[65]

Some porn performers flatly rejected the idea that they should absorb a boss's low profit margins and so opted against performing in low-paid "ethical" productions. "Queer porn pays $300, but they get away with it by saying it's 'art.' Whatever," said one mainstream performer who identifies as queer and a feminist but prefers not to perform in films marketed as

Authenticity Work

such.[66] She went on: "You know what? You want to make a porn business, pay me a fair rate. If you want to have a hobby, have a fucking hobby. If you want to make it your career, you need to respect that it's also my career. I can't have my career if you're not paying me a fair rate. They don't want to hear that." The directors who prefer not to work with performers who make their living from porn are, indeed, making a living from porn (or at least trying to). They overwhelmingly identify more as activist auteurs than as businesspeople, but porn pays the bills either way.

Mainstream performers were quick to point this out and often described feminist productions as at once the most pretentious and the worst paid. Performer-director Lily Cade put it this way: "I always thought I'd end up in queer porn. . . . But I ended up here, being LA's token lesbian. Rates are better here, working conditions are better, and we're not full of shit. In LA porn, people know that we're here to make a product."[67] Not all mainstream workers experience mainstream this way. In mainstream, too, the boundaries between expressing oneself and making a product blur, and this eases some strains as it creates new ones.

Genres are often self-selecting, and performers who work regularly in feminist porn were generally satisfied with its terms. They did not express the idea that bosses were cashing in on their performances. "You're getting what they can give you," Chelsea Poe told me. Overwhelmingly, workers here connected the low pay they received to the authenticity of their performances. Poe explained that she has "never had an issue with wanting to ask for more money" for feminist porn performances. "Mainstream is very much work," she said. "I've had fun shoots with them . . . but it's work, where it's about the shots more than just going and fucking . . . compared to queer porn, where it's all about 'We're just gonna set the cameras up and you guys are gonna fuck and whatever's the product is the product.'"[68] When I asked how she felt about the genre's rate structure, Siouxsie Q, an activist, writer, and performer in feminist, mainstream, and BDSM porn, explained, "You get to have this exciting sexual experience that for me—the part of myself that's an exhibitionist—it's very fulfilling in that way. When the camera is there, it is hotter for me. And then at the end of it, I get paid, too. I don't think that's a very sustainable model, and if we want feminist porn to move forward, I hope it's not always like that. But speaking from my experience, I've always felt great about how much I got paid."[69] Sometimes, authenticity does feel like less work.

Not long after our interview, Q published an article in which she wondered whether "'authentic' is just another genre of porn, like 'MILF' or 'casting couch' that places performers in a box for marketability."[70] Echoing fellow performer Arabelle Raphael's concern that the language of authenticity "erases the fact that performing is labor and not just 'fun,'" Q offers this challenge to queer and feminist producers: "I would like to see more emphasis placed on fair labor practices than on whether or not I have a 'real' orgasm." Porn work for Q is an exhibitionist pleasure for which pay is tertiary. At the same time, labor practices are more important to her than the (real or perceived) authenticity of that pleasure. Such both/ands populated my interviews. Workers representing various porn genres spoke about the authentic self-expression and pleasure they experienced on set and yet consistently critiqued discourses of authenticity around their work.

Workers and worker-managers acknowledge this contradiction. "It's hard in the indie, feminist, and queer scene," explained Maxine Holloway, "because there isn't a big budget, and I really am super behind a lot of the things politically and want to support feminist and queer and indie pornography. It would be really nice if we got paid a little better."[71] "But then," she added, "as someone who produces and directs, I get it. It's not easy to come up with those funds." She went on to describe her own process coproducing and performing in the "porn theater" performance group Cum and Glitter: "Being able to pay people as well as we could was really important to me. Not just giving people this stage for artistic expression and all these things that are important to us—I want to give people that, but I want them to be compensated and feel valued for their performance and their time." Holloway made a commitment to being straightforward about the show's funding and to dividing ticket sales evenly among all performers. "I think being very transparent with your finances, especially when there may or may not be a lot, is key," she explained. The show did well, and performers' pay was more than the typical queer porn rate. "I think it was a good feeling," Holloway said, "to have total creative control over your performance and really be doing something that you want to do and receive good payment." But this perspective—workers are entitled to creative control (authenticity, if you will) *and* good pay—was uncommon among interviewees in decision-making positions, even those who are also performers. No other directors told me they share profits evenly with performers. And many see autonomy and sex for pay, or being oneself and doing a job, as conflicting. Again, this sense places them closer to anti-sex-worker feminists than either community would like to recognize. When directors describe authenticity as a kind of supplementary payment, they also come to sound like nonprofit and creative-industry (not least academia) managers in the world of straight work.

And yet "authentic" feminist porn performance *is* often a different sort of work. Courtney Trouble suggests that, in contrast to mainstream porn, "you aren't really working as hard" in feminist productions: "It's still sex for money, but most of the time, there's no script, there's no formula, you don't have to do a soft-core version, then a hard-core version, you don't have a director telling you which sex positions to be in."[72] Feminist productions can also have fewer preparatory demands: "You're not going to have to get waxed, you're not going to have to get fake tits to work for me, there's so much money you're not spending as an independent contractor to do queer or feminist porn. You don't even have to shave your legs. You can just show up and be hirable, with no investment." Mainstream's conventions and work flows can indeed be labor intensive and tedious, and feminist and queer directors (especially those who also perform) have a real political commitment to forging alternatives. But autonomy as it exists in "less manufactured" productions can create new areas of strain as it alleviates others. Performers in unscripted, authentic porn labor on a different register, but most workers do not share the perception that they are "not really working as hard" in these contexts.

Authenticity has a particular look, and it takes work to achieve. Even the authentic orgasm becomes a visible site of good, ethical work. Self-styled ethical producers, writes Stardust, expect a "certain type of orgasmic performance," and porn professionalism requires orgasmic performances that model "being versatile, identifying what is needed to complete the job, and executing it convincingly."[73] Likewise, performer, director, and producer Gala Vanting writes about an unpaid training in "paradigm porn performance" required of performers who hope to work for a production company that boasts natural, unscripted, and amateur content.[74] One can be trained in the practice of realness.

Workers' calculations of wages and hours in different genres illustrate how hard it is to define what "working as hard" means. Because they typically aim to produce scenes that appear less manufactured, and because some directors are more mindful of performers' time, feminist productions tend to make for shorter workdays—"they have never been the type of people to keep you for twelve to fifteen hours," said Danny Wylde.[75] But when working conditions are part of the brand, modeling those positive conditions can mean more work. Working at authenticity means helping the viewer feel good about what they have seen. Feminist sets, Wylde explained, "have this process of 'Oh, we'll interview you, talk about it, go over everything, and then at the end we're gonna decompress.' And the process of the films seems very important to those producers. Because they want to make sure that everyone is okay with what they're doing and they also want to capture that on tape." Most performers appreciate this attention to consent both because it improves their own experience and models explicit consent to viewers. Sometimes, though, they simply want to shoot a scene and go home. Directors take more time to discuss consent not only for performers' benefit but also because this is part of the brand—they want to capture it on tape.

Sometimes, marketing narratives around explicit consent fail to reach performers on the ground. In 2018, a performer disclosed sexual assault on the set of a feminist porn studio that explicitly trades in its "ethical" production practices.[76] In response, Erika Lust, the studio owner, reaffirmed her commitment to consent practices on set and published a capacious "performer's bill of rights."[77] Performers "have the right to call off a scene at any moment,"[78] but ethical directors' imaged place outside the dirty power dynamics of mainstream can lead them to forget that feminist sets still have a boss, a check at stake, and social hierarchies that may constrain workers' comfort with exercising such a right. Likewise, in the postscene interview, some workers are reticent to discuss negative aspects of the work process directly after shooting a tiring scene, on film, and before they have been paid.

Feminist porn performers at once framed their porn work as an extension of their personal politics and desires and spoke about the strains of authenticity. Holloway described pleasure and sexual exploration as job benefits alongside more flexible hours and higher pay than she could find in other fields. She acknowledged, too, that the pleasurable, political, and artistic aspects of performance sometimes encouraged her to overextend.

> The first scenes I did were mostly for queer, indie, [and] feminist
> productions, so all about authenticity. So I brought it, I brought
> everything I had to these scenes. And it wasn't [until] about a year
> into it where I started to realize that I needed to set boundaries.
> I didn't really know where my porn began and my personal sex life
> ended. Which I think made for some really awesome experiences,
> amazing performances, but it wasn't until later that I realized
> I kind of needed to separate those things. Which I feel like has
> been good for sustainability of doing sex work.[79]

Her description of the emotional work required to maintain a self outside of work is a concern echoed by a range of workers in jobs that put the self to work.[80] Sex work scholarship already offers vibrant discussions about whether such boundary work is indeed necessary for workers.[81] My aim here is to show that, for workers who do desire such a boundary, authenticity can be experienced as a strain. This is as true in mainstream as it is in "ethical" alternatives.

Performers across porn genres describe authenticity as labored, even as many also resist an economistic understanding of their work. During the same conversation in which he gently pushed against my use of the term "porn work," Conner Habib described making a conscious choice to "go in and like it" on gay mainstream sets. Habib remembered making a similar decision while working at a bookstore: "There was a moment where I started hating my job, and I was like, 'Okay, there are two choices, aside from quitting. I can either be totally involved and try to make this store the best store in the world, or I can just not give a shit and just come and put my time in, and those will be my two ways of enjoying this.' [In porn] the people who check out when they come in are choosing the latter choice, which is fine."[82]

Choosing to "go in and like it" does not, however, require giving oneself totally to the work. In the same interview, Habib talked about the value of "creating a healthy detachment from your physical self." But, he added, this is "not just a 'survival strategy' like antiporn activists frame it. It can be that. But it's also a skill that can sometimes really give you something and even reframe sex work." Dialectics of detachment and investment trouble any neat boundaries among strategies for managing emotional labor. One can be "totally involved" *and* cultivate a "healthy detachment from [one's] physical self." Performers' emotion management strategies shift fluidly, changing throughout their careers and even during a given workday. Such flexibility is important in part because porn performers are called upon to perform on multiple levels: for the camera, for management, and for and with coworkers. Emotion management strategies function differently according to the context in which workers deploy them.

Realness here is multilayered. While producers may be satisfied with faking it for the camera—what might be understood in Arlie Hochschild's terms as "surface acting"—most performers pursue something that feels realer in their own practice and hope that coworkers will do the same.[83] The scenes performers talked about feeling most proud of and energized by were those in which they experienced a connection with their on-screen partners. This connection need not be based on sexual desire. Performers also describe camaraderie between friends and respect between colleagues as *real* connections that facilitate the work of performance.

Performers across genres suggest that manufacturing realness is easier when all screen partners are willing to participate. Refusing to do that work withholds labor from management but can also make work harder for coworkers. This is also true, of course, when workers in straight jobs withhold their labor—the comradely work resister has to carefully calculate how to shirk work duties without displacing them onto coworkers. But withholding effort in the sex work context has intensified stakes—it may be unpleasant to do straight work with withdrawn coworkers, but sex work with a disinterested partner can be straining or traumatic to a different degree. I asked Ela Darling, then a "girl-girl" performer, about her perspective on this. The reader may recall Darling's analysis, featured in chapter 1, that convincing one's partner of one's attraction, rather than the attraction itself, is what is most important. She went on: "What bugs me is when, before the scene, a girl is like, 'I never have a real orgasm, I always fake my orgasms.' . . . I'm a professional. . . . If you can't come on-camera, I understand, but if you're gonna fake it anyway, I don't need to know beforehand. . . . We're trying to reach a goal together."[84] Where the relational work of performance is concerned, the pretense of true authenticity is less at issue than coworkers' willingness to fake realness in the spirit of generosity.

On sets, I saw screen partners helping each other become emotionally and physically ready to perform, trading notes on each other's sexual preferences, flirting, and touching one another. These exchanges are gendered—cis women tend to do more of the work of helping partners maintain erections, for example—but performers of all genders manufacture authenticity together. These conversations often feel more friendly and playful than romantic and earnest, and performers suggest that this can be an asset. It might be friendly professionalism or comradely ethics, rather than a deep erotic connection, that animates a performer's interest in just how much clitoral pressure their partner enjoys. This kind of straightforward communication—a sort that partners in unpaid sex often struggle to achieve[85]—is possible because porn sex is work, not in spite of it. Conventional narratives around unpaid sex as organic and intuitive can make direct communication feel contrived. The contrived nature of most porn—indeed, its derided plasticity—means that on-screen partners are not limited by the pressure to maintain that illusion. The distinctions

Authenticity Work

between sex on set and off do not exist only in the negative. If bringing sex to the market introduces some limitations, it also alleviates others. Sometimes, straightforwardly commercial sex even feels better.

THE WORK OF INAUTHENTICITY

We know that mainstream scenes require a great deal of unpaid preparatory labor and, often, more physically strenuous performances. The physical work of a mainstream scene—hours of shooting in prescribed positions all while "opening up" for the camera—is different from the work one does on a feminist set, which commonly involves the partners, positions, and safer sex methods performers prefer. Mainstream scenes can also involve scenarios that run counter to performers' politics, ethics, or preferred self-presentations, less of a risk when performers are setting the terms of a scene.

While some performers care little about the final product so long as they get paid, most want to be part of projects they are proud of and which represent them and the communities with which they identify (and ally) respectfully. Importantly, workers' accounts do not line up with anti-sex-worker feminists' understandings of what makes a sex scene demeaning. Instead, workers told me they resisted faking orgasms, acting out cheating plots instead of ones featuring consensual polyamory, performing demeaning story lines, and using racist and transphobic epithets in scripted dialogue. Some refuse to perform in ways they find politically objectionable, but most cannot afford to turn down all such work. Instead, they develop ways of working within and against the conditions on offer.

Kelly Shibari talked about her frustrations with scenes in the BBW genre that caricature fat women. In one instance, she turned down work with a series called *Feed Her, Fuck Her* in which the scene called for her to order large amounts of what she called "unhealthy" food from a hotel's room service and have sex with the man who brought it to her room, eating all the while. From her perspective, the scene was "just more 'Oh, fat girls are fat because they eat a lot and they eat unhealthy food,'" not a representation she was comfortable being a part of.[86] Shibari, who also works as a successful publicist and draws royalties from novelty products marketed under her name, is among the performers whose access to diverse income streams allows them to sign on to film work selectively. Turning down work is a privilege not all performers have.

Eighteen-year industry veteran Lexington Steele talked about how he negotiates roles that require him to perform aggressive Black male sexuality:

> Very early in my association with adult, I knew that I fit what is called the "BBC" [big Black cock], I knew that I fit that mold. I chose to lean into the mold, make it my own, and change the stereotype and glorify in it. If you're going to be a bear, be a motherfucking grizzly. . . . So yeah, I've portrayed some roles in video where I was like, "Man, I really don't want to do or say this or be on the receiving end of this or that commentary," but maybe I decide to do it. . . . Do I understand that I facilitate the fantasy? Yeah! I completely glorify it and I base my whole brand upon it. But the important thing is, in taking the stereotype and embracing it, I'm now more able to change the mold.[87]

Steele, who majored in history and African American studies in college, spoke of being "very aware of what I deliver for what the market demands." "I fit a particular mold that existed before me and will exist after me," he said. "If you're not comfortable with the mold that you provide, you can either try to get into another slot, or you have to leave the business." Steele chose to "lean into the mold," refusing to be reduced to the trope by agentially inhabiting it.

As various porn scholars suggest, porn's narratives of female sexuality are more diverse than monolithic, but women still described demands to perform tired tropes of racialized femininity.[88] Ana Foxxx is unwilling to fully embrace the "mad Black chick" characters she is often called upon to perform. "That's not who I am," she said. But with limited alternative casting opportunities, she cannot reject all these roles either. Instead, "I just try to take the roles that want me to be that way and tweak them in my way, so that it's still me," she explained.[89] Here, workers' desires for authenticity cannot be reduced to the work ethic, and their insistence on "tweaking" roles to make them feel a bit more "me" might undermine bosses' power rather than entrench it. Cognizant of the simultaneous fetishization and devaluation of Black female sexuality, performers in Mireille Miller-Young's study of Black women in the porn industry deploy a similar strategy, what Miller-Young terms "putting hypersexuality to work."[90] This matters for textual analysis but also for taking porn workers at their word when they say that the performance of stereotype might mean something different to working people than it does to consumers or cultural critics.

As Jennifer Nash argues in her analysis of hard-core's "racial iconography," consumers and critics may read texts in various ways, too.[91]

Non-Black performers encounter a wider but still limited range of available representational molds. Tara Holiday, originally from Chile, talked about the fetishizing roles often available for Spanish speakers, but rather than as a burden, she described these as a "niche" that helped secure work—"people love that," she said.[92] As in media more broadly, the hypersexual Black woman's foil is the ditzy white one. People also love that, it seems, and white women talked about navigating that set of tropes both in their on-camera performances and behind the scenes. Lorelei Lee described her strategy for resolving disputes with directors: "If something went wrong or a director was just like, 'Well, I'm just gonna add another dude into the scene,' instead of being like, 'Fuck you, we can do math,' we were like [*here Lee's voice rose several octaves*], 'We're totally willing and excited to do everything all the time, I'm just gonna call [my agent] and make sure that's okay.' . . . I was like, '*I'm in this system; this is where I have power.*'"[93] Hard business dealings did not fit within the role Lee was hired to perform. Stepping out of the role of a submissive and sexually available woman who is "excited to do everything all the time" (and with no concern for pay) would have risked future bookings but also would have required the additional emotional work of shifting gears mid-workday. Instead, Lee maximized her power by pretending that she had none.

Such performances can be at once playful and labored, and porn workers describe both feeling put upon by managers who require them to perform emotionally straining, hackneyed, or politically troubling tropes and experiencing pleasure in subversive performances. This is, significantly, not the pleasure of a job well done in the classic sense of the work ethic but, rather, the pleasure of executing a power play in which being a savvy operator means mimicking the opposite. Performers' strategies here resonate with Danielle Egan's analysis of the "covert mimesis" erotic dancers in her study deploy, performing object status as a means of harnessing their power.[94]

Like the dancers in Egan's study, porn performers are acutely aware of their locations within economies of fantasy. But these locations are shifting and blurry in porn to an extent they are not in the world of erotic dance. Egan discusses the calculations dancers make, calibrating resistance in view of economic pressures such as the threat of termination and fines levied by management. Porn performers do weigh the risks of being denied casting opportunities and, in the rare event that they refuse to perform in a scene after first agreeing to do it, confronting fines from agents. Some performers who deploy "covert mimesis" as a resistive strategy do so simply to sustain themselves economically, but more common among the performers I interviewed was a matrix of motivations that included both a waged worker's economic need and an entrepreneur's desire to win market share and generate profit. In porn's gig economy, those priorities might be fused.

Profits, in addition to wages, are part of the calculus. Even for performers who worked at the time only as waged workers, top-down pressure from management is not the only force that pressures workers to perform physically and emotionally in ways they would not otherwise choose. Workers also answer to their own desires, as gig workers, to maintain their personal brands. The promise of pay (for a particular scene and in the gigs that might come after) balances these and other strains of inauthenticity, and workers have their own calculations about what makes a scene "worth it."

MONEY MATTERS

Contrary to anti-sex-worker feminists' and some managers' perceptions that money makes sex worse, many workers said that clearly defined and monetized performances help protect boundaries and stave off burnout. VJ is a retired performer who worked in atypically rough scenes. We know by now that the final product of a scene is not necessarily reflective of how workers experience making it—conditions on a hard-core BDSM set can be better than those on a romance one, for instance—but in this case, rough scenes did make for an exceptionally rough workday. The scenes "pushed [her] mentally and physically," and VJ turned the work of weathering that strain into a "game": "I figured out really quick that it was a mental game, if you could get past the so-called verbal abuse and physical abuse and push past that and understand that you signed up for this, to basically sell yourself for whatever period of time. . . . How do you play the game, how do you make it safe for you, how do you make the most money? It's all strategic."[95] Marking her performances as *performances* with a clear beginning and end and a defined price tag—expressly not "sharing sexuality with the camera"—made physically and emotionally straining work tenable.

Workers' experiences of effective emotion management strategies are closely tied to the extent to which they can leave set feeling that a

Authenticity Work

performance was worthwhile. Money matters. Performers describe experiencing the same work processes differently when they are differently monetized. Scene rates are closely tied to specific sex acts, so performances that are inappropriately valued (performing anal sex at the rate one expects for vaginal sex, partner sex for a solo rate, and so forth) can feel exploitative regardless of one's unpaid sexual preferences. Some performers told me they enjoy anal sex in their private lives, for example, but refuse to perform it on-screen unless they are compensated appropriately. When new performers ask her how to set scene rates, Sara Jay told me, "I always say, 'Close your eyes and think, "How much would it take for me to do that?" That's probably what your rate should be. If you do it for less than that, you're probably not going to feel good.'"[96] Maxine Holloway said, "Knowing your price and your value is something that's really important and helped me sustain my career."[97] When performers spoke about feeling "exploited" or "taken advantage of," it was in reference to being underpaid, not compelled to have sex in the ways some outsiders assume. What is more, a well-paid scene might actually *feel* better.

Performers describe higher scene rates as one factor that helps them feel good about the work they have done. Ana Foxxx waited to sign on to her first anal scene until she was able to command the fee she felt was reasonable: "It was $5,000 for the movie. I had two scenes. And I was excited. There was a company that wanted to shoot me, and I was like, 'Well, if I do it, man, it's my butthole on the screen. I want to walk away happy not just because I had good sex; *I want it to be worth it.*' And I'm still keeping to my same rate. It's harder work for me. It's not something I do all the time. I want it to still be special."[98] The $3,500 Foxxx charged for one anal scene is far above the standard rate of $1,200. She had been told as much by a number of directors and even some agents she consulted. That she is Black no doubt contributed to directors' and agents' initial refusal to take the rate seriously. Her insistence on a high rate is antiracist praxis in addition to savvy negotiating.

Payment shapes the experience of porn work. Some performers describe authentic pleasure as part of what makes work satisfying for them, but for Foxxx and others, payment makes a scene "worth it." Some even said money makes for better, more pleasurable sex. For Tara Holiday, payment brings not only work satisfaction but also a pleasure that eludes unpaid sex. Holiday, who began performing at forty-three, described her first porn shoot as transformative:

It wasn't until the moment I got paid that I got hooked. . . . The moment I got paid, in my inner being I felt, "This is the best thing sex has ever given me." Why? Because any other time I'd had sex, I either wasn't sure if I wanted to have it or I wanted the guy to go longer. It wasn't satisfactory, for many reasons. And at the end of the day, I always felt empty afterwards. This is perfect for a woman like me. I loved it. And I got hooked from then on. "Fuck, this is it," you know?[99]

Holiday flips on its head the narrative that paid sex brings feelings of emptiness or disconnection from one's "real identity and real self," as anti-sex-worker feminist Kathleen Barry puts it.[100] Instead, paid sex brings mutual benefit in a way unpaid sex rarely does. Writing about the workings of consent in the context of escorting, Charlotte Shane reminds that desires for cash are still desires: "I am enthusiastic about earning money," so sex work is "wanted sex" because it brings cash.[101]

From a perspective that views market sexuality as antithetical to authentic sexuality, the idea of money as "the best thing sex has ever given" would be decried as evidence of how market sexuality disconnects women from "real" pleasure. From managers' perspectives, money as the best thing one might expect from sex could be lamented as evidence of workers' lack of authentic investment in the job. Anti-sex-worker feminists and managers agree here. Both readings rest on the assumption that natural sexuality exists, a premise that social theorists have long critiqued as a mode of social control rather than a reality observed across time and place.[102] If there is any historical continuity, it is that sex has long been a central space of both social regulation and market activity.[103] Recalling that the marking of the intimate as discrete from the commercial operates precisely to obscure unpaid labor, we should be wary of any move to posit authentic sexuality as incompatible with the market. What is notable in the sex work context is that sexualized exchange is transparent. That transparency can, for some workers, mean more power to negotiate the terms of sex exchange and, as Holiday suggests, more control over what one takes away from a sexual encounter. This is not to suggest that commoditized relations neutralize power imbalance. Rather, all relations are commoditized, and those that are more straightforwardly so can be less extractive and taxing.

And so, while performers' on-scene emotional labor strategies vary, most describe self-conscious performance as a protective factor. This trend aligns with what sex work scholars in other contexts have documented as the ways self-aware, commoditized performance can reduce job strain.[104] In her study of middle-class sex workers in San Francisco, Elizabeth Bernstein identifies "bounded authenticity" as both a key emotion management strategy for workers and a central component of the services rendered to clients.[105] Bounded authenticity ranges from executing superficial performance to maintaining real, but circumscribed, intimacy with clients. Teela Sanders finds that British sex workers craft workplace sexual identities that enhance earnings by performing femininity in a manner that appeals simultaneously to customer demand *and* to emotional health by encouraging workers to put on a sort of performance that is clearly distinguishable from their nonwork selves.[106] Likewise, erotic dancers in Susan Dewey's study describe emotional labor similar to "surface acting": Diamond, a dancer, notes, "You have to keep smiling and pretending you're having a great time, but the minute you forget it's just business, you're really in for it."[107]

Many porn workers echo this sense and at the same time insist that sex work is not "just business." Sexual pleasure *can* make porn different from other jobs. Indeed, it can make porn feel less work-like. This is not a tension that can be resolved by marking two discrete groups (as most studies of emotional labor do) where some performers see porn as "just a job" and others strive toward authenticity. Some workers fit neatly into either camp, but most hold this tension in the same story.

PLEASURE AT WORK

Porn workers refuse any neat divisions between the real and the performed. They also suggest that realness can make performance easier, though not in the simple way many managers assume. "What worked for me as a sexual performer is that I'm basically a romantic," Herschel Savage told me when I asked how he sustained a thirty-nine-year career: "The time I was with a woman, assuming that we connected on some level, it was a romantic scene. I was in love! And then it was over. I never crossed that line. I could find beauty in anyone, especially women that didn't feel very attractive. I would make them feel beautiful. That meant something. And it meant something to me."[108]

Thinking about the work of falling in and out of love hundreds of times—Savage is credited with having performed in over 1,000 scenes—I offered, "That's such an incredible skill!" Savage responded, "I wouldn't think of using that word—it's who I am. I always try to make people feel good about themselves. But I believed it, I wasn't *just* performing." This approach worked—Savage proudly told me that women in the industry voted him most popular male performer to work with, and many women I spoke with who worked during the same period volunteered (unprompted) that he was a favorite costar. "That's important to me," Savage said. "I don't want to be with someone who's suffering to get the job done." That porn work is sex intensifies these dynamics; it was especially important to Savage that he not be in the position of having sex with women who did not want to have sex with him. But he also took aim at the drudgery inherent in a lot of jobs and said he wanted no part of it.

In the video that opens this chapter, Sovereign Syre disidentified with the language of work, because to her "work" signified "falsity."[109] Later, when I was a guest on her podcast, she said porn performance is "not work." "One part of me is performing, but it's still happening to my body. When I'm fucking on-camera, the sex is happening. My vagina is getting lubed, my Skene's gland is producing lubrication, my muscles are opening up and relaxing to accommodate a penis, my nipples are getting hard, my skin is getting flushed, my pulse is lifting, I'm sweating, my heart is beating faster, oxytocin is being released—all of that is real."[110] It is real and also a big part of the draw—a major departure from her previous work as a graduate student, a job that turned the writing she loved into a chore and required fending off an advisor's advances while also protecting his ego. Syre was proud of making a living doing something that did not require that kind of performance, and she wanted to be sure that stories about her job did not paper that over.

This says as much about straight work—and why many porn workers reject it—as it does about porn. One problem with work is indeed its "falsity," the way it alienates workers from their own bodies and relations with others. For Savage, "skill" is alienating in much the same way. Syre's and Savage's correctives speak to the trouble with trying to fit porn into a work language (and, as we will see, a legal architecture) that was built to exclude labors just like this—feminized, intimate, and at once real and false. To the extent that work and pleasure, performance and authenticity, get positioned as antithetical, these concepts cannot accommodate a job that is emphatically both work and sex that is happening, really.

On the backdrop of a discourse that sets up the real against the performed, terming Savage's ability to fall in and out of love at just the right time a "skill" cheapened the meaningful connections he had with coworkers. Trying to fit such connections into the existing language of waged work might help people get coverage if they sprain an ankle on set, but it does not tell a whole story. Beyond this, a job is, for many workers, something one suffers through, and it mattered to many interviewees that their sexual labor not be framed in this way. Sometimes, even with a bad contract, a long day on set, and the demand to open up for the camera, porn work also feels *authentically* good. Bodies respond, connections are forged, and orgasms are forthcoming. All of this matters for how workers experience their jobs. For some, it is part of what makes porn worthwhile even with its diminishing economic returns. As Shira Tarrant suggests, authenticity can become a kind of supplementary payment as porn's cash wages continue to shrink.[111] For others, money (and the sense of power it confers) enhances sexual pleasure. In both cases, pleasure is a working condition.

Some readers will see this as a matter of storytelling rather than experience—it makes sense for workers to resist narratives of their sexual labor that frame them as cogs or victims—but assume a disconnect between these stories and the day-to-day experience of making porn. But workers' "interpretive intervention[s]," as Juana María Rodríguez terms them in her analysis of porn star Vanessa del Rio's memoir, also shape the experience of actually doing the work.[112] When del Rio insists that, even with its racialized, gendered, and classed hierarchies, porn work was a source of pleasure, not injury, because "I would always find some way to be in on it," Rodríguez urges readers not to assume that they know better.[113]

For most workers, the "always" is murkier, and pleasure coexists with tedium, artifice, and, sometimes harm. During the same interview in which he pushed back on work-like language because it suggests "suffering," Savage suggested that there is plenty of suffering to be had in porn, too. Directors treated him like a disposable "piece of meat," he said, and blacklisted him for trying to organize a union. At sixty-two years old when we spoke, Savage was struggling to pay the bills, having received no royalties even as his performances in blockbusters such as *Debbie Does Dallas* had made millions for producers. This sounds a lot like the worst straight jobs, and yet Savage still resisted a language that reduced porn to work. He also said that the connections he forged with coworkers and the pleasures those made possible, kept him in the industry even as conditions in other ways were quite poor. Sometimes the things that make work tolerable also get us to do more of it.

How do we talk about authentic pleasure while still acknowledging that, for the vast majority of workers, porn work is a way to make do and get by? Porn workers' refusal to resolve this tension is instructive given that those engaged in critical theory's discursive/material battle have spent the last thirty years seeking tidy resolution. The debate over whether we should be talking about pleasure or the hard, daily work of survival has occupied a great deal of academic energy.[114] Indeed, the stakes are high. Marxist critic Teresa Ebert critiques what she calls "ludic feminism"—"a validating, affirmative, and pleasure-full cultural studies."[115] A focus on pleasure, she argues, is a "very class-specific inquiry," one that privileges "classes that have the relative luxury of displacing the body as a means of labor onto the body as a pleasure zone."[116] This depoliticized focus on pleasure will not help us make sense of the urgent material struggles facing working-class people, she says; worse, it might actually distract us from those struggles. I do think this helps explain why porn studies scholarship grounded in cultural studies has so strikingly avoided questions of labor. This chapter's discussion of authentic pleasure as a managerial tool gives us ample evidence of how "validating, affirmative, and pleasure-full" porn analysis might be weaponized against workers.

But porn workers are working-class people, and many insist that pleasure matters for how they think about the body as an instrument of (and beyond) labor. Taking pleasure seriously is also crucial for making visible the creative ways that workers manipulate work norms, win autonomy, and as Black feminist and queer of color porn theory suggests, take something from porn performance that exceeds what racial capitalism intends. Jennifer Nash insists that pleasure matters because it contests the construction of Black women performers as "evidence of agency's absence."[117] This is not a bourgeois conceit. Porn workers resist constructions that reduce them to bodies that labor and insist that pleasure makes working livable. Thus, in this book's introduction Savage described his decades-long career this way: "I've enjoyed it and hated it. . . . It worked for me in that I was able to survive. It was fun."

Rather than take working-class struggles for survival on their own terms, orthodox Marxist repudiations of pleasure can flatten them. Whether one "believe[s] it" or is "performing" has little impact on the reality that connecting in this way helps management and workers alike make money, as it may both produce more saleable scenes and ease the production process. But these connections are tools of not only production and exchange. Deeply felt connections among performers can also help build relationships and solidarity that work against labor discipline. Much of the informal organizing and information sharing that comprises collective resistance in the industry begins when performers connect on set and off. Such connections can also make work less straining, a dynamic Bernstein details in the escort context.[118] In Savage's case, real connections "meant something," allowing him to construct an identity apart from the hypermasculine "stud" roles he lamented being typecast in. Relationships among workers can mitigate the alienation some performers, like workers in other industries, experience in their work. Finally, as Syre reminds us, they can also feel good.

The same strategies can both help workers resist the tedium of work and facilitate the commodification of intimacy. But as Michael Hardt and Antonio Negri put it, "Resistance is prior to power."[119] Workers' desire for pleasure in work precedes capital's desperate efforts to capitalize on it—it is a mistake to assume that workers are only in the reactive position here. Sexual pleasure pushes this even further—for those performers who experience sexual pleasure at work, choosing porn is not the same as opting for artistic over corporate work, for instance. For many workers, sexuality *is* different, not because it is more vulnerable than other capacities but because it is more powerful.

In her classic piece on the pleasure/danger dialectic, Carole Vance suggests that we need pleasure in order to forge better futures. Against claims that pleasure is a distraction from politics, she insists: "Feminism must increase women's pleasure and joy, not just decrease our misery."[120] Speaking to the prefigurative power of pleasure, L. H. Stallings argues that sex workers "represent a radical spirit of revolt against antierotic, sex-negative, and workcentric elements of society."[121] Stallings warns that scholarly and activist framings of sex work as simply *work* risk "contributing to the production of more machines."[122] I think this lines up with Syre's invitation to resist the sanitizing power of "work" and Savage's gentle pushback at terms that risked reducing deep connection to clocking in. Our task is to take this seriously without forgetting that, for many porn workers, porn is still a way to pay the bills and a tedious one at that.

When performers talked about porn as work, I did not take this to mean they were saying that it was not real or that it was the same as assembling widgets. For most, calling porn "work" signaled just that this was how they made a living. "Work" also reminds us that, somewhere, there is value being extracted. Pleasure can be "real," as Syre says, and also work. Marxist feminists highlight this double life across reproductive labors. Breastfeeding, cooking for loved ones, emotional intimacy, and sex can very well be motivated by authentic (even good!) feeling and still repro-duce capital.[123] This, writes Camille Barbagallo, is why we cannot refuse reproductive labor in the same way we might refuse work in a factory—it reproduces us as workers "but, at the same time, as people whose lives, desires, and capabilities exceed the role of 'worker.'"[124]

Critiques of pleasure at work that see it only as something that makes us more exploitable reduce subjects entirely to their relationship to pro-duction. They miss this excessiveness. But under capitalism, there is no clear boundary separating pleasures that reproduce us in excess of capital from those that operate in its service. Nor, as feminist DIY practitioners learn the hard way, is there a clear boundary between workplace authen-ticity that represents an ethical alternative and that which extracts more labor. Getting to pleasure that serves everyday people, not capital, requires another mode of organizing life and labor.

If "performing authenticity" seems like a contradiction in terms, that is precisely the point—porn workers' relational and creative labor troubles boundaries between the real and performed, authentic and manufactured. The drive for authenticity shapes porn's production practices in key ways, determining both the content and form of porn work. And workers com-plicate long-taken-for-granted assumptions about authenticity as a liber-ating anecdote to commodified sexuality. Workers and managers alike suggest that authentic sexuality is work rather than an escape from it. For managers, authenticity is work because it produces capital. For workers, authenticity is something one works at. But what of the those for whom au-thenticity remains a powerful tool in resisting the ceaseless grind of work?

If workers who have sex for the money run afoul of the rules feminist critics and porn managers alike set up, those for whom authentic desire and pleasure are central break another set of rules. They refuse to do what critics of late capitalism suggest we should to guard ourselves from extraction: care less, leave your self at home, reclaim a kind of alienation that is protective. That these groups are not discrete—pleasure matters to workers sometimes, and at other times, the check is what counts most—highlights the double bind rigid approaches to authenticity set up for work-ing people. A dialectical view avoids this trap. Authenticity is protective, and it creates vulnerability, just like alienation. Porn puts the stakes of au-thenticity in relief, but its lessons are instructive for all workers hoping for pleasure at work and also knowing that this will surely be used against us.

Authenticity Work

3

A Scene Is Just
a Marketing Tool

Hustling in Porn's
Gig Economy

Interviews with porn performers often followed a similar progression. First, I asked how they got started in the industry, how on-set work is structured, and what they enjoy and would change about porn. Then, they explained that performing in porn actually occupies a relatively small part of their work lives. Few workers make a living on paid scenes alone. "I do everything. I'm the biggest hustler," said Sara Jay when I asked her whether porn performance was her main source of income. She went on: "I do affiliate programs, I have an online store, I have different kinds of internet revenues. I have my website, which is a big bulk of my income. I do everything from hosting nightclubs to signings at bookstores to feature performing. . . . My phone-sex line is going off as I'm talking to you."[1]

Porn workers tap a range of income streams as they navigate—and hack—an increasingly decentralized gig economy. Some take work in satellite industries to sustain themselves between castings. Others do paid scene work primarily to increase earnings in these other gigs. "A scene is just a marketing tool," explained longtime industry publicist and photographer Dominic Ace.[2] Here, waged scene work becomes less a site of straightforward value extraction than one of contest. Against framings of the gig economy as only ever a source of strain, this chapter argues that workers sometimes use it to take more from waged work than it takes from them.

Alternative income streams build and undermine workers' power at the same time. Workers use alternative income streams to creatively manipulate the conditions of porn work, maximizing earning potential, resisting burnout, claiming ownership over (some of) the means of production, and sometimes even making traditional managers obsolete. Yet by sustaining a reserve army of labor—workers willing to perform in waged scenes even when pay and conditions are poor—alternative income streams also subsidize employers and help maintain the status quo. This chapter explores how the gig economy is changing the pornographic landscape and what this tells us about the class relations of gig work more broadly. Most porn workers do not want to be only workers. In escaping worker status, they find themselves in shifting positions as entrepreneurs, independent contractors, employees, contracted and freelance managers, and producers. We need a politics of class that can account for this.

THE ECONOMICS OF THE HUSTLE

A multiple award winner, Kelly Shibari is a popular performer in the BBW genre. Still, good (well-paid, not fetishizing) scene work is sparse. Performers who meet mainstream's beauty rules have access to more casting opportunities, but they, too, struggle to make ends meet through porn gigs alone. For the vast majority of porn workers, there is simply not enough paid scene work to sustain an income. "These days I work maybe once a month as a performer," she explained. "[I perform] just to kind of keep things interesting, and so my performances don't look stale. And it's a little bit of mad money. But it's not what I depend on, what I bank on. . . . There's just not as much work as there used to be."[3] Later she added, "If I depended on this for a living, I'd be devastated."

This is characteristic of the broader gig economy. Here, "careers consist of piecing together various types of work, juggling multiple clients, learning to be marketing and accounting experts, and creating offices in bedrooms/coffee shops/co-working spaces," says Freelancers Union founder Sara Horowitz.[4] In this way, porn workers cobble together livable incomes; navigate shifting relationships with multiple clients, bosses, and fans; cultivate diverse skill sets; and blend work and home. Shibari gestured to these connections, guessing that her success juggling multiple income streams in porn is in part due to past experiences as a Hollywood freelancer. "I've always been freelancing," she said, "even before I got into porn. I was a roadie, then a production designer. Even the PR work I do. I've never worked nine to five for a corporation. . . . I think I had to clock in in high school." Like so many in the gig economy, she has never had a nine-to-five job, and yet she "always seem[s] to find [her] own work."

The timeline she plotted—the fact that "there's just not as much work as there used to be" and performers have to make do through other means—mirrors how scholars often historicize the dramatic emergence of the gig economy. In this narrative, the postwar security workers enjoyed would be slowly replaced by contract work, and by the 1990s, a gig economy would emerge in its place.[5] Scholarship on racialized and feminized labor suggests another story: the gig economy is only new for the predominantly white, middle-class workers who now find elusive the stability that once seemed an entitlement of their socioeconomic status.[6] Working-class people of color, and especially women, have always been gig working. Then and now, porn workers' reliance on multiple income sources should be understood in the context of the creative ways of getting by that those on the economic margins have long deployed—what Robin Kelley describes as the "hustle" in Black working-class communities (sex workers among them) in the midcentury United States.[7]

Even for workers with relative social privilege, postwar security was more elusive than stories of decline suggest. Auto work in the midcentury, oft held up as a prototypical example of good jobs gone bad, had to be supplemented by temporary work to account for the vagaries of production.[8] Likewise, porn's boom time sustained only the most elite performers on paid scene work alone. Its wages have not made for long-term security even for this select group; most of the performers I interviewed who were stars during that time are now facing extreme financial insecurity. Jeffrey Escoffier's history suggests that performers have long been using porn as a kind of "infomercial" for their other work, "triple-X version[s] of the traveling salesman."[9]

Contrary to narratives of decline, the hustle is not new, and not all workers experience it exclusively as a burden. The control and autonomy most porn workers say they want is at odds with the kind of routinized security many straight workers (or their industrial unions, at any rate) have historically sought.[10] Echoing many activists and scholars of straight work, one straight worker and activist described gig-based precarity this way: "We are hirable on demand, available on call, exploitable at will and fireable at whim. We have become skillful jugglers of jobs and contortionists of flexibility."[11] This was not, at least in our interviews, something porn workers identified as a problem. Many porn workers left relatively secure, full-time jobs precisely because they wanted the flexibility sex work affords. Workers may hustle in the gig economy not only because they cannot find steady work but because they do not want it. Put otherwise, it is not only that porn management has established a set of conditions that leaves workers no choice but to hustle but also that workers desire the autonomy—and class mobility—that the hustle permits. Others do wish for greater standardization but find that porn offers little. Varied income streams keep performers afloat in a mercurial industry.

One might be cast in twenty scenes one month and in two the next, a capricious agent could withhold castings, an injury or positive test result for a curable sexually transmitted infection (STI) could mean two weeks' unpaid time off, or a moratorium after another performer tests positive for HIV could result in weeks of work being canceled. "There were a lot of times where it was bottom-of-the-barrel scraping for me," explained VJ. "I would go from making $20,000 a month to making $3,500. . . . That's just how the business fluctuates."[12] Even in the best circumstances—an uninterrupted month with many castings that pay well—most performers cannot sustain themselves through paid scene work alone. "If a girl tells you she's only shooting for a living, she's lying," ventured Charity Bangs, who performs in straight gonzo films on average twice a month.[13]

Women (cis and trans) performers, who are generally paid more per scene but tend to work less regularly than men, typically rely most heavily on income streams from a range of sex industries. They also have generally higher earning potential in them. Women's career life-spans are generally shorter, and the employment discrimination they face upon retiring from sex work is greater. Cis men tend to enjoy longer careers in porn while also experiencing less intense stigma in straight jobs. With the exception of escorting in the gay market, men's incomes in satellite sex work industries are also limited. Cis men who do not work in the gay-sex-services sector are more likely to seek out alternative income sources as camera operators, postproduction editors, and directors of low-budget gonzo productions.[14] Trans men and genderqueer people typically work in queer and feminist porn—a genre that very rarely provides regular work—and their hustles in other sex industries are limited (but not foreclosed) by gender rules within.

For workers who can make significant incomes from porn and related gig work, making a living means not only paying the bills each month but also building both savings and a brand that will sustain them after retirement. At twenty-five years old when we spoke, Venus Lux was already working on a retirement plan. By building her own production company while she was still a performer, she hoped to move away from performing by age thirty. Lux explained, "You can't do porn forever. By the time you hit thirty, that's the point when you're considered a MILF. I do not want that under my title. Hopefully by the time I hit thirty I can say, 'I'm a Hall of Famer, I've got my award, I've got my company, and I'm making money off my brand.'"[15] Some performers said that the threat of "aging out" is overstated—performers can maintain careers well into their forties, and there are many proud MILFs. Whatever the timeline, alternative income streams are integral to porn workers' creative retirement plans.

Workers who use waged scene performances primarily as marketing tools hope to schedule scene gigs in ways that maximize a porn star brand. They suggest that the average performer can carry star status for about six months (exceptionally famous performers' brands can last much longer) after her last released scene, at which point fans—potential clients—lose interest. One interviewee who had recently decided to retire told me she delayed announcing this to her fans in hopes of retaining them as paying clients in her side gigs. Webcam clients, she feared, would not pay porn star rates to a retired performer, and website subscribers would cancel memberships to sites they expect will stop adding new material. In the meantime, she was slowly releasing previously recorded scenes in an effort to sustain the illusion that she was still a working porn star. Other performers announce retirement on social media and aggressively market one last self-produced scene, public appearance, or escort tour in hopes of driving fans' interest in these final opportunities to see their favorite star.

Satellite work can also ease transitions not quite planned for. After great success as a contract star, Raylene left the porn industry and pursued a career in real estate. But after the 2008 market crash, she found herself a single mother needing work and returned to porn. She had gained some weight in the years since she had been a contract star, and "nobody was hiring me. I had no way of making money and I had no idea what I was going to do," Raylene explained.[16] "I ended up jumping on the webcam and making tons of money." Webcamming helped make ends meet, and Raylene found she preferred its working conditions to porn's. "I kind of slowed down from shooting [porn]," she said, because webcamming made it possible to "work alone, in my house, during school hours, and then, you know, have the rest of the evening with my child. [I could] make a better living at home than when I was in front of the camera, and [I was] getting less hated, you know, for not looking good for the public." Erotic dance and escort work function in much the same way. "Later on in my career when I started to slow down, I did what a lot of girls did and segued into escorting," one performer explained. "That's just a natural transition for a majority of the girls."[17] As we will see, some find the conditions better.

Without satellite industries, it simply would not be worthwhile for most workers to maintain careers in porn. Performer and popular gay escort Christopher Daniels explained, for example, that he started performing in porn because he "noticed that the guys doing porn got better rates and did better as escorts. That was the sole reason I went into porn."[18] Across satellite industries, "porn star" billing can increase earnings substantially, even as the vast majority of porn performers are not regarded as having real "star" status in the industry. In some, such as the novelty business in which performers are paid to have sex toys modeled after them and marketed under their name, being a porn star is a prerequisite to securing a gig in the first place. For most workers (especially women) porn performance is their primary work identity but tertiary income source. In this context, porn scenes become more than individual gigs. Instead, like song singles in the post-piracy music world, they provide access to a host of other income streams.[19] Thus, sociologist David Schieber calls scenes "promotional labor."[20]

The industries in which porn performers pursue gig work function as satellites from the perspective of the porn film industry—managers (and some performers) talk about them as peripheral to the central work of porn making. At the same time, satellite industries destabilize the idea of porn as a discrete and cohesive *industry*. Boundaries separating adult film from other industries are increasingly porous as workers and bosses (and worker-bosses) seek new ways to integrate porn with other products and services in pursuit of greater profits and work in satellite industries gets folded into porn work under the auspices of promotion, exposure, and marketing. Porn studios, for instance, contract performers to do erotic dance gigs to engage fans during trade shows. Still, satellite industries are distinct from the porn film industry in a number of ways: they organize work processes differently, are subject to different regulatory schemes, and often (though not always) generate capital for different parties.

Porn employers nevertheless benefit from satellite work. Increased income potential in satellite industries incentivizes paid scene work in spite of its diminishing returns. Satellite industries, in turn, subsidize

Hustling in Porn's Gig Economy

the porn industry's wages and fund the costly maintenance, marketing, and other preparatory work required of performers. One might take erotic dance gigs to finance a trip to a porn convention or go on tour as an escort to fund trips to out-of-town porn shoots. When traveling for out-of-town shoots, one performer explained, "obviously, flying out there and paying for hotels, I broke even. For the sake of building my brand and my name, I told myself, 'If you make money, awesome. If you don't, whatever.' I had to sustain myself through escorting—how else am I going to pay for airfare and whatnot?"[21]

Porn managers know that satellite work sustains their labor supply. The low wages they pay and the travel and lodging expenses they displace onto workers must be offset somehow, and they know that performers do not rely on paid scenes alone. They also know that scene work helps keep other hustles afloat. This benefits managers—when workers are using scenes as marketing tools, they are less likely to complain when the conditions of those scenes are poor. If one performs under another person's management just two or three times a month and needs those performances to sustain a "porn star" brand, the incentives may be too meager and the stakes too high for making individual or collective demands for better working conditions or pay. But the power this gives managers is limited—workers who can make money in a range of ways are less dependent on any single boss.

Mobility in sex work gig economies lets porn workers command greater control over the terms of their work and, sometimes, the means of production. Performer Samantha Grace explained, "You have to do other things to make money. Film work is a form of marketing. I work with other companies so I can promote *my own* website, my own films, my own custom videos, pro-domming."[22] Grace's description of how she came to work in the porn industry—she chose sex work as an alternative to low-wage retail jobs that left her thinking, "Oh my God, I'm never going to get out of this"—helps contextualize her approach. Retail work meant being trapped, and sex work entrepreneurship promised an alternative. She refused to limit herself to the kinds of sex work that, in making money for someone else, looked most like retail. Porn workers have a keen understanding of the relations of ownership—they work for others so that they can promote *their own* websites, direct-to-consumer scenes, products, and services. Sometimes this lets them turn opportunities for extraction on their head.

Underwear dialectics provide a sharp example of what this looks like in practice. Producers increasingly displace the costs of doing business onto performers by requiring them to supply their own wardrobe—pieces that cannot be worn on film again—for scenes. The costs can be considerable, and not everyone needs a collection for personal wear. And so rather than absorb the cost, performers post online wish lists, inviting fans to gift them lingerie, clothing, and shoes. Fans can then see their gifts featured in porn scenes. Then, performers sell the lingerie and clothing they have worn in scenes to fans. These exchanges can recover performers' original cost and then some (twenty-dollar underwear might auction for fifty dollars once used), turning disposability into a virtue. Performers found a money-making opportunity where producers saw only an expense to be displaced.

Producers get scene wardrobes they do not have to pay for, but performers get advertising for which they do not pay production costs. In the meantime, performers seize another opportunity to build fan loyalty—not to the studio but to individual performers who can take their names elsewhere. This kind of direct exchange is something production companies cannot easily appropriate—the intimacy of the exchange is part of its appeal. A struggle emerges, where companies attempt to foist the cost of business onto workers, and workers, in turn, use scenes as advertisement for products from which they profit. In the underwear dialectic as in the use of scenes as advertisements for a wider array of side hustles, worker creativity unsettles the idea that paid scene work is only ever exploitative in the classic sense of the term. Producers who pay workers a fraction of the profits (they hope) a scene will garner are trying to extract value from their labor (and sometimes they succeed), but performers are savvy about ensuring that they take something in excess of the wage. Satellite industries are these struggles' terrain.

SATELLITE SEX WORK INDUSTRIES

In the following pages, I explore the sex work jobs porn workers most frequently take on: erotic dance, webcam modeling, escorting, and platform-mediated direct sales to fans.[23] Each has commanded dedicated scholarly analyses, and my focus here is on how workers describe these fields in relation to porn work. The porn industry and its sex work satellites have in common a degree of marginality in the world of respectable work. As technology studies scholar Georgina Voss elaborates, stigma tars management and workers alike.[24] Performers' visibility, however, makes them particularly vulnerable to it. When performers take on straight work (either as a supplementary income source or after retirement), they risk harassment from customers, coworkers, and management in the event that they are recognized, and they lack access to legal protections should they be fired because of their participation in even legal forms of sex work.[25] Most straight jobs pay less than sex work and have schedules incompatible with porn's inconsistent hours and last-minute scheduling. Being a porn star is a liability in straight work and an asset in sex industries. Understanding this, most workers focus on alternative income streams in which being a porn performer brings money and autonomy rather than insecurity and stigma. In so doing, they encounter a whole new set of rules.

Whorearchy structures the porn worker community's hierarchical valuation of the various income streams performers pursue. The overwhelming perception in the mainstream porn industry is that, as performer-director Lily Cade put it, "there is a hierarchy of sex work, and porn star is the top. Anything else is beneath that."[26] As such, while almost every woman I interviewed said it was impossible to make a living in paid porn work alone, most considered porn star their primary work identity. Some trade in the greater respectability afforded to a legal industry that is assumed to offer more fame and higher pay, distancing themselves from other sex workers (even when they also participate in these forms of sex work and porn often pays less). But identifying as a porn star (rather than as a webcam model or an escort who sometimes does porn, for example) is about more than simply staking one's position at the top of an abstract whorearchy. In so identifying, workers seek to control where they fall in relation to structures that differentially apply risk—of criminalization, stigma, workplace abuse, discrimination upon retirement, etc.—to workers according to the kind of sex work they do.[27] Porn star identification is also a tool for navigating gig work, giving workers who can claim it access to more negotiating power in satellite industries. Work in satellite sex industries thus places porn workers in community with other sex workers but one structured by deep hierarchies.

Erotic dance occupies a key place in the porn work cycle. Many cis women performers (and cis men who dance at gay go-go clubs) get their start dancing, and then meet touring feature dancers who help them break into the porn business. Others are already established in porn and take up dancing as a side hustle along the way. As porn careers wane, or as performers lose interest in porn work, performers again seek out feature dance work, this time to ease the transition to retirement. At each stage, a "porn star" brand gives workers access to a higher echelon of erotic dance.

Felicia Fox discovered this early on in her career as a dancer. She had been working as an erotic dancer at a local club, and then started on what she called the "kindergarten circuit"—the kind of tour available to dancers who could not bill themselves as porn stars.[28] She decided to perform in porn to raise her rates. Now a "feature dancer," her base pay climbed from $100 to $500 for a show lasting one or two songs. With better advertising and preferred scheduling, she also netted larger tips and could charge higher fees for lap dances.

As guest dancers with greater negotiating power, features can avoid some of the most exploitative labor practices regular dancers face, such the stage fees clubs charge and the tips managers expect for preferential scheduling.[29] This distance between dancers who market themselves as porn stars and those who cannot creates tension in clubs. Sara Jay explained her uneven experiences as a feature dancer interacting with a club's regular dancers: "At some clubs it's so bad that they keep you completely away from the other girls. Then there's other clubs where the girls are amazing and nice and they help."[30] Sharing a shift with a feature dancer can be good for regular dancers, Jay said, because features bring business. Porn performers with less name recognition work as regular dancers at a single club (under the same conditions as those who do not perform in porn) rather than features. A MILF performer in her forties, Tara Holiday gets cast in porn just a couple of days each month and relies primarily on dancing to pay her bills. "At this point in my life," she said, "I get the day shift. I'm not allowed to go at night, even though I'm a porn star—they don't care."[31]

Even with less desirable shifts, Holiday said she likes dancing. When I asked her why, she explained, "The freedom! The money you make. There are no rules. You make your own rules." That freedom meant that she could make day shifts work for her, establishing stronger connections with more sober customers who had not already spent all their cash on a night out. But that kind of relationship building requires in-person emotional labor not all performers can do. Accustomed to flat fees for porn performances, some performers found the transition to tip-based work jarring, humiliating even. "I feature danced once," VJ explained. "It wasn't for me. I looked at it as 'I can go do XYZ on set and get paid $2,000. Why would I go sit here and beg for dollars?'"[32] Chanel Preston told a similar story: "I love dancing—it's so much fun—but I hate hustling for money. It's not my style. I'm not very good at it. . . . I don't like to give people control over what I'm doing."[33] Workers frequently made distinctions between taking direction from porn directors and giving customers control and between negotiating over scene rates and the "hustling" or "begging" they associated with tip-based industries requiring direct interaction with consumers. Others feel they have more autonomy in satellite industries. Workers' diverse perspectives defy any universal ranking of satellite in relation to porn work.

Webcam performance is another core income stream for many performers and one that, like dancing, requires ongoing negotiations with customers. Webcam platforms operate by providing workers—"models"—with access to a centralized site used to drive web traffic and process payments. Webcam platforms do not pay models; instead, they take a cut of 30 percent to 70 percent of the payments performers earn. Like gig platforms in the world of straight work, they replace in-person with algorithmic management and organize their consumer interface to engineer competition among workers.[34] Workers, then, must navigate both the algorithms' always-changing rules and fraught dynamics with consumers.[35] Both are shaped by a glutted and sharply hierarchized labor market. Kink.com CEO Peter Ackworth put it this way: "If you're very popular, you make very good money. If you're not, then you have to learn how the system works . . . how to hustle the customer." But that hustle does not look the same for all workers—hierarchies of race, appearance, age, and so on shape what workers can ask for and how hard they have to push to get it, a reality Angela Jones details in her study of cam labor.[36]

At the same time, individualized micronegotiations with customers can give workers more power to set their terms than porn allows. Customers' valuations of models' time are structured by hierarchy but in less institutionalized ways. Whereas porn agents enforce common racist rate differentials, cam models set their own price. Some customers are willing to pay. In addition, while a flat rate in porn can obscure what exactly a scene requires, cam work makes plain exactly what is for sale, for how long, and for how much.[37] And where waged porn work requires building relationships with directors or risking lost future work, in camming there are usually more viewers waiting if hard bargaining turns some away. An interviewee who invited me to sit in on her cam session clearly stipulated terms such as "four dollars to stand," "six dollars to show ass," and "panties off in exclusive only."[38] "If you continue to make requests and do not tip, I will block you," she warned one demanding viewer. Later, when another viewer asked how much she charged for "exclusive" time, she responded, "$14.99 per minute. I know it sounds like a lot, but I only get 35 percent, guys. I'm not here to work for free." "Pay me, you little fucks," she later added. I never saw this level of directness, or such clear references to management's cut, on a porn set.

Protecting boundaries and reminding customers of their terms all while appearing approachable, sexy, and authentically engaged (that is, in a formulation that will now be familiar to readers, not "just for the money") is a delicate and potentially draining task.[39] Some interviewees are unwilling to do this kind of work, feeling that, as in dancing, negotiations with customers constituted a sort of "begging." "I feel like webcam is degrading," one woman remarked. "I know this is going to sound super arrogant, but I've worked really hard to not have to [cam]."[40] For others, camming feels like more control—when individual workers determine pricing, they can be less subject to the discriminatory scheduling and pay conventions of other sex work industries. Camming is both easily accessible (unlike in waged porn work and dancing, one does not need a manager's permission in order to work) and relatively low risk (in terms of health, safety, and exposure to policing), so workers often pursue camming even as they have critiques of how the work is organized. But here as in porn performance, lowered barriers to entry cut both ways: workers benefit from camming's accessibility but also contend with a flooded labor market.[41] The COVID-19 pandemic heightened this contradiction in camming and platform-enabled clips sales. These digital labors helped performers survive the loss of paid porn (and other in-person) work, but performers also contended with a glutted labor market and thus reduced bargaining power.

Escorting work, like camming, offers low barriers to entry and a greater degree of autonomy. Interviewees who did this work reported overwhelmingly positive experiences, appreciating escorting's high pay for few hours and control over scheduling and work terms. "Of all the possibilities that you have, I think escorting is the best. I love it," one performer told me.[42] "There's a difference between being a regular girl escort and being a porn star," she added, pointing to higher rates and the free marketing porn scenes provide. In less time, she could make more from escorting than from performing in scenes.

Independent escorts can also set the terms for sessions without managerial interference, and some said they had more autonomy over safer sex practices here than they do in porn scene work. "I think it's safer," one performer and escort explained. "You have these screened, older, married men that wear condoms. . . . I know a ton of escorts in the business and none of them go without condoms."[43] The sex is often less tiring than on-set sex. Even if escort clients think they want the "porn star experience" (an advertising term), most cannot begin to keep up with porn's actual requirements. "I like escorting because you have so much fun; no one is filming you, so you can have sex like you have in regular life," one worker told me.[44] Gesturing to the doublespeak required of workers in criminalized economies, she added, laughing, "Oh, did I say 'have sex' in escorting? No, you can 'accompany' people." Clients are not professionals, though, so sex in this context can be labor intensive in other ways—a bit clumsier and with partners who may struggle to communicate their needs.

Escorting's location at the margins of respectability and law, and the possibility that performers will find it a better alternative to waged porn work, makes it a particular target of porn manager criticism. When I asked agent Chris Caine about his perspective on performer escorting, he replied, "I don't like it because girls start getting lazy. . . . They start to evaluate everything by time instead of by the job. They'll say, 'I'd rather spend one hour with this guy for $500 than six and only make $1,000. In that six hours I could have done four guys and made more money.'"[45] What management sees as laziness, many workers see as an obvious business move. This conflict might help to explain why almost every straight-porn manager I interviewed cited escorting—doing "privates," in industry speak—as a scourge on the industry.[46] When I asked talent agent Mark Schechter about the stigma escorts face in the industry, he explained, "It's a very valid reason. . . . Because we have a very stringent testing policy, if we don't protect that pool from the outside elements, then we are [at risk of] potentially damaging or poisoning that pool."[47] This assumes either that porn performers never have unpaid sex or that sex with clients is riskier than unpaid sex. Of course, performers have unpaid sexual lives, and condom use is much more common in paid sex with clients than it is among unpaid partners. But while the idea of "poisoning the pool" does not reflect the realities of STI transmission, it does reflect the ways escorting, like other side hustles, can poison porn workers' willingness to work for the porn establishment.

Working in a privileged stratum of escorting, porn star escorts find themselves higher up on the whorearchy and largely free of the police harassment that street and parlor-based workers encounter. They nonetheless have to contend with the risks of laboring in a criminalized economy, and criminalization hurts workers more than it does managers. Many workers book escorting gigs through the same agents who manage their porn work but, because escorting is criminalized, have little recourse when agents push them to take work they would prefer to avoid, take a large cut of their earnings, or are otherwise abusive. In 2019, news broke of a reality porn workers had been talking about for years: one powerful porn agent routinely pushed performers into escort work, took a high percentage of their earnings, and then threatened to out them if they left his business.[48] Wanting to avoid such exploitative arrangements, many workers choose to operate independently and rely on online advertising platforms to draw clients. Attacks on sex workers' ability to advertise online have restricted their ability to operate autonomously in this way.

Restricted online freedom has also had seismic effects on workers' ability to make use of social media advertising and direct-to-consumer sales. In so doing, it limits another key means by which porn workers seize autonomy through alternative income streams. Ways of nurturing connections with fans have become increasingly specialized and personal as performers seek to distinguish the direct services they offer from the scenes fans can access for free from tube sites. With 150,000 Twitter followers, Siri has developed a significant fan following with which she interacts regularly. For fifty-seven dollars, fans can buy her unwashed "everyday panties" along with a photo of her wearing them. They can purchase signed DVDs directly from her, including a filmed event in which she and fellow performer Sara Jay give oral sex to their fans in celebration of the World Cup soccer championship. "Not only does it have all the footage of the entire TEAM BJ event," the product blurb boasts, "but there's tons of fun and interesting BTS [behind-the-scenes] footage, too, including before and after interviews with the real-life fans who got BJs from Sara and I."[49] Siri sends signed DVDs along with a message thanking fans for "#Pay[ing] ForYourPorn," as the Twitter hashtag goes.[50]

Personalization ensures that workers profit most directly from products and scenes, but most sales still require some sort of middleman. Most performers opt for third-party-operated sites, calculating that the initial cost—around $5,000—to set up one's own site is too high and monthly maintenance too labor intensive. Third-party sites also help protect personal information and drive web traffic. A universe of websites and apps, all with different payment structures, caters to performers who market digital scene access, DVDs, still photos, and worn clothing to fans. Fans can, for example, bid on performers' lingerie, clothing, or shoes on auction site BabeBids, and the site takes a 10 percent "transaction fee" of the final bid and charges additional fees for featured products and pages.

Performers also use mainstream services in ways their makers did not intend. One example of this is paid phone conversations through services such as Verified Call (originally designed for therapists and their clients). The company charges a "convenience fee" to clients on top of the rates workers set, a strategy its president, Kurt Vogner, hopes is more provider friendly than services such as webcam sites, which take a cut.[51] Workers also found ways to use the service that developers "hadn't even identified," Vogner said. Clients pay for a block of minutes in advance, and workers keep their fee regardless of whether the client finishes the call. Financial dominatrices (porn performers among them) instruct clients to pay for a block of 100 minutes only to hang up after one.

Ironically, Vogner told me about this hack just after explaining that developers designed the system so that the "below-average person can use it and understand it. As much as they're nice people, let's be honest, these girls have sex for money," he said. It was not uncommon for non-sex-worker interviewees to suggest that sex workers are not terribly bright, only to later describe a situation in which sex workers had outsmarted them. Performers have figured out similar hacks for a wide range of mainstream internet platforms (all engineered by people with higher-status jobs than sex work), putting applications such as Snapchat (for paid access to photos), Amazon (to publish wish lists for everything from clothing to books and home decor), and Zoom (to sell webcam shows without a middleman) toward creative use. And crafty uses of file-sharing sites and payment processors make it possible to produce and distribute content without established directors, producers, and distributors. In turn, this makes directors and producers out of performers, but ones whose class position is intensely vulnerable to platform discrimination and web censorship.

MANAGERIAL ROLES IN PORN

Workers want to produce their own performances for various reasons. For performers who have exceptionally large fan followings, owning your own scene can mean significant earnings. Anticipating what the internet would later make ubiquitous, 1990s superstar Asia Carrera opted to self-produce her first anal scenes, garnering $300,000 in profits. "She made as much money as a producer would have made off her," noted Bud Lee, the film's director and her husband at the time.[52] Anti-capitalists will appreciate that even managers acknowledge that when producers own a scene, they make money *off* the workers who created it. Performers want to appropriate their own surplus labor, and the internet makes this even easier to do. Performers can use direct-to-consumer porn platforms or mainstream file-sharing programs to produce and distribute their own content.

Today even big-budget features do not approach six-figure profits, but performers still have reason to claim the profits producers would otherwise make off their work. Kelly Shibari explained that in self-production, "if you're lucky, you might make an extra couple grand with every movie. It just becomes this kind of staying-afloat process."[53] In this atmosphere, self-producing is less about making massive profits than ensuring that "at least you get to stay in the business that you love," she said. Most performer-producers use self-production for this kind of maintenance.

The same technological advances that enabled the amateur content explosion that put downward pressure on professional performers' working conditions have also made professional performers less dependent on large production companies. Performers hoping to self-produce once had to acquire and learn how to use expensive and cumbersome camera equipment. They also had to handle distribution and marketing themselves and risked getting lost in a system that privileged large production companies who had existing relationships with cable networks and adult retailers. Today, performers can produce content cheaply and sell it using online platforms tailored for this purpose (such as OnlyFans, ManyVids, and Clips4Sale) and ones built for mainstream use. Some of these productions rely on solo content or trade relationships in which workers come together to coproduce content (and share both authority and copyright), while others place performer-directors in the position of contracting employers.

Self-producing (individual scenes or entire films) usually means financing one's own production. Costs typically range from $5,000–$20,000 for bigger projects to no cost for content produced using trade labor and a smartphone. Self-producers maintain copyrights for scenes and can repost them in a variety of venues. They also maintain decision-making power. "It's really easy to set the price to what you're comfortable with," explained Maxine Holloway. "People do try to haggle with you sometimes, but usually it's like, 'This is the menu, this is the price, do you want to buy it or not?'"[54] Performers may or may not view themselves as producers when they create such material. "When I got into the industry I shot things for my own personal website. . . . In a roundabout way, I was producing, I just didn't realize it," said Tanya Tate.[55] As chapter 5 shows, the state, too, may or may not view self-producers as *producers*.

Beyond claiming the profits they generate, workers seek ownership over their own scenes in order to command control over the production process. Performers self-produce as a way to hire themselves for performance work or in order to manage the kind of scenes they have access to. This is particularly important for workers who struggle to find good work in mainstream. Black performers, for instance, often self-produce in order to circumvent porn industry racism. Some struggle to get cast by established directors and want any kind of work, while others get plenty of paid scene work but wish to be free of the racism they encounter in negotiations, on set, and in the representations they are asked to carry out. Albeit with different stakes, this is also true for a range of performers who do not fit within the industry's narrow rules for appearance and gender performance. "I produce my own work because I can't get work elsewhere," explained genderqueer "fat femme" performer, director, and producer Courtney Trouble in an Adult Entertainment Expo panel.[56] Highly paid, frequently cast performers (who are more likely to have access to conventional erotic capital) are alone in being able to afford working only for other people. Even they choose to take on management positions to diversify incomes, wrest autonomy over their conditions, and ensure career longevity.

For others, producing scenes is the surest way to enter the industry in the first place. Cis men's appearances are less monitored, but work opportunity is still generally reserved for attractive, "proven" talent (those who have demonstrated their ability to maintain an erection and ejaculate as directed). And so, some self-produce as an entrée into porn. Their motivations for doing so range from making a living to accessing legal sex with sex workers. A universe of small-budget production blurs the lines between director-producers hiring others for work (or seeking out trade arrangements with them) and "guys with cameras," a phrase frustrated performers use to describe nonprofessional (and often unprofessional, too) performer-producers who simply want to have sex with a porn star. The democratization of production cuts both ways.

Performers can circumvent worker-manager dynamics by establishing trade relationships with others. Maxine Holloway described a "really amazing network of doing trade content" in which workers collaborate, often with friends or lovers from the performer community, to produce scenes and share content ownership.[57] Performers might share labor to produce original content for direct-to-consumer sales or collaborate to fulfill fans' custom scene requests. Some said that the possibility of doing trade shoots let them avoid traditional paid scenes: Why go to set, let a director tell you how to have sex, and forfeit the profits when a trade scene on OnlyFans will net just as much? Trade can offer more autonomy and, because it often features partnerships chosen at least in part because of mutual desire (or at least camaraderie), better sex. It is not, however, outside broader market pressures.

Working with established producers and studios still has benefits for those who can do it: budgets are bigger, the necessary infrastructure already exists, and someone else deals with paperwork and liability. When porn workers are also performing in the scenes they direct, working with a studio also makes it easier to focus on the scene rather than surrounding logistics. But contracting with a studio can mean less creative control. Typically, a production company contracts a director to film a scene on its behalf and pays the director either a fee on top of other production costs or a flat sum out of which the director takes their own fee as well as other production costs, such as performer and crew wages, set rentals, and the like. In both cases, producers typically maintain copyright and directors receive no royalties.

Performers' motivations for taking on this kind of directing work are gendered. Women and gay men, who tend to be better paid for performing work, said they crave the respect, creative control, and long-term income stability that can come with directing. Jessica drake "realized that the more creative control I had over my movies, the happier I am with them, the more I really get into it. With wardrobe, if I had script ideas, if I had sexual scenarios that I wanted to act out—I was given the creative control to do all those things."[58] Straight men were more likely to perform and direct for low-budget gonzo studios who seek out performer-directors as a cost-saving measure (in such productions, one person often performs, directs, produces, and handles lighting and sound) because this was the work they could get. Varied entry points into hybrid worker-manager identity shape performer-director-producers' approaches to the politics of class.

THE CLASS POLITICS OF THE HUSTLE

Porn workers approach the gig economy with the aim of controlling their incomes, the work environments, and the representations in which they are featured. In so doing, they sometimes become managers, wresting autonomy over their own work lives by becoming controlling parties in others'. I wondered how this shifted their perspectives, and when I asked, "Are you a different kind of director because you also perform?" most said that having performed made them better, more understanding bosses. This bore out in other interviewees' accounts of having worked with these same performer-directors only some of the time. One performer-director told me proudly about the ways she fights for workers' rights. She was one of the directors other interviewees complained about most. Once a manager, she became known for unpredictable outbursts and disorganized, poorly provisioned sets lasting upward of twenty hours.

Interviewees also spoke to a question I had not thought to ask: Are you a different kind of performer because you also direct? On this point they overwhelmingly said that occupying management roles shaped their perspectives as performers, sometimes to greater effect than the other way around. Performer-director and studio owner Lexington Steele, who got his start in the industry as a performer, explained, "The performer in me is managed by the executive in me."[59] He went on: "You look at everything from the top down. . . . So as a performer, maybe you do your scene and you take a break—you really only need a five-minute break but you take ten. . . . Now as a producer, you start to think about that fact that, okay, each time you guys stop for fifteen minutes, [you] stop twice, so [that's] half an hour. The location is $150 an hour, those thirty minutes cost me seventy-five bucks. . . . Time is measurable in dollars and cents." Later in our conversation, Steele discussed his opposition to producer-paid STI testing, likening a test to the tools an independent contractor must bring to work. It would be too simple, though, to suggest that Steele's loyalties to management overtook his identifications with other workers. Throughout our interview, he used language such as "we as performers," spoke candidly about industry racism, voiced support for a performers union (even as he said its success was unlikely), and even talked about performers as porn's "proletariat class." "The performer in me is managed by the executive in me" speaks to Steele's lucid analysis of internalized class conflict.

If mobility among performing and managerial roles promises workers greater autonomy, it does not free them from market pressures. Steele, who self-finances his productions, put it this way: "When I have to recirculate my profits, I've got to apply those with surgical precision. . . . If I put out a movie that I've spent $15,000–$20,000 on, I've got to ensure that the market is going to consume that in such a way that I can see that profitability."[60] Contract directors feel a similar squeeze, even as production companies put up the initial investment and win the spoils if scenes do well. The production company she directs for gives Lily Cade a budget of about $8,000 for a four-scene film, and she determines how the budget will be allocated. "It's hard to make that stretch," she told me, but "I have creative control. I'll sacrifice a lot for that."[61] This common arrangement puts significant pressure on directors to cut costs. I asked Cade about who covers pre-scene STI-testing costs, wondering if, given that she also performs, she is more likely to cover such costs when in a managerial role. "I kind of have to go along with everyone else," she explained. "I'm not enough of a power player to be like, 'I'm gonna pay for tests!' How? With what? I'm a contractor; I get a shitty budget and I have to try to make it into a movie." Cade's own fee is whatever is left over after she has paid everyone else, and like performers, she makes no royalties.

For some managers (both those who perform and those who only direct) these pressures engender the sense that managers are trod upon—worse off, in some ways, than workers who are only performing. Without the star power some performers enjoy, most managers simply take what they can get. I asked writer-director Jacky St. James if there was any discussion of contract directors organizing collectively. "Unfortunately, at this point people are so desperate for work, they'll take what they can get," she explained. "There's no solidarity with that."[62] The vast majority of those I interviewed who hold management roles shared the sense that money is too tight and their own power position too tenuous to make substantial changes in business practices. If big studios pay poorly or refuse to cover the costs of workplace injury because they can, small directors and producers say they have no other choice. They offer a similar narrative—we have to make what sells—to justify representational choices that conflict with their own politics, such as including racist tropes in scenes. In both cases, directors make clear that they are not the group we should look to for voluntary change.

Again and again, managers told me they simply play by the rules of the game. To the question of whether being a performer changed his perspective as a director, Dave Pounder responded, "Do you mean did I pay people more because I'd been a performer? No. For me it was purely capitalistic."[63] Pounder told me he pays the lowest possible rate that performers will agree to. This was not all I meant in asking the question, but Pounder's response gestures to issues beyond payment. For managers for whom the production process is "purely capitalistic," being a paid performer is merely a stop along the road to greater control and financial stake. In such a framework, there is nothing personal about the decision to extract as much from workers for as little as possible; that is simply how capitalism operates. Even when managers did not lay these dynamics out

Hustling in Porn's Gig Economy

quite so plainly, they tend to prioritize profits in their decision-making. Like bosses in other industries, most present this not as a matter of ideology or ethics but simply as following the norms of a system that pits their interests against workers'.

Other interviewees spoke about multiple roles in terms less of class conflict than of mutual understanding. Jessica drake, a contract performer and director for major studio Wicked, said, "I do feel like I'm a different type of director because I came from a performer background," and explained that because she's been on the other side, she always pays performers' full rate, adding $100 for features that require a longer day; works to make performers comfortable on set by providing quality catering; and is active with a performer advocacy group. When I visited drake's set, performers I spoke to privately said drake was a favorite director to work for. Sometimes, it *is* easier to work under someone who has done your job. Drake said this is true in both directions: "I'm more empathetic now as a performer. Because I can now put myself in both positions, and sometimes when I'm on set as just talent, I look at other talent and I wish they understood where the director was coming from. I think it works both ways. It works for me; it makes me both a better director and a better performer, being the other."[64] Throughout our interviews, performers suggested that directors who have performed are on the whole better to work for.

In turn, performers who also direct do tend to have a kind of empathy for their bosses, evidenced most clearly in a work ethic and approaches to policy that line up better with management's than workers' interests. It was performers who also direct who were most vocally opposed to employer-funded STI testing and workers' compensation, for example. Performers and managers (and performer-managers) also do organizing together, and only some see this as a barrier to political work. Most performers who do not currently have managerial positions hope to take them on eventually and align with managers in an anticipatory way. And so class mobility pushes workers to adopt managerial consciousness even as it also undermines established managerial class power.

Gig economies can mean autonomy for workers but often as individuals grasping at whatever advantages prevailing systems allow, rather than a collective working to topple them. Sinnamon Love explained that access to a robust gig economy makes it possible for some porn workers to demand better working conditions. At the same time, she said that not all workers have equal access to the benefits of gig work. Love relayed a recent conversation with a white friend who had expressed frustration that some performers accept pay below standard rates for scene work. "If no one worked for low wages, producers would not be able to pay them" was a sentiment many of the white women I interviewed shared, often alongside a critique of colleagues they perceived to be driving down wages.

"But not everybody has the advantages, especially women of color, in terms of working outside of porn and being able to make enough money off set in various different business ventures to be able to turn down work," Love noted.[65] She went on: "Your ability to market yourself outside of filming makes it easier to turn down work. If you have a successful webcam business or you have a toy line with a company or you're able to feature dance in clubs or you have big nightclubs that want you to do appearances, whatever the case might be—that will allow you to turn down work for less money. A lot of times, women of color don't have those advantages." As in paid scene work, income and work opportunity in self-production and in satellite industries are hierarchized according to race, age, gender presentation, sexuality, and other registers of embodiment and identification. Thus, those who can expect the best working conditions, casting opportunities, and pay in paid scenes—young, white, conventionally attractive, cis women who perform in straight scenes and cis men who perform in gay scenes—typically find their privileged status reproduced elsewhere.[66] In turn, these disparities reify porn's existing hierarchies. Racism in satellite industries "makes that [porn rate] disparity a lot bigger," Love said, "because there are a lot of women of color that are willing to take work for less money because they need it and they can't afford to turn it down."[67]

At the same time, alternative income streams sometimes offer opportunities for subverting porn's hierarchies. The workers most marginalized in the mainstream porn industry are both more likely to produce their own content and to pursue alternative income streams in which they have the greatest amount of autonomy (even when, as Love points out, such mobility is limited by hierarchy). It is easier to control working conditions when you are the boss, and workers who are dismissed by porn agents and producers because of their race, gender presentation, weight, or age often find success in self-production and satellite work. Clients and fans have a much broader range of desires than establishment managers can imagine, and products and services born of autonomous forms of sex work are overwhelmingly less homogenous than ones with top-down management. In the freelance future, as Sara Horowitz puts it, "management won't be top-down so much as grassroots-up."[68] That future is largely already here

Hustling in Porn's Gig Economy

in porn, and this has material effects on both the production process and the kind of porn viewers see.

The democratization of porn production—what Lucy Neville describes as a shift from "cultural production" to "participatory cultures"—means "the loss of elite control over sexual discourse."[69] New sexual stories sometimes emerge when different people get to tell them. A Black performer-producer told me, for example, that one of the extra-economic benefits of self-production is that she gets to show hot, loving interracial sex with her white boyfriend without any of the racist tropes this would typically entail on a paid set. The wide range of queer sexualities represented in DIY porn also attests to the ways that democratized production can change the representative landscape.[70] Democratized production changes the representational politics of mainstream, too. Jennifer Moorman tracks, for example, the ways that women filmmakers' approaches to "extreme" mainstream content resist conventional femininity.[71]

Some self-producers, however, choose to replicate the very same representations that once made their bosses money. This presents a problem for discussions of representation. Previous writing explores workers' creative strategies for navigating racist and misogynist representations *managers* demand. Taking this kind of resistance seriously requires reading porn's texts as open to multiple meanings and resisting what Ariane Cruz describes as paranoid readings that "invest a totemic power and control in white men as the authors and primary architects of *the* interracial fantasy."[72] Such readings did not make sense when white men directors *were* the primary storytellers—as Black feminist porn scholars make clear, they grossly underestimate workers' capacity to resist—and they make even less sense now.[73] But if porn workers have historically made calculations about the kinds of pushback they can safely undertake in the context of the wage relation, porn's changing class landscape unsettles this dynamic. Workers want to be the ones profiting from their own labor, however loaded its representational politics. Now, they can. Prince Yahshua, for instance, told me about his choice to name his production company Silverback Entertainment, a marketing nod to the racist association of Black men with gorillas.[74] This might be resistance, but it is a more complicated kind. In 2014, I argued that capital, not workers, owns the ethical burdens associated with labor—if labor (re)produces products, representations, or relations that harm, capital, not workers, is responsible.[75] This does not hold quite so well in the porn landscape as it exists now.

Most workers do not want to be workers. And class mobility is not evidence of privilege in any simple way. As Herschel Savage put it in this book's introduction, "Not owning your product, you're in a desperate place."[76] The stakes are even higher for multiply marginalized workers, whose conditions are poorest under a boss's control. For some performers, taking on managerial roles is a matter of survival rather than profit seeking. For most, the reality lies somewhere in the middle. This puts them at odds with much anti-capitalist theory and organizing, which focuses on a working class defined by its subordinate relationship in the production process. This working class is more sympathetic, and more conceptually wieldy, than one that includes people who sometimes stake out independence by extracting value on their own terms. But we should not hope that subjects remain in a "desperate place" only so that they might maintain ideological purity. To do so would be to prioritize a simple class analysis over workers' own desires and critiques.

Now more than ever, porn workers have access to the means of production, and most employ others at least some of the time—hiring other performers for self-produced scenes, contracting postproduction editors, and so on. Orthodox Marxist theories of class cannot accommodate this—in Marx and Engels's original terms, this places worker-managers squarely in the bourgeoisie.[77] Indeed, porn workers struggle not to be working class in the traditional sense of "selling their labour-power in order to live."[78] For many, selling one's labor to a boss is profoundly degrading; for others, it is simply unsavvy when you have access to the means of production: your body, a smartphone, a web connection. And so most porn workers are not just *workers*, but the language and politics of the bourgeoisie does not fit either—they do not, as the bourgeoisie traditionally has, have access to wealth that protects them from the daily work of survival. Instead, class mobility is a means of making do.

Trade relationships and self-produced solo scenes offer a potentially disruptive alternative to waged work, on the one hand, and becoming a boss, on the other. Here, performers might be understood as "appropriate[ing] their own surplus labor," a designation the Marxist feminist geographers writing as J. K. Gibson-Graham lends to the truly self-employed.[79] They argue that this makes self-employment a potentially noncapitalist economic relationship, and indeed, performers can use trade to circumvent the wage relationship. But if trade scenes are free of direct managerial control, they are not free of social hierarchy, and some performers said negotiating terms and boundaries in this less formal context presents

Hustling in Porn's Gig Economy

its own challenges. When performers share scene ownership but have larger distribution networks (more paying fans on a personal website, for instance), a shared scene could be extractive even if distribution rights are shared. Thus, performer and activist Jiz Lee's best-practices guide for trade quotes Siri's advice against trading with performers who would "profit from the scene exponentially more."[80] Murkier still are unpaid shoots not between professionals engaged in trade but featuring a performer with a "civilian" partner (a non-sex-worker partner or a willing stranger from hookup apps, for instance). Non-sex-worker partners may feel that sex with a porn star is a fair deal, but this also represents a dynamic in which performer-producers make money off of someone's unpaid sexual labor. This is not a wage relationship, but it is not noncapitalist either.

Less important than fitting this industry into language developed in another historical moment—a language that seriously undertheorized sex work and other forms of "nonproductive" labor even then—is making sense of how porn's actual class locations are ethically and politically charged.[81] If so much Marxist theory assumes a working and owner class and assigns both normative weight and political potential accordingly—the bourgeoisie exploits, the working class resists that exploitation—we need better ways to talk about exploitation and resistance when these classes are not stable. And so rather than a fixed working class, Gibson-Graham describe classed locations as "multiple and shifting."[82] These shifts are particularly mercurial in porn, where one could be a manager in the morning and a worker in the evening or both simultaneously.

In view of its democratizing potential, Mireille Miller-Young describes DIY porn as "an intensely politicized space where the line between exploitation and empowerment, pleasure and peril, community and alienation is totally blurred."[83] This is also true of work in satellite industries. But it does not follow that we should, in the spirit of much post-Marxist cultural theory, minimize that class dynamics carry political weight. Exploitation and resistance persist, even when their subjects are unfixed. While sitting with the messiness of porn's class relations, I also want to make clear that that messiness does not make class less politically charged. Even if managers are not always the same people, managers enforce workplace discipline. Even when producers are not good-old-boy studio magnates, sole ownership of a scene (in contrast to solo or trade arrangements in which all performers own the final scenes) means making money from someone else's labor. A boss is still a boss, even if only for two hours.

Class is, as Marxist economists Stephen Resnick and Richard Wolff argue, "an adjective, not a noun."[84] Class positions are not fixed identities, but they are something we *do*, and that unfixedness does not make the doing any less material. When in managerial roles, people tend to act like managers. Lexington Steele put it this way: "Being a check writer gives you a whole different perspective."[85] Porn's class mobility means that most performers have access to that different perspective, but unless they abandon performing for producing, they also have access to the perspectives born of working for a living. This is how we get to worker-managers who at once strenuously advocate performers' labor rights and undermine them on a set the worker-managers direct.

To acknowledge the transformative potential of autonomous production is not to celebrate freelance gig economies as a frontier for the unencumbered. Even when one is able to be free of a direct boss, asymmetries persist. And a constellation of value-extracting intermediaries and third-party providers, as well as the porn managers who profit because of the industry's symbiotic relationship to gig economies, remains. Romanticizing this is, I think, quite dangerous in a labor market—in porn and beyond—characterized by growing contingency. The disappearance of direct managerial control can signal less retreat from capital than its obfuscation behind the veil of tech development. This is a market in which self-employed workers are often readiest to work more for less and one in which hybrid class locations present real—but not insurmountable— barriers to solidarity and collective action among workers *as workers*.

Porn's class story is not a simple one of workers against bosses. Rather, working people struggle for autonomy, sometimes in ways that undermine that struggle for others. With the exception of totally horizontal trade arrangements, it is impossible to free oneself from managerial control without visiting it on others. This is an ethical crisis that is irresolvable under this system. And yet, porn's greater class mobility gives workers—as individuals and as a community—real power. It actively seizes that power from porn's traditional managerial class of studio owners, producers, and the freelance and contracted directors who act as middle management. For Conner Habib, porn's DIY spirit means that "we don't need your corporations' money to do whatever we want. We're gonna do it, and we're gonna pay each other somehow. . . . The more of us that do that, the more the system will fail."[86] Managers know this.

In 2018, director Mike Quasar tweeted about performers' use of time on set to distribute content to fans on OnlyFans and Premium Snapchat, which allow fans to purchase access to performers' self-produced photos and videos: "If you're going to use my set as your personal studio and probably make more money than I do, maybe I should at least get a discount or leave your phone in your fucking car!!!"[87] A popular management-side attorney liked the tweet. Quasar added, "I've been doing this over 25 years and I have a 16 thousand dollar camera but some girl with an iPhone is probably making more money than me."[88] In some cases, he is right—performers can make more money producing their own content than the career directors and producers who once claimed these profits.

Performers have done a better job of adapting to porn's changing market, identifying a range of income streams and marketing personalized content fans are willing to pay for. Meanwhile career directors and producers, who have largely failed to do the same, watch their content be pirated and their profit margins shrink. When I started this research in 2012, producers and directors talked about direct-to-consumer scenes as a relatively minor threat dwarfed by the specter of privacy. Today, they identify direct-to-consumer scenes as an immediate threat not only to market share but also to access to labor. In 2019, a producer worried to me that he could not compete with the direct-to-consumer market. Performers who can make a living on their own terms, with partners they choose, and from the comfort of their own homes, are less willing to work regularly under others. Instead, a scene here or there—to use as a "personal studio," as Quasar put it, and advertising tool—will do. This is the risk, from managers' perspective, of conditions that require workers to work multiple gigs in order to get by: workers may find that they prefer side gigs and come to be less and less available for waged scene work.

As paid scenes have transitioned from being primarily vehicles for extraction to (also) marketing tools for performers, even the class dynamics of traditionally produced (rather than self-produced, by performers) scenes have shifted. In these cases, directors are still management in that they control the production of the scene itself, but Quasar is right that in some cases (especially for contract directors who do not own the content they produce), they are making less than performers. Even when producers own the rights to a scene, they may make less from it, over time, than performers do. Waged scene work might not, in this case, be exploitative in the true spirit of the term—where bosses accrue surplus value in excess of the wage they pay. Directors insist that the work they do is more skilled—with twenty-five years of experience and an expensive camera—and that they should therefore command higher profits. Craftily navigating porn's gig economy, performers upend these assumptions.

This is remaking the porn landscape. Even with studio profits at a low, scene rates are going up among performers who can make significant amounts through other means. At the industry's trade convention, major studios take up less and less space and are slowly being replaced by booths advertising webcam and direct-to-consumer scene sales. The porn industry's trade group is struggling to raise member funds as the traditional employer class gets replaced with a dispersed community of performer-producers, many of whom do not believe their interests are represented by the same organization built for their former bosses. The Marxist line that capitalism sows the seeds of its own destruction is crystallized here.[89] Workers use the internet as a tool for helping this process along.

THE CLASS POLITICS OF CENSORSHIP

Porn workers' access to that tool, however, is being progressively undermined. Policy makers, in concert with anti-sex-worker lobbyists, have been systematically working to prevent sex workers from accessing the open web. In the years in which I conducted fieldwork, three major sites that sex workers used to advertise and screen for in-person services were shut down and seized by the FBI under the guise of preventing sex trafficking. Then, in the spring of 2018, Congress passed the Allow States and Victims to Fight Online Sex Trafficking Act together with the Stop Enabling Online Sex Trafficking Act (SESTA), which threatened new federal penalties for third-party websites accused of providing a platform for traffickers to advertise.[90] This was in spite of a lack of evidence that such platforms are a major avenue for traffickers; leaked documents showed, for example, that federal prosecutors knew that Backpage did not actually facilitate trafficking even before its pre-SESTA shutdown.[91] SESTA's passage was also counter to the urging of sex workers, sex trafficking survivors, and many service providers, who said that the law would make trafficking victims and workers in the sex trades more vulnerable to violence.[92] As this book was going to press, EARN IT threatened to intensify the state surveillance that SESTA made possible.[93]

Like other forms of criminalization, SESTA hits multiply marginalized workers—people of color, trans women, and migrants—hardest.[94] Within a month of SESTA's passage, at least 135 websites had shut down or barred users they suspected of engaging in paid sex.[95] These included sites in-person sex workers use to advertise and screen clients but also a range of payment processors, file-sharing programs, and social media platforms. The relative privilege of porn-star status protects performer-escorts from some, but not all, of the risks of criminalization. Porn workers' built-in visibility (through scenes used as marketing tools, large Twitter followings, and access to fans at conventions) makes them somewhat less reliant on sex-work-specific online advertising to connect to escort clients. But SESTA's deliberately broad definition of trafficking meant that a whole range of websites beyond those that facilitate direct contact between sex workers and clients either closed down or restricted access for anyone suspected of being associated with sex industries. Workers had already been navigating the internet's more dispersed anti-sex-worker restrictions for years, as platforms randomly changed terms of service agreements to bar sex workers or, without warning, started enforcing existing ones. But in SESTA's wake, this became organized and sweeping. Video conferencing, payment processing, and social media platforms, among others, are now less available to porn and other sex workers. Google Drive erased performers' video files without warning, in some cases destroying workers' only scene files.[96] The reader will recall that these are the very platforms porn workers used to reduce their dependence on managers and other third parties.

In the wreckage, some workers have been pushed back to the same extractive relationships they had become so good at circumventing. When they cannot advertise and safely screen clients on their own, some in-person workers turn back to managers (or "pimps") to do this for them. When social media platforms close sex worker accounts, they lose a key tool for building a fan base independent of whether established porn managers think they are worth being cast. When file-sharing services close sex worker accounts, it becomes harder for porn workers to sell content directly. And when free video conferencing services shut sex workers out, they must rely on webcam sites that take 60 percent of their earnings. Conventional porn managers—those who worry that alternative income streams restrict their access to willing workers—are in many ways well served by these shifts.

Supporters of web censorship sell it as an attack against powerful operators who use the internet to exploit women and girls. In reality, it empowers those very operators. Internet censorship is a boon for capital, threatening to reassert a dynamic workers have fought so hard to topple.

Web censorship also reasserts the old rule that sex must be free, undermining workers' efforts to be paid for their sexual labor and tipping the scales of power in favor of clients. Thus, porn industry journalist Gustavo Turner describes the ways censoring policies on sites such as Instagram and Facebook encourage abusive fans' "entrapping and 'revenge reporting' on sex workers."[97] Performer Kendra James faced an account closure, for example, when a fan reported her for solicitation after she replied to his demand for free nudes with a link to her paid site.[98] Feminist studies scholar Anne McClintock observes that, historically, sex work criminalization "places power more firmly in male hands"; censorship operates in the same way.[99]

The power to make a living outside the wage system and to avoid unpaid hetero sex is, as Silvia Federici has long argued, central to what has always made independent sexual labor so threatening to capital.[100] Capital requires the "separation of the producer from the means of production" through enclosure, and this is "something that has to be continuously reenacted, especially in times of capitalist crisis, when class relations are challenged."[101] Internet censorship does exactly this kind of work, hardening old rules about who's in charge. Even "cyberspace can be enclosed," writes the sex worker theorist Tamara MacLeod.[102]

What comes next is still very much in flux and will remain so as long as the contradictions of capitalism persist. What is at stake is a potentially seismic redistribution of control over both profit and work processes. Workers want that redistribution. They also want flexibility. We have seen what this looks like in the porn context, but porn workers' correctives here should also give pause to those who see only loss in the move away from the single boss and the cubicle farm. Gig economies can offer workers meaningful control even if they do not constitute a radical alternative to the wage relation (and even when they sometimes reinforce it). Porn workers' creative interventions in porn and its satellite industries—and managers' grasping reactions to their growing obsolescence—bear this out. Few straight workers today have figured out how to hack their industries to the same extent, but we can imagine that the desire to do so is generalizable.

The economic form that once preserved porn's status quo—flexible, precarious work in which workers shoulder the costs of doing business— could also be its undoing. Taking this tension seriously can shift how we

Hustling in Porn's Gig Economy

think about late capitalism more broadly. It suggests, first, that we should abandon backward-looking politics that seek a return to systems that were comparatively stable but also stifling. And it reminds us that workers are often one step ahead, driving change, even when it seems that capital is exerting control in straightforwardly top-down ways. Reading workers' creativity as merely a reaction to managerial power assumes too much of capital and too little of workers. Workers use gig economies not only to respond and adapt to management's rules but also to refuse and recraft them.

4

I'm Kind of Always Working, but It's Also Almost Always Really Fun

Porn and the Boundaries between Life and Work

Stoya was finishing a work call when I arrived at her home for our interview. She was launching her own production company at the time, and we talked about the demands of behind-the-scenes labor. I asked how she separated work from the rest of her life when so much work was at home. "I don't. I'm just me," she responded. "Any hobby gets turned into work, and all of my work, because I'm such a pain in the ass about 'Well, it has to be fun for me, these are the people I'm willing to work with,' my whole life is a really awesome hobby. So I'm kind of always working, but it's also almost always really fun."[1]

Royalties from the sex-toy line modeled after her made it possible to pick and choose her other paid work, Stoya told me. Such freedom to choose only fun projects is rare among most porn workers (and most working people, for that matter). In a compressed market, most performers take the gigs they can get. But the experience of almost always working is nearly ubiquitous. Porn workers spend countless hours trying to get and keep work. Being work-ready means preparing for scenes and resting after them, marketing oneself, and networking. For some workers, it also means activism—fighting the anti-sex-worker stigma and policies that make it harder to make a living. Together, these labors lead to workdays without a clear end. And because the work looks, and sometimes feels, like things we elsewhere do for fun and for free, the boundaries between work and life blur. The late-capitalist tendency to bring daily life to the market—what Marxist feminist theorists Christina Morini and Andrea Fumagalli call "life put to work"—is intensified in porn work.[2]

This chapter explores how porn workers navigate lives "put to work." Its premise is that the question I originally asked Stoya—how do you separate work and life?—is the wrong one. Rather, we might begin with the understanding that such boundaries do not exist in the way labor scholars have traditionally understood them. Then, we can ask more interesting questions: What does it feel like when life is so thoroughly put to work? When workers wish to protect small pieces of life from work, how do they do this? What are the stakes of claiming that a thing that looks like (private) life is really (public) work? Who profits, and who pays? Rather than try to recover a way of working that more cleanly separates work and life, a Marxist feminist read on porn work asks how these categories come to be attached to payment in the first place.

The stakes of porn's blurred boundaries between life and work are heightened because freedom from work that consumes life is a major reason workers seek out porn work in the first place. "Fuck overtime!" workers told me and explained that one of porn's major draws is that one can make more money in less time, leaving space for a life not wholly focused on earning next month's rent.[3] But porn, like much feminized, freelance, contingent, and creative work, pervades one's life in other, more diffuse ways. Here, porn work is a microcosm of the tension so many workers have found in the transition to late capitalism: we flee traditional employment in search of more autonomy but find that work that looks less like work can be all consuming. The racialized and feminized workers who have historically been excluded from and have opted out of straight work of course knew this long before we arrived at *late* capitalism.

Unlike overtime, life as work is not paid at time and a half. Instead, it is typically not paid at all. "If you are not paid by the hour," Marxist feminists have long noted, "nobody cares how long it takes you to do the work."[4] As we have seen, much left labor analysis finds a miscalculation in workers' pursuit of jobs that feel less like work—workers thought they would find freedom but found commoditized life instead, and bosses (including algorithmic ones) profited heartily. Porn workers sometimes echo this sense. But most also say they would trade porn's "almost always working," but usually in ways that are more fun, for straight work alternatives. If Morini and Fumagalli describe "life put to work" as the process by which capital derives profit from daily life, rather than standardized production as in a factory setting, it is also true that porn workers describe this relation as potentially profitable for them, too.[5] Time, as cultural theorist Sarah Sharma suggests in her study of business travel, taxi, and office work, is "a site of material struggle."[6] And while employers manipulate time to get more out of workers for less, workers also use time toward their own ends.

"FUCK OVERTIME!"

"I've worked my entire life," Tara Holiday told us in this book's introduction, "and this is so much better."[7] Before porn, she had worked as a massage therapist. "You have to go to school forever," she said, and when you can finally start working, spas pay just fifteen dollars for a one-hour massage. Porn gigs might be inconsistent, but in one scene (which typically involved around five hours of work) Holiday could make $800–$1,200. In addition to pay, porn offers "freedom." "You get to be your own boss," she said, and this means more control over scheduling and gigs. "You don't have to be a rocket scientist to see what's better there," she added. Porn is still a job, and one has to "see the business as a business" to get by. This means not just performing in scenes but also preparing for work, self-marketing, and cobbling together varied income streams. Porn work is "in this gray area, because you're having fun *and* you're working," Holiday explained.

Throughout my interviews, workers echoed Holiday's calculation. As freelance work, porn promised flexibility and autonomy. "My degree in art was taking me nowhere," said Ana Foxxx. After a few promotions, she was managing a grocery store but "still barely making enough to live."[8] When she found out that porn would pay in one day what the grocery store did

Porn and the Boundaries between Life and Work

in a month, she thought, "Why would I go back?" A month later, she quit the grocery store. "I was just like, 'Fuck overtime!'" she said. "I'd rather be on overtime humping a hot dude or chick. The stress of this is way easier to trade over a nine-to-five." Straight jobs meant economic insecurity for many of the porn workers who left them, but they also consumed too much of life. For most, porn's pay is simply "decent," as Danny Wylde put it.[9] The freedom to pursue a life outside work is what sets porn above straight work. In Wylde's case, this meant time for school, playing music, writing, and politically engaged porn projects. "I found some ways to make this politically interesting to me and found some ways to make it art for me," he told me. "Other [times], it was just like, 'It's a job, the pay is decent, it gives me time to pursue these other interests.'"

Unencumbered time is crucial for workers who juggle caretaking responsibilities, school, creative projects, activism, and chronic health conditions. All were things that workers said were incompatible with the flows of straight work. For Sinnamon Love, porn meant that she could "maintain some economic freedom and still be able to provide for my kids and take care of them myself without having to quit school."[10] Before it, balancing school, childcare, and two minimum-wage jobs had been deeply taxing. Interviewees echoed this, returning again and again to the high cost of trying to reconcile straight work with life. Paying her way through college while working full-time at a coffee shop and part time as a "cigarette girl" circulating local bars and selling cigarettes and candy at a steep markup, Lorelei Lee was "exhausted."[11] "That's really it. I was just tired," she said. "So I quit my job and started looking in the back pages of *SF Weekly* and *Bay Guardian* for nude shoots."

Even workers without particularly intense demands on their time resisted the control inherent in straight work. They, too, cited "quality of life" as porn's major draw and talked about freedom over time as quality of life's primary measurement. When the option of performing in porn presented itself to Lexington Steele, then an investment banker, he realized that he "had an opportunity to pursue some sort of journey that had only been fantasy."[12] "The second thing was quality of life," he said. "For a twenty-eight-year-old, I was ballin'. But the converse of that was that, as a Wall Street broker, the work rate is ridiculous. It was very easy to make the leap." Again and again, workers said that faced with straight work's regimented schedules, it was easy to make the leap into freelance porn work. "I can basically do whatever I want," Chanel Preston said of her porn work schedule. "I go on vacation when I want, I take off any time I want, I can go see my family at Christmas."[13] Even when she is in town and working, porn allows freedom from a set schedule. Unless she has a gig scheduled that day, Preston has total control over the pace of her day. Among other things, "I can wake up at whatever time I want," she said. This basic freedom is something porn workers consistently found lacking in straight jobs. In his porn work memoir, Tyler Knight talks about the straight job he imagines is waiting for him after porn: "Some MBA . . . tells me when I can do life-sustaining things such as eating lunch or peeing."[14]

There is a limit to the freedom porn work promises. The demands of on-set work also mean that one cannot eat lunch, or pee, whenever the mood strikes. And as we have seen, unpredictable schedules on set limit control over one's day. This makes it difficult to schedule other paid work, time with friends, classes, childcare, or interviews (as I learned during one five-hour wait at a sports bar in the Valley). Only one interviewee said she worked on a standard schedule. Lorelei Lee, formerly an independently contracted performer, was employed as an in-house performer-director at Kink.com when we first interviewed. Kink.com films from ten to six, and Lee explained that while "sometimes that feels like a much longer shoot, other times I'm like, 'It's six o'clock, I'm going home.' I never have to be on set until 2 A.M.—that's nice. You can plan a life."[15] A common complaint among porn workers is that unpredictable schedules make it difficult to "plan a life." This was a priority when I asked what they would change about their work. But only a fraction of the porn workweek is spent on set, and as workers' calculations reveal, one can make in those few hours what would take days in most straight jobs.

This does not mean that most performers are netting exponentially more than they did in straight jobs. "There are very few places outside of the medical profession, or specialties, where you can make the rate per hour that you make performing," explained Richie Calhoun, "but then there's always the question of how often you perform."[16] Most performers shoot only a few scenes each month, making their overall pay comparable to what it would have been in straight jobs. It is time, sometimes to a greater extent than money, that makes porn worthwhile. Materialist critiques of work that focus wholly on money and on-the-job conditions are missing something. Time is material, too, and workers want more than shop-floor control or a larger cut of the profits. Here again, porn workers echo the autonomist demand not just for better work but for less work.

Workers come to porn in search of a reprieve from the mundane work that consumes so much of life. In some ways, porn delivers. But, as elsewhere, the double bind of freelance work is work hours that are potentially limitless.[17] This goes beyond long hours "on the job." Instead, it reveals a much deeper boundlessness around where work begins and ends. This is a question of time: If most porn work takes places off set and off the clock, what is a workday? It is also a matter of porn work's content, which blurs the lines between working, preparing for work, and cultivating the kind of self that makes work possible.

WAGES FOR PORN WORK

By piecing together a range of income streams, workers can make money—or at least build a fan base that might produce income in the future—almost anywhere and at any time. Workers described this hustle as a more or less constant set of labors. When one knows there is money to be made on the phone while hanging out at home or that the strip club near your vacation destination will pay $1,000 for a guest appearance, it becomes clear just how much discrete time off work costs. The cost of taking time away from preparatory and self-marketing labors may be even higher—personal brands need constant tending. Porn workers know very well what Nicholas Ridout and Rebecca Schneider describe as "the constant audition that has become the work of getting work" in the mainstream creative sector.[18]

When she first moved to Los Angeles, Lorelei Lee worked "constantly," shooting five to seven days a week, sometimes twice a day. Some weeks, though, she was scheduled for just one scene. "I never knew where I was working the next day or if I was working, so I could never plan anything," she told me.[19] During the three weeks she was in LA each month, Lee shared an agent-owned "model house" with a number of other performers. Her agent lived at the house, accompanying performers to jobs and industry events as well as taking them to dinners, shopping, and to the movies. For agent and performers alike, the workday had no finite end point. Industry heavy hitters would visit the house throughout the day, or performers hoping to make contacts would go with the agency's driver to pick up other performers from set. This meant that even on days when no shoot was scheduled, one had to be "on" and ready to be seen. "You're constantly auditioning," Lee explained.

Performers are free to take days off, but the nagging sense that work might dry up made planning time off feel too risky for Lee. This was not because pressing financial need compelled her to take as many bookings as possible. At the time, Lee said, "I had more money than I'd ever had in my life and I wasn't spending it at all. I was hoarding it, actually." While the workweek is potentially boundless, freelance careers have boundaries always looming: aging out could mean forced retirement, one might get injured and need time off, demand for a particular look might dwindle, or a colleague's positive sexually transmitted infection (STI) result might mean an industry-wide moratorium on filming. In stark contrast to the boom-time sensibility of the 1990s, a sense that porn production might irrevocably change at any time seems to grow deeper by the year. Stricter laws might make it impossible (or cost prohibitive) to shoot, or the forward march of piracy might mean that shoots could not be funded at all. This is not unlike the situation of freelancers in other industries in crisis; adjuncts in the humanities, journalists, and freelance editors, among others, describe similar pressures to take work while they can.

Porn workers realize, though, that constant work is unsustainable, and many seek out ways to create distance from work. When it won't do to clock out within the space of a week, some create even stricter lines by leaving town for days or months. Lee kept an apartment in San Francisco and scheduled a week each month in which she would go home and rest. Other performers leave home to find work rather than to take a break from it. Performers who live throughout the United States travel to Los Angeles once or twice a month, booking as many gigs as possible. Performers sometimes live away from major filming locations because of proximity to family or cost of living; this is also a way for workers to establish some separation between their lives as performers and the other roles they occupy. Rates and opportunities for multiple bookings are declining, but savvy performers schedule trade shoots and cobble together as many income sources as possible to make the trip worthwhile. Christopher Daniels, one of these commuting performers, explained that during work trips, "you're hustling the entire time."[20] Then, he flew home to rest and prepare for the next one.

Keeping filming and living separate does not address the constant labors of self-making and marketing that porn workers undertake in workspaces ranging from gyms and salons to homes and vacation spots. Perceptions of what constitutes time off vary among workers and over time and place for individuals. For most performers, time off means taking a break from filming and other paid gigs but continuing to maintain websites, interact with fans on Twitter, pursue bookings, and undertake the countless other unpaid tasks porn work comprises. One is rarely off the clock from the labors of self-making. A performer might take a break from full makeup and hair removal in between shoots while continuing a rigorous gym schedule, for instance. And much of what workers described as "time off" is spent resting from the physical wear and tear of the job. As many straight workers well know, time away from in-person job duties rarely translates to a reprieve from the labors we carry out in private, whether they are express functions of the job or required to maintain ourselves as employable. Porn workers undertake these expansive labors of self-making and marketing "for the privilege of being eligible to be hired," as Richie Calhoun put it.[21]

Marxist feminists argue that capital profits from the unpaid work required to reproduce ourselves as workers (literally, as in childbearing and rearing, and more expansively, as in readying oneself and other wage earners for paid work through cleaning, cooking, emotional support, and the like).[22] Without it, there would be no workforce. "The wage," for Silvia Federici writing on the Wages for Housework movement, does not pay for the work we do but rather "hides all the unpaid work that goes into profit."[23] In marking this, Marxist feminists lift the veil of (nonmarket) privacy from exchanges they argue were always already public. While Wages for Housework theorists focused on unpaid work in the home, thinkers inspired by their critique, Morini and Fumagalli among them, mobilize it to make sense of the broad range of labors we do to reproduce ourselves, and others, as workers.

The theory of reproductive labor is increasingly relevant to all workers to the extent that labor in the contemporary economy takes on the trappings of feminized reproductive work in its tendency to reproduce people, ideas, and desires rather than durable goods.[24] The Italian autonomist movement, in conversation with allied Marxist feminists from the start, draws out these connections. Paolo Virno suggests that, in late capitalism, "the old [Fordist] distinction between 'labor' and 'non-labor' ends up in the distinction between remunerated life and non-remunerated life. The border between these two lives is arbitrary, changeable, subject to political decision making."[25] Marxist feminists make clear that that distinction never held. Here, as in our previous discussion of precarity, they push back against the argument that these conditions are new. Under Fordism and the economic models that came before it, working-class women and people of color still did work that blurred the line between labor and nonlabor, and the boundary between paid and unpaid life was indeed changeable and a matter of politics. Porn workers of all genders perform feminized reproductive labor, and this is both a continuation of timeworn realities of feminized work and a microcosm of late capitalism's increased tendency toward blurred work-life boundaries in a wide range of jobs.

When work is feminized in this way, its direct relationship to value, and the wage, gets murkier. For this reason, Eva-Maria Swidler urges a move beyond an orthodox Marxist search for quantifiable surplus value. It remains true that "capitalism actively manipulates what is submerged and what is visible, what is and what is not paid for," but surplus value cannot be understood as simply "paying a wage that is less than the full labor value of the products of workers, skimming the difference for profits."[26] When the boundaries between work and life blur, it becomes less worthwhile to mark out exactly which activities produce surplus value. It also gets harder to quantify just how much value is being produced. When self-brands, ideas, and desires come to the market, their value is less clearly measurable than that of durable goods. And so surplus value also exists "beyond the wage."[27] The dynamics of reproductive labor persist in self-employed work. What is and is not paid for is as murky in a self-produced scene as it is in a waged one.

Does a scene fee cover one's time filming a sex scene, a whole day on set, or the hours spent readying oneself for work and recuperating from it? Is interacting with fans on Twitter paid time because it might generate more customers for paid side hustles? Is a vacation unpaid life time except for those moments in which, transformed into a fee-based Snapchat photo opportunity, it becomes paid work? Porn workers make different calculations in answering these questions, and most have given up the task of drawing hard boundaries around what counts. This carries risks for workers, but it also, crucially, answers their own demands for work that lets them also do life.

Exposure

Work tasks bleed into life for porn and other workers seeking to reproduce themselves as workers. The day-to-day gets folded into the matrix of the self-making and marketing that workers do in hopes that exposure will pay off at some future moment. Venus Lux put it this way: "You have to embed yourself into social media. Every single day. I hated it in the very beginning—you just sacrifice so much privacy. You're eating dinner, take a picture. You're going to the bathroom, take a picture. You're sitting on the toilet, take a picture. . . . Sometimes you lose a sense of enjoying the moment."[28] Soon after our interview, Lux tweeted a photo of herself in the bathtub. She explained that social media is the most time-consuming and invasive kind of marketing but also the most accessible to workers. At this stage in her career, in addition to maintaining a social media presence, Lux has taught herself marketing and web management, and she can afford to hire a publicist, web search optimization service, and tech person to manage online content. But even someone without start-up capital or technological expertise can use bathroom selfies and the like for self-marketing.

If the typical late-capitalist worker is "like an advert for yourself," this is even truer for porn workers.[29] They are both freelancers who must constantly be on the lookout for their next paid gig and self-marketers who cultivate a fan base to whom they market products and services directly. Across porn and satellite industries, social media is a major avenue for self-marketing. Workers build their personal brands (and, at the same time, those of their employers) on Twitter, Instagram, and other social media platforms, interacting with fans, sharing photos (both pornographic and otherwise) and anecdotes from their daily lives, and advertising the goods and services they provide. They blog about their work and other aspects of their lives and answer fan questions through their personal websites and with Ask Me Anything events on social media. Many offer more personalized exchanges with fans through private message functions on social media apps. Here, platforms for self-marketing can become sales platforms in their own right when performers sell access to more direct forms of social media engagement.

Self-marketing blurs the boundaries between work and nonwork time, between being oneself and performing a character. As Lux says, turning the everyday into work in this way can, among other things, make it difficult to enjoy the moment. To negotiate these boundaries, some workers present an online persona matched with their porn film performances, complete with discrete tones of voice, and even birthdays. Workers who opt for this approach might post photos only in full makeup and tweet about how much they enjoyed the sex on set that day, for instance. The moments one might be less able to enjoy, then, are not your own, but a character's, and this can make it feel like less of a loss to interrupt them with a selfie. Others break character strategically with candid photos of themselves going about daily activities, posts about their families and hobbies, and even fourth-wall-busting commentaries about their workplace frustrations. Still others, such as Stoya, are "just me," refusing the separation of self and character entirely. Again, the same worker might deploy all these strategies at different times—one might feel inclined to be "just me" at some moments and more guarded at others.

Performers are acutely aware of how intensely their social media presence is scrutinized. Still, many refuse to present one-dimensional online personas. "The best thing about Twitter," Vex Ashley tweeted in 2018, is that "in 1999 you could pretend that your favourite porn girls were perma-horny, passive, and amenable, but now it's unavoidable public record that we're all basically acerbic, snarky communists who do not stand for bull-shit."[30] Social media is disruptive, and not just in the employer-friendly way "disruption" is often understood. It can also create opportunities for forms of expression that critique the porn industry rather than just adver-tise its wares. Just before the January 2015 Adult Video News Awards, Ela Darling initiated the #realpornawards hashtag on Twitter. The hashtag ex-ploded, with tweets that tell a not altogether flattering story of the industry. Proposed awards included "Best Blowjob in a Xanax Haze," a nod to work-ers' use of performance-enhancing drugs; "best justification for not doing interracial while not sounding racist," a comment on white performers' role in reproducing industry racism; and "Dr. Riggs Award of Excellence (Most self-diagnosed cases of chlamydia in one year)," naming the San Fernando Valley doctor frequented by many in the industry and disclosing the prevalence of STIs on set.[31] Workers may sometimes be "advert[s] for [themselves]," but this is not as straightforwardly controlling as laments of personal branding and the panopticon of social media would suggest.

The expectation that porn workers maintain a carefully curated online presence creates real strains for porn workers, but in this case it also opens space for an alternative to the rule-following polish expected of many straight workers. Straight workers get fired for online expressions much milder than acerbic, no-bullshit communism, and yet Ashley has an active career both performing for others and producing her own content. Porn workers can and do criticize management, share controversial political ideas, and complain about fans, all without lost work. Of course, the line between charmingly unfiltered and unhirable troublemaker is blurry and changeable. One might also make oneself unhirable through too much filtered-ness. While many workers seek out porn to avoid the rule-bound world of straight work, they discover that brand management (online and off) has its own invisible rules. The explosion of self-production mitigates some of these strains (the costs of angering a director are lower when you can hire yourself) and generates others to the extent that fans sometimes behave like a legion of microbosses.

Porn and the Boundaries between Life and Work

Online interactions with fans can require heavy emotional labor as performers must at once create relatable personas and establish boundaries. Most do this by posting somewhat personal photos (of themselves at home, on vacation, or with friends and pets, for instance) and musings (about day-to-day activities, news, politics, or their workdays) but minimizing direct engagement with fans (including those who comment on their posts or otherwise address them directly). Direct engagement is often available for a fee, and performers are quick to point this out. When a fan asked for a free private chat for his birthday, the generally cheery Tanya Tate replied, "You do your job for free too? #thoughtnot."[32] Cultural products such as these may be hard to quantify in orthodox economic terms, but performers know (and communicate) exactly how much they cost.

Workers face porn and satellite industries' ubiquitous calls to work for free. "Constant marketing is the key to success," Verified Call's recruitment materials remind prospective providers for the platform.[33] Such demands of constant—and unpaid—work trouble claims of easy and fast money. One can "get started now!" and "make your own schedule," perhaps even earning "up to $10,000 per week," as webcam platform Streamate advertises, but the company's claim that webcam work is "easy and fun!" does not bear out in performers' experiences of the work.[34] Instead, workers must engage in constant marketing, be consistently online and available for work in hopes that someone will be ready to buy time, and vigorously court prospective buyers in free chat rooms. Each satellite industry has its own conventions tying free work now to paid work later. Independent escorts, for example, navigate potential clients' expectations that they will discuss fantasies at length (and for free) before an appointment. As with free work in straight jobs, sometimes the paid gig never comes.

Some workers explicitly adopt free work or other giveaways as part of a marketing strategy. "There's a lot of free stuff that I offer so that when I do have something that costs something, then [fans] feel like that's an okay trade. I think it's called 'freemium,'" Kelly Shibari explained.[35] More commonly, free work is framed as exposure one cultivates in hopes of securing work. As in the porn film business, workers in satellite industries may spend more (unpaid) time campaigning for paid work than they do working (at least to the extent that working is defined by remuneration). But if we define work as activity that makes money for someone, it becomes clear that self-marketing is work, in addition to something workers do to facilitate more work.

Self-marketing produces capital for producers who make money from scenes. It is also productive for social media platforms; scholars of digital labor argue that social media engagement is a form of labor since it, too, produces capital.[36] But just as performers creatively appropriate waged scenes as marketing tools, transforming a site of extraction into something else, they appropriate the unwaged content creation social media platforms expect toward unexpectedly remunerative ends. This might be part of why such platforms are so eager to ban sex workers. Facebook police may not like visible nipples, but one wonders if they like the subversion of unwaged digital exploitation even less—profit here is only supposed to flow one way.

Workers calculate approaches to self-marketing according to their own comfort and also the knowledge that exposure impacts hiring and firing, as it does in other sectors of the economy.[37] In an Adult Entertainment Expo seminar for aspiring directors and producers, a well-known director-producer recommended observing prospective performers' social media presences before casting, looking for those who engage with fans and who market their scenes. "We do make a lot of money off social media. We want girls that are going to promote their scenes; they're not just going to come in and do it and we're never going to hear from them again," she said.[38] In a now-familiar turn, she recommended hiring workers who are not "just there for the money," suggesting that workers who are overly focused on money will stop working after the paid workday ends. Because performers are paid a onetime fee and do not receive royalties, managers hoping that they will work even after they have been paid look for performers who are willing to promote scenes for no direct material gain. And so, exposure and promotion are at once integral to the work and defined as outside work in that they do not count toward paid work hours—"extra" work in both senses of the term.

At the same time, porn workers use self-marketing to build brands that facilitate mobility in the gig economy and make them less dependent on managers. Porn workers are savvy about whom exactly their self-marketing benefits, and many said they hustle harder to promote scenes, products, and services they own or those they felt would build their brands most substantially. On one set, I heard a director chide a performer for not retweeting her last scene. The performer later told me she thought the scene's premise was tacky and would alienate her paying fans. She did plenty of promotion for scenes she produced herself. Hers is the opposite calculation from the one the director quoted above assumes.

Money-focused performers do not promote less than those who perform for other reasons; they simply promote more strategically. Meanwhile, fans are often willing to pay for self-produced content. In trading in fans' access to what porn scholar Daniel Laurin calls "subscription intimacy," direct-to-consumer services such as OnlyFans let performers monetize intimate access.[39] Promotional labor brings inconsistent and unpredictable returns. Stoya described a host of unpaid labors—interviews, conventions, Twitter—that she undertakes "because hopefully somehow it translates into sales."[40] When marketing scenes someone else owns, she can expect no royalties, and so the benefits of self-marketing are even harder to trace. "[Producers] already gave me my paycheck," she explained, so "how much do I actually care?" But the Stoya-branded Fleshlight male masturbator device does draw royalties, and self-marketing helps to sustain its popularity. And when Stoya started her own production company, her social media following was crucial to building a paying fan base. Stoya is also a writer and journalist, and a strong following helps secure paid gigs in those economies, too. A carefully cultivated fan base can pay dividends.

At the same time, constant marketing and cultivation of fan relationships do not always have the rewards one expects. Theresa Sneft describes "the paradox of late capitalism": paid labor markets are contracting just as access to "microcelebrity" status opens up.[41] With opportunities for waged scene work waning just as opportunities for exposure widen, this is especially true in porn. For porn and other workers, "microcelebrity" has no reliable connection to material security. One publicist complained that a client with over 100,000 Twitter followers had only ten paying subscribers to her website. Likewise, the free webcam shows performers offer in hopes of driving paying clientele do not always yield paying customers. In fact, they can work as a kind of scab labor, raising expectations for what other performers will do for free and making it more difficult for everyone to charge for interactive time.

The exposure porn workers are offered in exchange for their participation in a host of projects and events (including interviews for online and print media, television, and radio) also promises benefits that are difficult to measure. Workers' calculations of the delicate balance between giving too much and too little away must be understood in the context of porn piracy, which has, they suggest, conditioned many consumers to feel entitled to performers' labor at no cost. In this context, it is particularly important to nurture a fan base whose members feel personally connected to you and are motivated to, as Tanya Tate described her fans, "go out of their way to be good to me, look out for me."[42] Relationships with fans can also be crucial for workers who need political allies. Here, performers ask that fans "look out" for them by calling their representatives when the latest anti-sex-worker legislation goes up for a vote. But here, too, fans push boundaries—activist performers complained to me about self-styled allies who were more interested in demanding their sexual attention than helping to smash the state.

The demand to work for free to sustain the possibility of future pay is not unique to porn and its satellite industries. Workers across industries are implored to offer unpaid work in exchange for the promise of potential future employment. Calls for job seekers to expand their "human capital" through unpaid internships set up unpaid work as a precondition, but not a guarantee, of paid employment.[43] Free work is a popular feature of job interviews in industries ranging from academia and food service to corporate sales, where the sample syllabus, "stage" (unpaid shift), and research presentation, respectively, are normalized aspects of the hiring process. As a *Fortune* article unironically put it, "How to get a job: work for free."[44] For independently contracted and freelance workers, especially those in creative industries, demands to work for free persist throughout a career.

Porn workers encounter similar demands to work for free in hopes of building brands and securing future work, but the industry's more porous class boundaries mean that promotion is more likely to benefit workers directly. Freelance writers enrich publishing platforms with "free promotion" packaged as currency in the "attention economy" and have little hope that readers will someday pay them for content directly.[45] A carefully cultivated Twitter presence, however, is as likely to draw fans to a porn performer's self-produced scene as it is to bring attention to one owned by a large production studio. The common freelancer slogan "exposure doesn't pay the bills" does not quite fit here. Exposure *can*, eventually, pay the bills. Porn's work of unpaid promotion is exploitative but also something else. This makes it harder to refuse.

Self-Making

The same is true of the reproductive work of self-making—workers do extensive appearance work in order to be hirable, but this work also supports various hustles from which they profit directly. While there is more aesthetic diversity among performers than the stereotype of a "porn star" suggests, performers spend time and money making themselves attractive

Porn and the Boundaries between Life and Work

to hiring managers and fans alike. Mainstream straight, trans, and gay productions tend to have the strictest beauty rules and require the most time and money of performers preparing for shoots. As we have seen, these gigs also pay more than those in genres that require less intensive beauty work, such as queer and amateur porn. Their conventions also carry over into self-managed scenes and services marketed to the same audience—a mainstream star whose fans expect coiffed extensions in her performances under a studio will likely maintain that same look in scenes they sell to fans directly.

Performers in genres that do require beauty work spend hours of unpaid time and hundreds of dollars each month readying themselves for scenes. For those cast in multiple mainstream gigs every month or who make a significant amount from self-produced scenes and side hustles, such costs are negligible in comparison to a month's wages. For others, the costs of remaining hirable consume a huge portion of their earnings. "I only shoot three times a year," explained Devlyn Red, a performer in the big beautiful woman genre who talked about the lower rates and fewer casting opportunities in that genre. "If you're only shooting once, and you're only getting $400, and your [STI] test is $165, plus the gas to drive to LA, plus you've got to go get waxed, get your hair and nails done . . . I'm breaking even sometimes. Or I'm making $100 on something I'm spending five hours shooting."[46] Other regular costs include cosmetic treatments such as Botox, tanning, and facials and body treatments designed to stand up to high definition's unforgiving gaze.

Some appearance work is explicitly required, especially of (trans and cis) women performers. Exclusive contracts with production companies include clauses indicating that the contract will be terminated if the performer changes her appearance with a new hairstyle or color or with weight gain "without written consent of the producer."[47] After she went off birth control for medical reasons, one performer told me she lost a contract because of the cystic acne she developed. Agents are straightforward in telling new talent what sells, some recommending particular cosmetic procedures and even providing an advance to cover their cost. Directors often give their own specific self-presentation instructions before a shoot, alerting self-booking performers or agents about these upon casting. An agency schedule might include the note "straight hair, natural makeup, bring sexy business looks" alongside other booking details, for instance. In addition, hiring norms constitute their own implicit appearance rules. Performers in non-BBW genres are overwhelmingly thin, and most workers maintain hirable body types with regular trips to the gym, restrictive dieting, and sometimes cosmetic surgery.

Preparatory demands are heightened for workers who fall outside the white, cis-feminine norm. In order to be hired as a trans woman, Venus Lux explained, "we have to look pretty, *and* we have to do what it takes stay hard."[48] "Looking pretty" in prescribed ways means performing a kind of conventional femininity that often requires a hormone regimen, a dynamic that porn scholar Sophie Pezzutto details in her study of trans porn work.[49] At the same time, those hormones make it more difficult to "stay hard," so trans women are caught in a double bind of preparatory labor that requires erectile supports to counter the effects of hormones. They must cover the cost of both. Many trans women would of course take hormones even if these were not required for work. The point is not that porn compels appearance rules that performers would otherwise avoid (this is only sometimes true) but rather that such work is reproductive because it makes performers work-ready and helps capital profit from their labor.

Mainstream beauty standards are also defined by a systemic devaluation of Blackness.[50] Appearance work for women of color thus means doing what one can to manipulate racialized markers. Kimora Klein, who identifies as half Black and half Asian, explained that shifting her beauty work routine gives her access to different kinds of work: "With my hair curly and I look slightly more 'ethnic.' If I tan a little bit, I do look like a light-skinned Black girl. But otherwise, if I put on the right eyeliner and straighten my hair, I look Asian. I can play to both."[51] "I mostly market myself as Asian," Klein added, noting the higher pay and greater work opportunities available to mixed women who can pass. Black performers who cannot pass encounter the contradictory expectation to conform to white beauty norms for some productions and to emphasize "exotic" traits for others. But even as they navigate such norms, Black performers find apertures for creativity and experimentation. Skin Diamond rose to prominence as one of the most popular performers of her era with a half-shaved hairstyle and tattoos, both things agents told me they advise Black performers against. Again, agents and establishment directors tend to have narrower visions of what sells than what the realities of the market bear out.

Beauty work's demands shift over the course of one's work life, and changing one's look can be an important tool in prolonging one's career. New performers often work for a core list of productions when they start

Porn and the Boundaries between Life and Work

out in the business and struggle to find work once they have made the rounds. Performers will fade out, explained Dominic Ace, "unless something is changed—maybe you got smaller boobs, bigger boobs, dyed your hair, gone postal and killed twenty people in the post office."[52] Christopher Daniels charted this trajectory for gay performers who hope for career longevity: "Start as a twink. A year later, start doing steroids and going to the gym, beef up, and be a big strong man."[53] In her early thirties—the marketing limbo in which a woman is "not a Teen, not yet a MILF"—once hugely popular performer Dana DeArmond found her bookings dwindling.[54] Together with friend and fellow performer Asa Akira, she launched Project MILF, a crowdfunding campaign organized to raise enough money for the breast implants she hoped would reinvigorate her career.

In addition to these long-term labors of upkeep, porn work can require extensive preparation just before a scene. At the close of our interview, I asked Ana Foxxx if there was anything she wanted to add. "Man, we really do work hard," she said. "The day I realized how hard it is to work in the industry is the day I did my first anal scene. All the preparation I had to do. . . . The scene was fine, just the preparation for it."[55] Preparing for work (fasting and using enemas, in this case) is, for Foxxx and others, often more labored than the scene itself. Getting ready also means doing one's own research—Foxxx solicited advice from experienced performers and asked her gay cousin what she should do to prepare for anal sex. This is what on-the-job training for porn work most often looks like, and performers are ready to share tricks of the trade with newcomers. Performer groups confronting the industry's often isolating structure have for decades worked to centralize such information sharing.

Pre-scene preparation for many performers extends beyond a paid day's work. Performers often organize their schedules the day before a scene in hopes of performing and looking their best on-camera. These goals are sometimes in conflict with each other. Performers may fast or restrict their food intake before a scene in order to appear the most slim and also to prepare for receptive anal sex but then must contend with fatigue and a lack of stamina during a demanding scene. Performers in higher-end scenes also restrict activities in the days leading up to a scene to be sure that they do not have sunburn, scrapes, or other blemishes when they come to set. BDSM performers have to be particularly careful, since an old bruise or rope burn could result in being sent home from set with no pay. Here, being work-ready means showing no signs of having recently worked.

Unless a scene demands a highly specific costume such as those required for big-budget porn parodies and BDSM shoots, performers are usually expected to bring their own wardrobe. Wardrobe costs are higher for women, who are expected to come to set with various outfits and sets of expensive lingerie. "Once you shoot in something, you retire it and replace it," explained Charity Bangs, who estimated monthly wardrobe costs of upward of $200.[56] "A dead give-a-way that you're in porn is buying 20 pairs of matching bras and panties at once," joked Chanel Preston.[57] As in other jobs, consumption is itself a central part of the work of porn.[58]

Performers often abstain from both paid and unpaid sex just before a scene. For receptive partners, abstaining before a shoot can mean less risk of coming to work already sore or with microfissures that might make them more susceptible to STIs. Cis men and trans women who perform as insertive partners (or "tops") hope that abstaining from sex before a shoot will help them stay erect and provide for a more explosive ejaculation shot. Before the advent of erectile support medications, topping was a particularly specialized skill—few tops could meet the demands of screen sex. After Viagra's 1998 arrival on the market, "any[one] could be a porn star," explained Carter Stevens.[59] This is not quite true—topping is still hard work, and "the pressure to have a hard dick gets in your head, it's really difficult," as the current performer Christopher Daniels explained.[60] But erectile supports did make this part of the job easier and, in the process, both undermined existing performers' bargaining power (by increasing the pool of those who could do the work) and made the work less anxiety provoking to do.

Now, erectile support medications are ubiquitous, and directors assume that performers will come prepared and on their own dime. "[Studios] need to provide that stuff," Daniels said. "Most performers don't have health insurance." Five vials of injectable erectile support cost about $350, he said, and each "could do like one and a half hard-ons." It can also be difficult to procure such medicines as a young person with no medical indexes for erectile dysfunction. Many performers see the same doctor, whom they call the "candy man" because he is willing to prescribe off-label. In this case, being work-ready carries significant risks.

Resting

The work of reproduction also includes rest. Scene work is, after all, intense physical labor. If getting hair extensions and STI tests is porn work,

Porn and the Boundaries between Life and Work

so, too, are curing an infection, nursing a sprained ankle, giving the heart a reprieve from Viagra, and abstaining from penetrative sex while mucous membranes repair. These labors made up a great deal of what interviewees described as "time off."

Workers across industries can identify with taking time away from paid work simply so that we can return to it, what Sarah Sharma calls "recalibration."[61] Social workers are advised to undertake "self-care" in order to avoid "burnout" and "compassion fatigue."[62] Athletes use days off to heal torn ligaments and prepare the body for another round. Here, too, the characteristics of the "new" precarious economy are not all that new. Mid-century steelworkers (paradigmatic workers of the Fordism many labor scholars mourn) found their off-work hours consumed with adjusting the body to unpredictable scheduling, healing from grueling conditions, and even adjusting their diets to favor strong-tasting foods—the only things workers could taste because the work destroyed their sense of taste and smell.[63] Here as in porn, the workday ends, but the work remains.

In porn, recalibration's demands involve the diffuse labor of "self-care" but also targeted healing from the particular risks scenes present. As we have seen, workers' concerns here are not, as many outsiders assume, limited to STI transmission. Noting the connections between porn and other work, Conner Habib pointed to stress as "probably the biggest health problem in the industry. You're stressed out about going in, you're stressed out about looking good, you're stressed out about eating the right thing, you're stressed out about how people are going to perceive you, how you're going to perform."[64] Alongside the daily toll of stress, the concerns workers noted most often include the physical wear and tear of intense athletic labor and the more mundane aftereffects of sex. Thus, reflecting the experience of many other cis women performers, one performer described "a carousel of yeast infection, bacterial infection. . . . That puts you out of commission, and no one pays you for the days you have to take off of work. No one pays for the yeast infection medicine or your trip to the doctor."[65] This is, of course, not unique to paid sex—yeast infections are a common aftereffect of unpaid sex, too—but here they are directly related to paid work and yet displaced into the realm of the personal.

In the vast majority of cases it goes without saying that workers will bear the associated costs, including testing, treatment, and time off work.[66] While filming a camera-friendly but cumbersome shot, Prince Yahshua's partner's weight came down on his penis at the wrong angle. It "broke," as Yahshua described it, requiring multiple surgeries and four months off work. His medical care alone cost $120,000. Except for $20,000 the production company volunteered, Yahshua covered the costs as well as the wages lost during four months off work. When I asked him if the producers had production insurance, he explained, "Most companies don't. They're supposed to."[67] Yahshua seemed neither surprised nor particularly bothered by this. Trying to figure out why, I ventured, "It's funny, what seems outrageous to me versus what actually bothers workers. To me, this is one of the clearest workplace injuries imaginable. It's on film!" Laughing, he responded: "It really is on film. But we're independent contractors, and we've never had a union or anything. It's a competitive industry. We can say we're going to get together till we're blue in the face, but it never really happens. . . . *It worked itself out.* [The company] was there to bring their people around to make sure I was okay. As soon as I was good enough to come back, my first job was with them." Chapter 5 explores the policy questions around contractor status—here, we'll keep our focus on healing as a kind of reproductive work.

During her first month performing, Lara was hired to do a four-day location shoot with one scene scheduled each day and no time to recuperate between scenes.[68] As a result, she explained, "I was torn so badly I had to have surgery."[69] "The last two days I almost could not do the work at all," she said. "I just kind of gritted my teeth and went through with it." The compressed scheduling was the studio's call, reducing the costs associated with crews, locations, and hotel stays. Now, Lara schedules rest days at her own expense to give her body time to heal. Workers managing their own schedules describe similar calculations, though their own bottom line, rather than management's, is at stake. Performers who live out of town and travel for scene opportunities try to compress as many scenes into a trip as possible, as Lorelei Lee's and Christopher Daniels's earlier stories suggested. And even workers who do not have immediate time constraints struggle to turn down gigs in a market in which the work could dry up at any time. They schedule recalibration accordingly.

Resting can also mean recuperating not only from the scene but from the side effects of medicines that made the scene possible. The erectile aids performers who "top" use to facilitate on-screen sex present potential risks of dependency, cardiovascular stress, and priapism.[70] Receptive partners often use muscle relaxers to more comfortably accommodate particularly large or multiple partners (as in double and triple penetration) and sometimes experience dependency and side effects as a result. Others use a variety of antianxiety aids to help quell performance anxiety.

As Jeffrey Escoffier's history notes, this is not new—performers have long used substances, from pot to poppers, to help get the work done.[71] It is also not exceptional to porn. That workers need external supports, sometimes chemical ones, to coax our bodies and minds into performing according to job rules is another area in which porn resembles other forms of work. A body's functionality has long been measured against its ability to productively labor,[72] and a central aim of modern medicine is to enable such functionality. This is also true of emotional function—drugs are among the tools workers and institutions use to manufacture feeling.[73] Rather than view priapism or Xanax dependency as evidence of the special harms of porn, these cases call for a reevaluation of how the heavy costs (financial and otherwise) of *functionality* across work are distributed.

The question here is not about the normative value of these interventions—I trust workers in their calculations about what they need to get the job done. Instead, I am interested in the question "Are these interventions *work*?" This matters for making sense of porn work, but because porn does not hide its recalibration costs quite so well as many straight jobs, it also urges a reconsideration of how healing operates in work cycles more broadly. When I asked about healing from work, interviewees stressed that this book should not present the risks associated with scene work as evidence for porn's unique horrors. Most have worked other jobs, and they remembered experiencing risks in those, too. Chanel Preston made a point of saying that she did not see physical strain as exceptional to porn work. "It drives me nuts," she said, when outsiders approach the strains of porn work in "shaming" and sex-negative ways.[74] "What's the big deal? You go to another job, you might get sore. It's not a big deal to me."

Christopher Daniels also hoped to destabilize the idea of porn as an exceptional site of workplace risk. "There's a risk in my job just like any job," he said.

> I have a friend who worked in the VIP lounge for American Airlines, and he has horrible problems with his shoulder because the setup of the desk in these lounges is too low. It's the same thing with any job, you know? I'd rather deal with being exposed to chlamydia than be scalded by hot coffee. You take a pill and you deal with it. It took me years to realize the really horrible, negative stigma around any sexually transmitted disease. It's been very recent that I'm just like, "Okay, it's a part of life, it happens, you get taken care of and move on."[75]

Workers do not necessarily view possible STI exposure as more severe than other occupational risks. As Daniels suggests, this certainly carries more stigma but is not necessarily more hazardous to one's health than the more mundane harms work visits on the body. Some STIs are as yet incurable, but so, too, is the less stigmatized but much more dangerous asbestos-related cancer. It may be that what Gayle Rubin calls the "fallacy of misplaced scale"—the frame that burdens sex "with an excess of significance"—is the thing that makes these risks seem to exist on separate registers.[76] Or rather it is not so much that risk in sex work is burdened with outsized significance than that risk in straight work is less burdened than it ought to be. As straight workers die because their employers forced them into unsafe pandemic working conditions, perhaps the anti-sex-worker myth that risk is what separates sex work from straight work will finally break.

Work hurts.[77] The fact that workers get hurt in the process of capital accumulation is a "big deal" but a quotidian one, not the sensational story those who wish to exceptionalize porn work like to tell.[78] Robert McRuer cautions against the tendency to position disability as *the* evidence of what is wrong with capitalism, using "disability as the raw material against which an imagined future is formed."[79] We need ways of talking about work-related injury that resist this. In charting them, we might interrogate the ways the porn worker body is "deemed available for injury," as Jasbir Puar puts it in her discussion of ability and capital flows more broadly.[80] The profit motive (or, for self-employed workers, the realities of bills to pay) favors ways of working that expose workers to injury and places the costs of treatment on their shoulders. Then, workers do the reproductive work of healing and become work-ready again.

Self-Preservation

Working to maintain "the privilege of being eligible to be hired" also means agitating for the right to do the work and to ensure that one can do it and still go about the rest of life.[81] Porn workers navigate anti-sex-worker discrimination and its diffuse implications for everything from housing access to banking rights. Those who choose to engage politically devote countless hours to protecting the right to do sex work at all. Stigma, argues Georgina Voss, shapes the porn work cycle at every stage, from office work to the point of technological intervention.[82] And so porn work combines

Porn and the Boundaries between Life and Work

mainstream creative labor's constant work of trying to get work with the stigma management required of those associated with "dirty work."[83]

In making other work possible, antistigma activism becomes part of the porn work cycle. Porn workers focus an enormous amount of activist energy fighting hostile policy. The historical memory of censorship campaigns—what historian Whitney Strub calls the "long struggle over sexual expression"—lingers, and workers describe their industry as perpetually under siege.[84] But porn at the height of the obscenity wars of the 1970s and '80s was more centralized than it is now. The major producers who once spearheaded free-speech lawsuits have a fraction of the power and wealth they once did. Self-producing performers now face more direct financial costs if production becomes impossible and more liability if they produce outside the boundaries of the law. As social media and direct-to-consumer platforms have taken the place of porn theaters and peep shows, censorship becomes both more diffuse and harder to combat through a traditional free-speech lawsuit. This is magnified by antiporn forces' strategic move away from a politics centered on obscenity and toward one centered on the language of protection, especially under the guises of public health and preventing sex trafficking.

The 2010s were a period of constant policy battles for porn workers. In California, workers organized broad campaigns against 2012's Measure B and subsequent efforts to impose external health regulation in 2014 and 2016. Chapter 5 explores the politics of these regulations, ones workers said would make their jobs disappear (and become less safe in the meantime). Here, the point is that many workers felt that fighting such state intervention was essential to their ability to make a living, a kind of pre-scene work without which the scene would never come. During the same period, internet censorship intensified, restricting individual workers' ability to advertise and distribute their work and to do sex work in satellite industries safely.

We have learned about the 2018 passage of the Stop Enabling Online Sex Trafficking Act (SESTA). In the months leading up to the act's passage, sex workers responded with urgent organizing campaigns such as Survivors Against SESTA. Later, Hacking//Hustling would emerge as a response to the law's passage. Such organizations provide harm-reduction education for workers who are made vulnerable by the law, organize workers around lobbying campaigns, and provide media training for workers hoping to shift the dominant narrative.[85] Activists reported an influx of workers forced to work under dangerous conditions and with predatory third-party managers who seized upon the increased power SESTA brought them. Within days of SESTA's passage, several workers had already reported violent assault, and a least two workers had been killed while doing less secure street-based work. Survivors Against SESTA's slogan, "Let Us Survive," gestures to the premature death criminalization brings and makes a basic claim for the ability to do the work that helps people make do and get by. Against a false dichotomy between survival sex work and freely chosen sexual labor, activists argued that most workers under capitalism, porn and other sex workers among them, work in order to survive. Their campaigns hinge on the fundamental demand to "let us." Here again, workers made clear that organizing was crucial to doing the work at all (and being okay afterward).

At first glance, this seems to have little to do with porn apart from the reality that many porn performers also do escort work. But activist performers saw the connections immediately, highlighting the need for solidarity across industry sectors and also understanding that internet censorship would find its way to legal sectors of the sex industry soon enough. Sex worker organizers Liara Roux (also a porn producer) and Ashley Lake developed the crowdsourced Liara's List, an archive of post-SESTA tech discrimination against sex workers across industries.[86] Meanwhile, performer activists fight more diffuse forms of web censorship. The Adult Performers Actors Guild, a performers union, has focused its efforts on combating performer account closures on platforms such as Instagram. Again, "being eligible to be hired" requires also fighting for access to the platforms that make hiring possible. This makes organizing a kind of reproductive labor but one that benefits workers more than it does their bosses. As chapter 4 argued, censoring policies can actually benefit managers. Not all work outside paid work enriches capital.

The same is true of workers' efforts to fight anti-sex-worker stigma that impacts their ability to move in the world far beyond the set. This is another way the boundaries between work and life blur for porn workers—sex work stigma follows you, and it shapes what it is like to do the rest of life. Stigma brings discrimination even when one is not presently engaged in sexual labor. One's status as a current or former sex worker is enough. Before SESTA and in intensified ways after it, web platforms sex workers use not just to exchange services but also to simply exist in the world routinely shut them out. Vacation-rental site Airbnb, crowdfunding platform GiveForward, payment site Venmo, and social media sites Twitter, Instagram, and Facebook are among the dozens of sites that regularly enforce anti-sex-worker terms of service provisions whether or not one is using them for sex work. Workers rely on social media platforms to build community, share information, and do mutual aid, and censoring policies undermine these strategies. In a circular way, they also make it harder to organize against bad policy. In her study of anti-sex-worker web censorship, sex worker activist and public health scholar Danielle Blunt writes, "If you are unable to find someone [online], you are unable to build community with them, and if you are unable to build community you are unable to organize."[87]

Porn workers also encounter less formalized and all the more insidious exclusions. Interviewees struggled to find housing, encountering discriminatory landlords and leering ones and also experiencing the more mundane struggles of freelancers trying to provide proof of income. They fight stigmatizing medical care—practitioners who reduce every complaint, ranging from migraines to depression, to sex worker status. Even basic banking privileges are elusive. In 2014, Chase closed multiple performers' bank accounts without explanation.[88] One interviewee found out about the account closure only when her rent check bounced. Later, in 2018, workers faced another spate of sex worker account closures, and the End Banking for Human Traffickers Act threatened to formalize such exclusions in law.[89] Interviewees talked about how sex work stigma impacts child custody cases, hiring in jobs outside sex industries, and access to legal protections when sex workers are victims of violence.

After retirement, sex work stigma remains. Years after transitioning out of the industry, VJ described a "permanent haunting."[90] She was moving up the ranks in a straight job but experienced persistent anxiety that her new boss or coworkers might connect her to her past porn work, risking harassment or dismissal. The porn work cycle extends years beyond the last scene filmed. Interviewees told me they warn new performers of this and suggest that a scene rate should be enough to compensate not only for the work you do on set but also for what might come next. Here, one is "almost always working" not only because doing and preparing for porn work can extend to every corner of the day but also because one continues to be marked as a sex worker long after the last check clears. Ironically, the same thinkers who say that they do not want sex work to exist circulate stigma in ways that keep workers in the industry even when they would rather not be. Anti-sex-work lobbying never focuses on provisions that would protect former sex workers from discrimination when they try to do something else.

Considering the antistigma work sex workers do as reproductive work urges new questions about the category. Antistigma and organizing work are reproductive in the traditional Marxist feminist sense that they facilitate porn work (and thus the profit derived from it). Workers' unpaid activist labors can subsidize the industry, most obviously when workers lobby alongside their bosses to combat policies that would render porn production impossible. But they also bear out the contradiction Marxist feminists have described of the family—an institution that reproduces us as workers but also ensures our survival as people who do more than work.[91] Organizing also undermines capital in key ways. Workers agitate against bosses as much as they do in concert with them, so activist labors are not work that keeps the porn industry afloat in any simple way. And because stigma and censorship help managers even as they also target them—an isolated workforce is a more pliable one—working against stigma is in some ways antireproductive of capital.

Calling marketing, activism, preparation, and rest "work" makes a political claim. As Marxist feminists have long argued, reproductive labor is work because it makes other work possible.[92] When porn workers labor under another's management, managers profit from time they do not pay for and expenses workers shoulder. Producers and platforms join other late capitalists in operating more as parasites than as managers in the conventional sense, since much of the work gets done away from management's direct watch.[93] When performers do self-directed work from which they reap the profits, they themselves, in addition to a host of third-party platforms, derive profit from all the work that makes work possible. This is true even when one enjoys such labors or would do them even if they were not attached to economic survival. It is possible, of course, that performers would maintain their bodies in similar ways, have sex that presents similar risks, and incur similar costs regardless of their status as porn workers. Workers in straight jobs get their nails done, too. This was a common refrain among management and some workers when I asked who covered the cost of services such as hair extensions and STI testing. While it is true that porn workers might go to the gym, get tested for STIs, or need to rest after acrobatic sex "for themselves" rather than just for work, it is also true that these activities produce value. This makes them work.

If work status is taken to suggest that value-producing activities should be waged (and thus covered under the purview of the regulatory state), most porn workers would prefer that their reproductive labors remain in the shadows. Through the lens of hybrid class locations, many see having the "equipment necessary to execute the job," as Lexington Steele put it, as a matter of personal responsibility.[94] Many performers spoke of their bodies as "tools" and saw maintaining them as evidence of a good work ethic. Beyond this, when workers come to porn in search of a job that also lets them have a life, calling life "unpaid work" can negate the very thing they came for. Precisely because porn puts life, and especially sexuality, to work, workers want the privacy they hope will come from calling off-set labors something other than "work." "Work" implies "discipline," write labor scholars Eileen Boris and Noah Zatz, and people have a stake in resisting that baggage.[95] Of course, one could read workers' stories of all they do to prepare for work and conclude that that discipline exists whether or not we name it.

This tension speaks to the realities of porn as work in the traditional sense but also as something in excess of it. It is a tension feminized workers have long navigated and one more and more workers will encounter as all sorts of jobs become feminized. Most jobs do not fit within parameters that mark work and life as separate. And there are no neat distinctions to be made between care for self and community and reproduction of a workforce. The ubiquitous assumption in the current economic moment is that workers should absorb the costs (financial and otherwise) borne of these blurry boundaries. A Marxist feminist perspective instead insists that these burdens belong to capital. But the demand for wages for the work that makes work possible is performative, not literal. Wages for Housework's goal was not to win pay (and certainly not to elicit employer or state control) but rather to illustrate that capital could never afford this.[96] How much does porn cost, and how many hours does it take, if we include all the work that makes it possible?

5

Maybe the State Should Pay

Sex, Work, and the State

Porn workers do not trust the state. "We know that we're pariahs. We know we're a cockroach," Nina Ha®tley said when I asked what she thought of mandatory condom legislation in porn.[1] She went on: "We're pornographers; we know that you hate us." This gives lie, she thought, to the idea that the state wants to protect porn workers *as workers*. Instead, Ha®tley said, state approaches to porn work go "back to the idea that no healthy sane person would choose sex work, so therefore [we] must be in need of protection." That is, protection not from workplace harm but from one's own unruliness. The workers, managers, and worker-managers I interviewed disagree on a lot, but one point on which they overwhelmingly agree is that policy makers, lobbyists, and the concerned public "don't care about us." When I asked them what they wanted from the state, some said they wanted to be consulted about the policies that impact their lives. Others simply wanted to be left alone.

At the same time, porn workers tell a story of violent state neglect. Porn workers are among the millions of U.S. workers who, to employers' benefit, labor on a contingent basis and in employment relationships that policy cannot account for.[2] In labors defined by what precarity theorist Isabell Lorey calls "the privatization of risks and cares," workers absorb the risks (financial, health, and so on) of doing business.[3] Yawning gaps in employment law make this possible, and one response to this is an appeal to the state to fill those gaps with better regulation and stronger enforcement. Indeed, this is the approach most left labor scholars take to the crisis of the shrinking state. If privatization is the problem, making public seems to be its cure. But sex workers—"public women," as the old saying goes—have long found their lives and labor framed as matters of public concern.

To the extent that appeals to reverse the "privatization of risks and cares" involve a kind of making public, they are a poor fit with what sex workers say they want. Most workers say they want privacy. While this is not the same thing as privatization, they cannot be neatly separated out either. But workers also describe the high costs of a dynamic in which employers make sex public when extracting value and introducing labor discipline but private when disavowing responsibility for its risks. This chapter takes both these claims seriously and plots an alternative. What might a regulatory apparatus that does the opposite—make work private when privacy works for workers and public when it does not—look like?

WORKING AT THE LIMITS OF THE LAW

One problem with employment policy is that most employers (in porn and straight work alike) ignore it. Jon Rodgers produces and directs low-budget scenes. He offered to show me the paperwork he requires performers to sign before filming a scene. One form, a modeling release giving the studio distribution rights to the scene, was stamped "this is not a contract." It was, indeed, a contract. "I understand that I am an independent contractor," it read. "As such, I understand that the benefits of workmen's compensation laws and pension plans do not apply to independent contractors."[4] This, too, is not quite true. Rodgers films in California, where the state's labor code and film commission both define temporary employees (such as porn and mainstream film actors) as *employees* and require employers to secure workers' compensation insurance.[5] Waged (rather than self-produced) porn performance meets the standard legal definition of employment, even as the state of California enforces this unevenly.[6]

I asked about this. "I can talk about that because I was in the trucking business for thirty years, and the state has been trying to get owner-operators classed as employees—same type of situation," Rodgers said.[7] He went on: "If I hire a talent, I'm supposed to follow all the employment laws. We're supposed to do withholding. That's not gonna cut it. It's nothing but a bureaucratic money grab to get more withholding taxes. . . . When talent comes to work for me, my paperwork specifically states that they're an independent contractor and that talent is responsible for all taxes and that kind of stuff and that there are no known STDs."

Rodgers's contract terms are standard—producers insist that performers are independent contractors, and the vast majority do not carry the required insurance. "Here's the grim reality," replied Christian Mann, then company manager of Evil Angel. "Performers, even if the state of California says that they are employees, they are independent contractors. They are performing in a way that looks like independent contracting."[8] Likewise, managers maintained that calling performers "independent contractors" solidifies this status even if the state says otherwise.

This is in part the old story of bosses flouting the few protections that do exist. Because employment law is so rarely enforced (and carries anemic damages when it is), industry norms have a greater impact than the letter of the law.[9] Thus, labor scholars talk about a "'gloves-off' economy, in which employers are increasingly breaking, bending, or evading laws and standards designed to protect workers."[10] The 2000s saw a highly successful effort to gut a workers' compensation system that was, as Nate Holdren's history of workplace injury details, already stacked in employers' favor.[11] Employment discrimination remains widespread half a century after the passage of the Civil Rights Act.[12] And minimum-wage law often goes unenforced.[13] Policy that is supposed to protect workers is written in ways that all but ensure its limited ability to do just that. Austerity-minded cuts to state services intensify this. To an audience member's question of whether she was concerned about a just-announced Occupational Safety and Health Administration (OSHA) case involving the production company she represents, an attorney on a trade convention panel replied, "OSHA is overworked and just wants this off their desk. They just want to hear, 'This lovely girl is a corporation and not an employee.'"[14]

Employers in all industries flout the law, but those in the gig economy exploit a foundational loophole in doing so. Employment law governs the distinction between independent contractors and employees and grants rights and protections to the latter. On paper, independent contractor status allows for reduced legal protections for workers, but it also assumes that the work is truly temporary and grants workers significant autonomy in deciding how the job gets done.[15] A plumber hired to do a onetime job at a bookstore, for example, would legitimately be an independent

Sex, Work, and the State

contractor under these rules. This is unlike the situation of porn workers or app-based delivery drivers, for instance, and so courts sanction employers who misclassify workers as independent contractors.[16] In addition, independent contractors in creative fields own intellectual property rights for the work they create.[17] In waged porn work, producers claim these rights. Bosses cannot legally have it both ways.

Regardless of what the law says, management has been successful in rendering performers' classification as independent contractors a largely unquestioned industry norm. Interviewees representing a range of class positions told me that performers are independent contractors because producers treat them as such. This is so common in the broader world of work that state agencies alert workers that being told by an employer that one is an independent contractor, or signing an agreement stating that this is the case, does not make it so.[18]

Nonetheless, managers insist on workers' independent contractor status—that is, except when they are simply not sure. I asked contract performer-director Alex Linko about his own employment status, as well as that of the performers he shoots: "When you shoot a commissioned film, are you a contractor or an employee?" I asked.

"A contractor," he responded.

"And the performer you hire is a day employee?" I asked, referring to the employment classification used in mainstream film productions and the one technically required of porn productions.

"I don't think so. She fills out a 1099 and I don't do her taxes," Linko replied.

OSHA had recently ruled that porn performers are employees, so I asked, "But for OSHA, is she an employee?"

Never losing patience with my wonkish questions, he answered, "Is that what it is? I don't know."[19]

This is the state of employment law in the United States—some bosses actively ignore the rules, others do not know what they are, and workers exist in limbo. Even when strictly applied, those rules leave workers without protection.

Stoya described her frustrated attempts to nail down her status when she worked under exclusive contract with a large production company. "I think I'm gonna have to pay the government money with taxes, it's not being taken out, I don't know," she remembered thinking. "So I go into the office and I'm like, 'Am I an employee or an independent contractor?' In my entire time with that company, I never once got a straight answer."[20] Stoya went on to describe the various features of her work that send conflicting messages about employment status.

> You tell me when I'm being shot, but I pay for my own transportation from the East Coast. You do pick me up from my hotel and take me to set, but then when I get to set, there's a script. The contract said I wasn't allowed to take outside jobs without [the company's] approval, even in nonconflicting fields. . . . The whole thing is really fucked up. They have the benefits of dealing with an employee as far as telling us what to do, but then they also have the benefits of an independent contractor as far as not paying payroll tax, social security, all those things.

Likewise, when I asked Charity Bangs, who performs for multiple studios rather than under an exclusive contract with one, whether she worked as an employee or an independent contractor, she responded, "It seems like directors want to get the benefits of both."[21]

There is no legal means of getting the "benefits of both." And yet control on the one hand and a lack of protections and benefits on the other characterize the experience of waged porn work. The conditions workers have described throughout this book can often be traced back here. We learned, for example, that performers make the same rate for a scene regardless of whether they work two or twenty hours—exclusion from overtime protections makes this possible. The law says that customer preference does not excuse racism in hiring or pay, yet producers use customer preference arguments to explain racist hierarchies in casting and pay.[22] The postretirement poverty performers experience is connected to studios' failure to do social security withholding. "The thing with being an outlaw is that the retirement package sucks," veteran performer-director Carter Stevens told me.[23]

Finally, the health risks porn work can present—and the costs they place on workers—are born of porn's liminal place in occupational health and workers' compensation policy. Employers have little reason to change production practices so long as they can be confident that they will avoid any costs that come from them. As Christopher Daniels explained, "Some studios during location shoots won't use silicone lube, and that really angers me because water-based lube dries up and tears your skin. But they're like, 'We don't want to damage the furniture.' . . . I've left some shoots bleeding because of a little thing like water-based lube."[24] When rental agreements are stricter than workplace protections, damaged furniture costs studios more than workplace injury. Porn workers also lack actionable protections from retaliation if they do sue for workers' compensation. I asked another performer whether she considered suing when an on-set injury left her in need of an expensive surgery and weeks off work. "I guess that I could have," she explained. But she remembered thinking at the time, "'If I do anything with workmen's comp, they're not gonna hire me again. I'm burning that bridge, and I kind of need that exposure right now.' It's a really tough position to be in."[25]

Policy, rather than exceptional callousness on the part of porn managers, gets us here. "The hard hat is not about the boss personally giving a shit about the worker," said Juba Kalamka. In construction, bosses "figured out that with liability 'it's cheaper for me to give you basic protections for my long-run bottom line.' I think that's the difference in porn. The economic bottom line is affected in a different direction."[26] This distinction is blurring, though. Straight workers who once enjoyed some level of protection increasingly find that their bosses, too, face few consequences for putting them at risk. As one studio owner at a porn-industry legal panel jokingly reminded the audience, OSHA cannot keep track of construction workers falling off roofs. Surely, they do not have time to deal with porn. The COVID-19 pandemic makes clearer still how unexceptional porn is in this regard. The same academics who argue that porn is special in that workers either take risks or lose work now find their own university administrators offering up the same choice. In both cases the state does nothing, and workers, not employers, pay the costs.

The regulatory state is shrinking. Beyond this, employment law was designed for a workplace defined by stable employment at one business, managerial direction from a single employer, and clear boundaries between work and the rest of one's life. We know that this has never been the reality for precarious workers in service-based, agricultural, and creative economies.[27] Indeed, regulatory systems were explicitly designed to exclude these workers in favor of a white masculine norm.[28] These exclusions are not so much anachronistic as they are foundationally racist, xenophobic, and sexist. Now, the forms of contingency that exclusion bore are spreading from margin to center. Porn workers are part of the one-third of U.S. workers in contingent employment relationships.[29] The state knows this, and the problems of the "new economy" are not in fact new. In 1994 the U.S. Department of Labor issued a report calling for a "modernized, simplified, and standardized" legal definition of employment in light of the reality that "more workers now find themselves in contingent employment relationships than ever before."[30] Decades later, such "modernized" policy is not forthcoming, and employers continue to evade their legal responsibilities to workers by exploiting the law's loopholes.

Among the areas most out of touch with the realities of working life is the law's assumption of a single responsible employer.[31] Even if we can say that performers are employees (as courts have), this does not answer the equally important question "Who's the boss?" For porn and other contingent workers, such clear lines of managerial control do not reliably exist. The porn work process can be organized in a number of ways. Directors *or* producers may control hiring and firing, set workplace policy, and be responsible for payment. The same person may or may not perform these various roles. To the question about his perspective on laws requiring producers to pay for sexually transmitted infection (STI) tests, one contract performer-director asked, "[Would] I pay myself?"[32] And trade relationships make such distinctions irrelevant. Kimora Klein described her experience of getting injured on a trade set. She did not have private health insurance at the time, and without a boss, there was no one liable for the workers' compensation insurance that should have covered her care. "These people are working with me; they're not working under me or above me," she said.[33] In these cases, performers absorb the costs of workplace injury not because they're afraid of retaliation from a boss but because there is no boss.

As scholars of domestic labor, the sharing economy, and other sites of contingent labor suggest, a more nuanced set of policies could help to make sense of who the responsible employer is in the many cases in which there are multiple people in charge who may or may not represent the same business.[34] In what policy scholar David Weil calls the "fissured workplace," employers outsource job tasks to various contractors, thereby evading direct responsibility to workers.[35] Porn production companies that contract with freelance directors are one example of such an arrangement. The policy changes that would address this situation in mainstream fissured workplaces could also help here. But the fissured workplace still assumes an employer hiding somewhere, and as we have seen, porn workers take pains to free themselves from just this. Here, the "workplace" is not fissured so much as it is diffused beyond recognition. Again, most workers do not want it reconsolidated.

A more sophisticated means of identifying a controlling employer would also fail to address work-related health problems that build over

Sex, Work, and the State

time and are difficult to trace. What *is* work-related injury in the gig economies of late capitalism? Injuries that take place (at once or over time) while workers prepare for work, as they undertake the self-making and marketing activities that make them hirable, or as they pursue alternative income streams that subsidize the work are, to be sure, related to work. But they are not, at least by prevailing standards, "work related." Like so much employment regulation, OSHA determines employer responsibility based on measures of place and payment that do not fit flexible economies: work-related injuries are those that take place "in the work environment" and for pay.[36] Most porn work takes place off set and off a boss's clock, and as we have seen, many performers prefer it this way.

A public conversation between performer and Adult Performer Advocacy Committee (APAC) board member Ela Darling and AIDS Healthcare Foundation's (AHF) Michael Weinstein illustrates how little outsiders understand what porn work actually looks like. In a public comment at an AHF press conference regarding the foundation's advocacy for the California Safer Sex in the Adult Film Industry Act, Darling addressed the act's proposed "whistle-blower" clause, which allows private citizens to sue "producers" who violate the act by failing to use condoms during filming.

"How would you address adult performers who are afraid of the provision that allows private citizens to sue us for the work that we do?" she asked, speaking to workers' concerns that the provision would make performers who produce their own material vulnerable to civil suit and provide stalkers access to performers' personal information.

"The right to sue is not [to sue] the performers, it's [to sue] the producer," replied Weinstein.

"But performers create their own content," Darling replied.

Weinstein's response was flatly "They're subject to the same laws as anybody else."[37]

Weinstein's response—and the fact that Darling had to explain that "producer" could mean something other than a porn kingpin—speaks to outsiders' troubling conviction that they need not understand the particulars of porn work in order to regulate it. Outside lobbyists present interventions such as this act as pro-worker, but workers must give up class mobility in order to be included in that community (these are "protections" workers do not want even then).

Policy forces workers to choose between autonomy and protection. As their origin stories show, workers often come to porn to escape the inflexibility and lack of autonomy of straight jobs, many of which do come with employee status. They *want* to "be their own boss," and many associate independent contractor status with the kinds of freedom they hoped to find in porn work. Lorelei Lee had recently transitioned to full-time employee status in her job as an in-house director for Kink.com when we first spoke. "I have health insurance and a matching 401(k). I've never had benefits before. Oh my God, I get sick days now, vacation time! It's great. . . . But I also loved being an independent contractor. I loved having the total freedom, being like, 'If I want to, I can never come back. I have no responsibility to you.' . . . I made my own schedule."[38] Before porn, she added, when she worked a straight job for an hourly wage, "I didn't want to be an employee. *I hated being an employee.*" Policy prescriptions that ignore this cannot pretend to be actually pro-worker.

But it is not self-evident that workers should have to choose between protection and autonomy. Instead, policy makers manufacture this choice by tethering access to basic benefits and protections to employment status. This is disciplining—when working-class people accept the terms of waged work, this is not just because they have rent to pay but also because the very foundations of social citizenship are contingent on being a worker.[39] In this way, the state hopes to force people to make themselves available for waged work. Sex workers upset the status quo in part because they so often refuse.[40] But the contradiction of the capitalist state is that, sometimes, organized working people wrest significant concessions from it.[41] There is a lot to lose in refusing the employment relationship to which these concessions are tied.

When I asked Chelsea Poe her perspective on the STI-testing mandate that was up for a vote when we spoke in 2014, she critiqued the motivations of those behind it but also gestured to policy makers' decision—in 1935— not to protect independent contractors' right to organize collectively.[42] "What should really be done is not having us be private contractors, so we can actually unionize like any other sort of athletic entertainment. I feel like having porn performers unionize and have their own testing is the best possible way, not having a government mandate."[43] The common perception that the porn industry leans libertarian flattens what is for many workers a more complex critique. Rather than oppose state intervention as such, workers resist a particular kind of state—one that offers poor remedies for vulnerabilities it created in the first place. Demands for privacy are the most available tool for articulating that resistance.

Among interviewees representing varied class positions and sectors of the industry, the idea prevails that porn is sex and therefore an inappropriate site for state intervention.[44] When I asked her about mandatory condom policy, Poe told me that queer porn's convention of leaving safer sex methods up to individual partners was "the only fair way." "You're addressing it like it's actual sex," she explained. "It's just between you and your partner. I don't see why other people need to get involved." To the same question, mainstream performer, director, and producer Prince Yahshua told me, "There's no way that another person can tell two grown adults what to do with our bodies."[45] Meanwhile, the Free Speech Coalition (FSC), an employer-funded trade group, advocates for the "constitutionally grounded rights of adults to make their own decisions regarding private sexual behavior."[46] This is unremarkable—most employers prefer that the state not meddle in their "private" exchanges with workers. But while workers typically prefer the protection that comes with publicness, this does not bear out in porn and other sex work. Sex work's unique situation, in which workers and employers often come together around the discourse of privacy, is born of histories of policy that is *both* anti-sex-industry and anti-sex-worker. Like sex workers in other sectors, most porn workers have little faith in the power of the state to redress harm, even when they are critical of the conditions a regulatory vacuum lets their employers impose.

Porn workers demand privacy because they have so often received only stigmatizing surveillance. "The people protesting and saying, 'You're taking my rights away,'" don't understand that "the legislators don't give a fuck. You're a sex worker, you're a whore, they don't care," Poe said. Poe gestures to the long history of policy approaches to sex work designed to criminalize commercial sex rather than improve working conditions in it. "Protection" here is framed not as defending against workplace abuse but as safeguarding the public from the contagion of bad women on the one hand and shielding wayward women from their own poor decisions on the other.[47] This history, grounded in efforts to control women's mobility (often in racist and xenophobic ways)[48] and punish sexual rule breaking, informs both sex workers' historical memory and the realities of current policy. These traditions are deeply rooted in the state's interest in policing racialized gender norms, but the policy they shape impacts sex workers of all genders. It is no surprise that state surveillance hits multiply marginalized workers hardest.

In criminalized regimes, police routinely perpetrate physical and sexual violence against sex workers, the prison system is abusive by design, and prohibition makes workers more, not less, vulnerable to client violence.[49] While workers overwhelmingly say that legalized regimes are superior to criminalization, they, too, have had negative consequences for workers, making them vulnerable to state surveillance, public outing, and a two-tiered system in which workers who cannot meet the standards of legal work are pushed even further into the shadows. Legalized regimes frequently force STI testing, bar those who have tested positive from work (even when safe sex methods mean there is no risk of transmission), and require workers to disclose their legal names[50]—all aspects of proposed legislation for the porn industry. In contrast to decriminalization, in which sex work is regulated as any other form of work, legalization is grounded in what sociologist Yasmina Katsulis describes as the idea that sex workers are "a particular type of people, people whose private lives are made public, whose bodies are subject to regulation, and who are important only insofar as they present a threat to the public health."[51]

Porn workers know this history. When the AHF proposes regulation to "minimize the spread of sexually transmitted infections resulting from the production of adult films . . . which have caused a negative impact on public health and the quality of life of citizens living in Los Angeles," it is clear who counts as a citizen here.[52] And so Juba Kalamka described AHF's campaign as "[taking] advantage of the general public's perception of the porn industry." He went on: "People were invested in it in a politic-of-respectability, public-morality kind of way that didn't have shit to do with the welfare of the performers. It was about fear and people being able to keep these freaky cooties in the San Fernando Valley and out of my house or my bedroom."[53] This, in spite of the reality that no evidence of such an impact exists.[54] More to the point, though, is that even if a negative impact on public health were clear, it is profoundly antiworker to assume that this trumps performers' claims to safety and bodily autonomy. "Being described as a 'public health risk' feels a lot like being called a 'dirty whore,'" Stoya said.[55]

Compounding this is porn's history as a target of obscenity prosecution.[56] Just as it was for conservative politicians and antiporn feminists in the obscenity wars of the 1970s and '80s,[57] championing antiporn policy now is a career builder. "I think it's a way for Michael Weinstein to put money in his pocket and build his own career," Raylene said of the AHF president's efforts to lobby for a condom mandate. "It's really an easy business to attack."[58] But she was not against regulation. Even as she did not want this mandate, she said, "I also don't think it's fair for the directors or the people in the business not to band together and say, 'You know what, let's protect each other.' I believe that there should be a mandatory condom thing; I just don't think it should come from an outside source." Many workers agreed—they want real changes but do not trust the state to administrate them.

Sex workers have never experienced the "privatization of risks and cares" in quite the same way as workers in straight jobs. "Bad citizens and disruptive subjects," writes public health scholar Valerie Webber, porn workers defy the public-private divide.[59] Nor do they have any evidence that the state will offer relief. Instead, they confront the violence of publicness without any of its benefits. Faced with this double bind, many sex work thinkers make a calculation that workers are better off without the state.

With a framework legal theorist Adrienne Davis describes as "erotic exceptionalism," they argue "that the sexual nature of their work trumps its role as labor."[60] Making privacy claims, erotic exceptionalists maintain that sex work's status as sexual should make it exempt from state oversight. An exceptionalist stance can line up with conservative labor politics, ones that play to employers' interests by shielding workplace relations under the banner of privacy.[61] "If its sexual nature exempts it from regulation, then people will certainly call it sex, and not work, and fairly so," cautions Davis.[62] Thus, sex work scholar Julia O'Connell Davidson is both skeptical of the state's capacity to be a reliable ally and critical of a hard antiregulation approach—"the sort of minimal regulation on industry that even Milton Friedman would approve."[63] For reasons ranging from marketing to skirting labor law, calling porn "sex," and not "work," is exactly what employers want. Many are, indeed, hard antiregulation Friedmanites. But where other workers have historically organized against "privacy," porn workers overwhelmingly evoke it. As a popular protest sign reads, "U.S. out of my underwear!"

Privacy is an unsteady foundation for politics. Feminist activists and scholars have long pointed to the failures of privacy rhetoric, for example, for poor women of color in their struggles for welfare[64] and reproductive[65] justice. They show that privacy is a luxury loaded with whiteness and class privilege. Queer theorists, meanwhile, suggest that recourse to privacy betrays commitments to normativity and liberal citizenship—"there is nothing more public than privacy," remind Lauren Berlant and Michael Warner.[66] The demand for sexual privacy "reinforces class differences by presuming people have access to private space," reminds Melinda Chateauvert.[67] The exclusions such a frame brings to sex work policy are clear—workers who labor in massage parlors and on the street (who are more likely to be poor, undocumented, gender nonconforming, and women of color) find themselves excluded from the protections of privacy and subject to magnified state violence.

Employers' interest in representing paid sex as private is rather un-complicated; public employment relationships are subject to regulations that get in the way of profit. In intimate labors such as domestic work and childcare, privacy rhetoric is an especially powerful tool for employers hoping to escape regulation.[68] Intimate workers have long struggled against the notion that work in private spaces (such as home healthcare), or work that involves exchanges coded as private (such as childcare), should escape state oversight.[69] For Marxist feminist theorists, the very idea of "private life" naturalizes reproductive labor, making it appear as an exchange between individuals rather than one between workers and capital.[70] This is good for capital.

The dominant alternative to exceptionalism—what Davis calls "erotic assimilationism"—does not quite hold either. Here, the idea is that sex work is work like any other and that the risks associated with it can be addressed by regulating sex markets just as other workplaces are. This is the premise of less nuanced calls for sex work decriminalization.[71] Assim-ilationists fail to ask "*which* type of labor sex work would most likely be assimilated to."[72] The protections they imagine formal work status would confer are almost exclusively reserved for employees, and as we have seen, the status of sex workers as employees versus independent contractors remains hotly contested. In reducing workplace policy to a monolith, as-similationists ignore "how much of standard workplace law will almost certainly fail sex workers."[73]

Calling porn "work," however, can mean more than one thing. This book uses "work" not because that language makes anything tidier but rather because it brings contradiction to light. Here, "work" highlights not vulnerabilities easily remedied by regulation but risks the state can amelio-rate but never fully fix (and sometimes actually manufactures). If standard workplace law will fail sex workers, this is in part because it fails all work-ers, most especially multiply marginalized ones. What assimilationism cannot accommodate is the fact that publicness offers no guarantees and plenty of risks. Regulation will fail not only because sex work is sexual but also because it is work.

What is more, the boundaries between sex and work *are* blurry for some sex workers. Porn work is work, but it also exceeds the boundaries of work. Some workers at some times experience porn sex as *real* sex, and this demands autonomy in particular ways. As such, Zahra Stardust argues that prohibitions on filmed sexual acts such as fisting—policies ostensibly put in place to protect performers—serve to limit queer sexual speech.[74] And Chauntelle Tibbals cites performers who experience mandatory condom use as a form of not just symbolic but also physical invasion—"anything that forces itself into my vagina is by definition raping me," one performer says.[75] Resistance to regulation does not mean the same thing here as it does in Milton Friedman's world. It also, without a doubt, helps bosses.

The following sections unpack this dynamic in the context of occupational health regulation, taking workers' antiregulation claims seriously while also critiquing the alliances such claims enable and the voices they exclude. While the experiences that inform appeals for privacy center largely on occupational health regulation, they set the tone for workers' perspectives on state intervention in other areas, even when workers are critical of the conditions their employers impose. A state that "doesn't care about us" in matters of health is also, many porn workers believe, not a reliable ally in the fight against workplace discrimination, contractor misclassification, wage theft, or other areas of classed struggle.

OCCUPATIONAL HEALTH REGULATION

Workers' critiques of state intervention focus on health policy because the state is far more interested in sex workers' bodies than it is in other aspects of their work. This is out of step with what workers say they want. As we see throughout this book, interviewees have a whole range of concerns, yet policy makers tend to reduce porn work to sex and sex to HIV risk. Overwhelmingly, performers said they were comfortable with the HIV prevention methods typical of their genres, especially since modern HIV treatment and prophylaxis options can reduce transmission risk to zero. Workers voiced more concern about common health risks such as bacterial and yeast infections, the long-term effects of performance-enhancing medications, and acute injury, yet regulatory attention has focused almost exclusively on HIV. When workers do see room to improve STI-prevention procedures, their own proposed remedies are very much out of step with what outsiders prescribe. This is symptomatic of the bigger problem with regulation—policy makers do not recognize workers' expertise. "We're the most important part of this discussion, and yet we're routinely shut out," noted Madeline Marlowe as performers urged California's Occupational Safety and Health Administration (Cal/OSHA) to include them in the policy-making process.[76]

Indeed, an outside organization, not workers, has been behind attempts to transform occupational health policy governing porn sets. Arguing that industry norms set a poor example for viewers, encourage the spread of STIs, and fail to fully protect workers, the AHF has lobbied, sometimes successfully, for a series of reforms.[77] Mandatory condom use for vaginal and anal intercourse and porn-specific permitting are at the core of these proposals. Some also include provisions for mandatory testing and vaccinations, barrier methods for oral sex and facial ejaculation, and employer record keeping of performers' medical records. Proposals have also included worrying provisions for enforcement, such as a "whistle-blower" clause that would allow private citizens to sue anyone involved with the production of scenes that fall outside regulatory guidelines.[78] Under president Michael Weinstein's leadership, AHF has undertaken this fight without input from current performers and against their repeated claims that proposed regulation would make them less safe. The organization's crucial mistake, as Richie Calhoun put it, was that "they tried to represent performers without getting with performers."[79]

There is no clear consensus among workers about ideal protective measures. Some workers prefer to work with condoms, while others find that condoms make it harder or more dangerous to do their jobs. This diversity of perspectives is, indeed, why workers' resounding call has been for performer autonomy rather than a broad mandate. Some who usually perform as receptive partners, especially women who film straight scenes, suggest that condom use in the very specific context of on-set sex can cause chafing and fissures that are painful and, counterproductively, make them more vulnerable to STI infection. Thus, in response to the common argument that condoms on set are no different from any other required protective gear (such as hard hats for construction workers), Lorelei Lee countered, "Construction workers usually aren't injured by their protective gear."[80] "Condoms break," some workers insist, and this is particularly worrying for some workers given that chafing could increase the risk of infection should an exposure occur. Other workers would be unable to work at all were condoms required. Some insertive partners suggest that condoms make an already difficult job that much harder: "Once I put a condom on, no boner."[81]

Many gay and queer performers oppose a mandate but also find anticondom arguments baffling. Recalling LGBTQ communities' struggles against quarantine mentality during the early years of the AIDS crisis, they were also critical of the straight industry's reliance on testing in lieu of barrier protection. Juba Kalamka saw a homophobic "fearmongering" in the straight industry's line that condoms don't work: "I see that as specious," he said.[82] Kalamka wanted to make clear that he was not suggesting that performers who make anticondom arguments are not entitled their perspective. "But," he added, "it's a positionality that's not supported by the actual evidence. It's called lube, really basically." "Implicitly homophobic," said Conner Habib; the straight industry's standard anticondom argument disregards that gay sets have been successfully using condoms, not quarantine, for decades.[83] For some straight performers, too, the purported drawbacks of on-set condom use paled in comparison to the risks of STI exposure. "I'd rather get a rash" than an STI, said Tiffany Fox.[84] For Herschel Savage, "personally, you've got to be crazy not to use condoms. I agree it's not as pleasurable."[85]

If there is no consensus about ideal STI prevention protocols on set, most workers do agree that proposed regulations could mean a loss of work or at least push the work underground. Producers (including many performer-producers) insist that they cannot sell content with condoms, let alone the other barrier methods some proposed regulations require, such as gloves and dental dams. "Those movies don't sell. . . . Obviously, you have to look out for the performers, but you also have to consider your bottom line," explained director-screenwriter Jacky St. James and a chorus of others.[86] Workers see their fates as tied to employers' and not only because they sometimes also are employers. Hit by online piracy, workers and managers together are worried about their fragile industry. "Studios can barely afford to keep their lights on," said performer Christopher Daniels, "and people want bareback content. You have to care about models' health and safety, but you're also trying to sell a product."[87] "We welcome safety standards," explained performer Ela Darling during public comment at a 2015 Cal/OSHA meeting. "We only ask that you hear our voices and implement sensible regulations that allow us to continue to do our jobs."[88]

Alongside the concern that proposed regulation will put porn out of business is the worry that it will drive production underground. With barrier methods that may hurt sales, burdensome record-keeping requirements, and expensive testing and vaccine provisions, most workers assume that management will ignore proposed regulation. Aware of the tremendous risks of working in underground economies, many say they would rather have an imperfect but legal workplace than a de facto criminalized one. "The actual effect of condom mandates is to drive the industry underground," explained Lorelei Lee, a central voice in organizing efforts against the proposed regulations.[89] "We simply are not in the same situation that a construction worker is in. Our industry is agile and was illegal until the '80s, not that long ago. And many people who work in porn have antiauthoritarian attitudes. The actual effect is to create fewer worker protections, to push people underground. Women who are performing in scenes then have less accountability for their employers because they're scared to report if something happens on set. If something happens worse than getting an STI. We know this from other avenues of sex work." Many workers share this concern—producers will not abide regulation, they say, so to impose it is to invite an even more precarious underground economy. Many are already wary of reporting on-set abuse because they fear blacklisting from producers and (rightly) anticipate that the state will not take sex workers' concerns seriously. Stricter regulation does not change that.

The choice between violent state intervention and none at all is an impossible one, and workers calculate rhetorical strategies in the context of this double bind. "The threat of further criminalization," Lee wrote in a 2019 essay, pushes many sex workers to say, "I love doing sex work. I only want the state to leave me alone."[90] What critiques of sex worker "libertarianism" miss is that workers are well aware that freedom from the state is merely, as Lee put it, the "less terrible of two terrible ideas."[91] If the state "doesn't care about" sex workers, workers are under no illusions that their well-being is management's priority either. They know that the bottom line, not workers' autonomous decision-making, guides managerial appeals for freedom from the state. "The producers don't give a shit about my health," Tiffany Fox told me. "They care about the content they can produce and how much money they can make off it."[92]

The "privacy" employers say they want is not a matter of performer autonomy. A major argument those in the straight porn community use in opposing outside regulation is, after all, that state intervention is redundant, addressing a problem stringent internal policy has already solved and targeting problematic bodies the industry has already weeded out. This is where privacy rhetoric runs up against itself. The industry's trade group, the FSC, has worked to rally online support with the Twitter hashtag #performertestingworks and described proponents of outside regulation as "fomenting a crisis where none exists."[93] If "it's not broken, why fix it?" said talent agent and FSC board member Mark Schechter. "The industry itself is very self-policed and regulated."[94] In an essay, Conner Habib argued against mandatory testing legislation on the grounds that it would "find HIV-positive people, expose their status to others, and ban them completely from any sexual representation or sex work."[95] The straight mainstream industry already practices a version of this. In the rare cases in which the industry's central testing system does detect an HIV-positive result, porn Twitter erupts with biphobic fearmongering about men who perform in both gay and straight porn or whorephobic outing of porn star escorts, and commentators are eager to out "patient zero." Performers confront positive test results at the same time as their access to income (and sometimes community) grinds to a halt.

Self-regulation is not characterized by a commitment to sex positivity either. For Prince Yahshua, "people on the outside, we call 'civilians.' The last four scares we had have nothing to do with the people in the industry. There were people on the outside trying to come in, but because of our lovely testing centers, they catch it before they ever get to people like me. . . . We have got to be the cleanest people on the planet."[96] This is why "law has no place in what we do; it's not needed at all." Alongside stigmatizing discourses painting those impacted by STIs as "dirty" and straight mainstream's tested population as "clean"—a common feature of both public and private conversations around these questions—is the suggestion that STI risk is a matter of personal responsibility. Diane Duke, then CEO of the FSC, put it this way: "Out of 4,000 people [the number of performers in the industry's testing database], somebody is going to come up [HIV] positive. I think performers are more careful with what they do with their bodies for the most part. But out of 4,000, you're going to get some who aren't. And those are the ones who are going to come to the top. If they haven't protected themselves in their personal lives, we're gonna catch it."[97] Duke deftly reconfigures the dynamics of workplace risk: careless personal behavior, not production practices, puts individuals at risk. If a long history of sex work policy has framed the sex worker body as a source of contagion, the dominant narrative in the straight porn community—the most visible voice in antiregulation arguments—flips this narrative by suggesting that the contagion is in fact outside. It follows that the task of industry policy is to weed out (individualized) external risk rather than to prevent (structural) workplace harm. Industry policy places the burden for doing so on individual workers but also gives them strictly limited means for doing so *at work.*

In spite of management's oft-repeated support for "performer choice," workers reported that they rarely get it when they perform under another's direction. Tiffany Fox described telling a producer, "I want to [use] a condom; I don't feel safe working," to which he responded, "You should pick another profession, then. We'll find someone else that will shoot without it."[98] From the opposite direction, performer-director Alex Linko explained that he cannot work for companies that do require condoms because he is unable to maintain an erection while using them: "I could not do the job I do if I was required to wear a condom."[99] Production companies that use condoms in scenes typically require them; those that do not use them typically require that performers forgo them. In sectors that use the industry's centralized STI-testing database, getting hired requires abiding by testing protocols. Partners cannot choose not to test or decide not to make their medical records accessible to the database the FSC operates.[100] On most sets and for most workers, if they want work, they submit to policies they had no part in designing. This is what choice means in practice. Freedom from regulation was never on the table. What is at stake, for the meantime, is whether that regulation will come from bosses or the state.

Employers work to protect their own ability to choose, and they do so in ways that pretend this translates into performer autonomy. Of condom use on set Diane Duke said, "If directors and producers want to do that, absolutely, go for it! We're not anticondom. We believe it should be the choice. And we believe that the performers should have that choice."[101] There is a lot of slippage at work here. Likewise, Mark Schechter explained that his perspective on on-set condoms is "pro-choice in the respect that if a performer or a company chooses to work with a level of protection such as a condom, we support that here; I support that personally. Likewise, if a production company or a performer chooses to participate without that level of barrier protection, I support that as well."[102] Again, this choice is not available to performers in practice. The basic dynamics of the wage relationship mean that performers *or* companies do not have the same power to set these terms.

Managers' commitment to their own freedom to choose reaches beyond on-set barrier methods to a spectrum of workplace practices. When I

Sex, Work, and the State

asked him who he thought should cover testing costs, performer, director, and producer Lexington Steele explained, "Porno performers are independent contractors who work for a number of people. If I want to voluntarily pay for your test, then okay, but by no means should it be obligatory."[103] When an errant penis pump chipped Lorelei Lee's tooth on set, there were no established channels through which she could seek care. Instead, her agent had to negotiate with the director. In the end, the director was "willing to pay for it, but I had to go to his dentist," Lee explained.[104] Also at the mercy of management's free choice were the women who contracted HIV on a 1998 set. One of ten men performing in a gang bang, Herschel Savage agreed only if he could be "the first one up." He would later discover that two women performers were exposed to HIV later that day. To my question of whether there was any system in place to ensure that their treatment was covered, he replied, "They may have gotten something, but it was out of the kindness of people's hearts."[105] This is what management choice means in practice.

One cannot vigorously advocate managerial and performer choice. Management and workers are sometimes the same people, but internal and external policies can either protect performer self-determination or empower management to set workplace practices. What workers want, they say, is freedom from *both* state and employer control. Stoya said that she "believe[s] in performer choice" and ventured that there are concrete shifts in policy that could make that choice meaningful.[106] Lee agreed: "If they passed a law that producers and directors have to have condoms on set available and that performers have the right to choose whether or not to use one, that would be a very helpful law. I think it would be a situation in which performers could then be empowered, if they're on a set and are denied a condom, or if they feel like they're being hired around, they can complain."[107] This is the kind of outside regulation that would actually support worker well-being and autonomy (especially if, unlike most employment policy, it was actually enforced).

But in spite of the line that "we [the industry] are not against regulation," there is no evidence that the *industry* would support regulations that protect workers' autonomous decision-making.[108] The "we" here is slippery, and while workers and managers have come together in apparent consensus when resisting proposed regulation, it is not at all clear that that same solidarity would apply if performers advocated for policies that would redistribute power from management to workers. After a major 2016 victory in which workers and managers successfully lobbied against poorly designed Cal/OSHA regulations, workers said that the next step was to design new policy that supports their ability to choose the protective methods they use. Years later, management has yet to show up for that party.

ORGANIZING AND MUTUAL AID

Workers are not waiting for management, or the state, to save them. They develop creative means of organizing on their own terms, forming worker groups modeled on traditional labor unions and ones focused on peer education and mutual support. Both are burdened with the slippery class politics seen throughout this book. Workers who advocate more militant forms of collective action see it as an important way to challenge power relations. Without organized workers, "the producers and production companies have the power," Herschel Savage told me.[109] Management agrees and has strenuously blocked such efforts at every turn.

Savage had tried to organize performers in mid-1980s San Francisco with what he thought was a modest initial proposal: "I was basically saying, 'No one work under $300.'" But production companies threatened to blacklist workers who held the line, and as soon as workers were broke, "they'd work for less. . . . There were so many hungry people." Decades later (we interviewed in 2013), Savage still regrets that the effort never took off: "It would have been the best thing to happen for health, security, retirement pay, everything. I mean, come on. I've done thousands of scenes and I have no residuals. That's the story for most people." Some thirty years later, the barriers to formal organizing Savage described persist—some workers cannot or will not hold the line, and companies do everything they can to block organizing attempts they view as threatening.

As Gregor Gall notes in his history of sex worker organizing, organizing efforts persist nonetheless.[110] After a series of on-set HIV transmissions in 2004 and the very public—and racist—scapegoating of one affected performer, Mr. Marcus told me he decided to get performers together. "Okay, maybe we should have some rights as performers," he remembered thinking.[111] He organized meetings but struggled to draw a consistent crowd. Performers do not remain in the industry for very long, he explained, and the community can feel fragmented. "The other hurdle was companies," he explained. With threats of retaliation, production companies did everything they could to cut the organizing drive off at the knees. "We would have formed a collective against something that up to this point had been an advantage to them," said Marcus.

Today, there is even less paid work to go around. To my question about the possibilities for organizing, performer-director Kelly Shibari explained, "Especially these days with the lack of work, we're more interested in making sure we can pay our bills."[112] Likewise, performer-director jessica drake explained that rate standardization is "highly improbable" since "there will always be that either super new person or super competitive or super desperate person that will buck the system. . . . It happens everywhere in all walks of life."[113] Indeed, the fact that scarcity complicates solidarity—and that bosses use scarcity to get more from workers for less—is not unique to porn. Alternative income streams lessen the strain of that scarcity, but organizing in decentralized economies presents special challenges. Managers are less powerful than they once were, but taking the place of visible bosses to make demands of are worker-managers who would rather not have bosses at all than organize collectively against them.

Most workers say that nontraditional forms of organizing have more significant impacts on their work lives than the union models that are more legible to those outside the porn worker community. Outsiders often advocate unionization through Hollywood's Screen Actors Guild—performer organizers told me leftists on social media routinely suggested this as though they had never considered it. But porn workers have already been there—the guild opted not to represent the porn community in 1974 and has held firm on this exclusion.[114] The mainstream labor movement has overwhelmingly followed suit. And workers said that organizing efforts that received much celebration from the outside, such as the 2010s' Adult Performers Association and Adult Performers Actors Guild, made limited difference in their work. Many had never heard of them. Others saw little purpose in organizing with an increasingly diffuse community over terms with industry managers who are becoming obsolete anyway. And still others gestured to political and personality clashes outsiders do not see. Some union officials were publicly homophobic, for example. Such models are not the only way of doing politics. And even when workers do not frame less formal kinds of organizing and community building as explicitly political, these undermine managerial prerogatives by arming workers with information and community.

In the absence of regulatory enforcement around wages and working conditions, it is performers who enforce standards by educating each other about what they can demand. Peer support puts performers' hard-won expertise to work. "In porno, a lot of times, you find out about a pitfall by falling into it first," explained Lexington Steele.[115] Workers use peer education to fill this gap. Lorelei Lee "always tried, if I'm working with somebody new, to tell them everything I know."[116] Performers say this makes all the difference. Jessica drake attributes her overwhelmingly positive experience of porn work in large part to the advice she got from veteran performers at the beginning of her career—"I went into it with my eyes open," she said.[117] These forms of community also build toward organizing that is more recognizable as such. Lee's practice began with sharing information with new performers, but it gave way to working "with other people on improving our situation" through collective organizing around worker health legislation and, later, the Stop Enabling Online Sex Trafficking Act.[118] Today Lee is a leading voice in sex-worker-policy activism.

Peer education helps workers survive the gaps bad policy creates. Performers do consent education on the fly, undoing the anti-sex-worker idea (one managers sometimes weaponize) that saying yes to paid sex negates your ability to negotiate its terms. On one set I visited, when a director tried to convince a new performer to shoot an additional blow job for the same rate, her costar let her know this was not normal—"you should say no," she said. The new performer did. Similar exchanges, performers told me, taught them how to extricate themselves from a bad contract, how to report wage theft when producers withhold pay, and what do to if an agent tries to take more than the legally allowed percentage of your pay. And in the regulatory vacuum that trade relationships intensify, "we've all had to reinvent the wheel," Maxine Holloway said.[119] In this spirit, performer and activist Jiz Lee's "Tricks of the Trade: Porn's 'Best Practices' for Content Trades and Shares" urges ethical decision-making, strategic thinking about distribution, and clear boundary communication.[120]

Mutual aid fills another set of gaps. Workers come together in crowdfunding campaigns to fill the void non-enforcement of workers' compensation creates when colleagues get injured. When workers struggle to rent an apartment—sex workers are not a "protected category" in fair housing law—they develop informal networks for securing housing. Also unprotected from employment discrimination in the mainstream labor market, when performers want to transition into straight jobs they help each other create legible work histories. Outsiders often assume that one of the industry's harms is pitting workers, and especially women performers, against one another. Competition for gigs, fame, and scarce resources, they imagine, makes solidarity impossible. Certainly, employers hope this is true. But the forms of community porn workers forge push against the idea that porn is viciously competitive. While competition, undercutting, and hostility among workers are features of the porn workplace, mutual assistance and solidarity are, too.

Workers also do peer support in more formal ways. Originally conceived as a collaboration between industry veterans Nina Ha⊗tley and Sharon Mitchell and reprised in 2014 by APAC, the *Porn 101* series educates performers about sexual health, consent, money management, and contract negotiation.[121] Such efforts hope to arm workers with the tools to protect themselves at work without directly antagonizing management or involving the regulatory state. They also include a professionalizing angle, urging performers to "take responsibility" for community health by exercising caution in off-set sex and reminding performers to show up to work on time. This combination of professionalization and information sharing earns such efforts industry-wide support (or at least relative noninterference from management). Nina Ha⊗tley came to *Porn 101* already wary of what directly antagonizing management might do. Faced with harsh retaliation when the Pink Ladies Social Club she helped to found in the late 1980s attempted rate standardization, the organization transitioned to a support model they hoped could improve workers' conditions without putting organizers out of a job.

Active performers spearheading subsequent organizing attempts have been careful to distance their efforts from models management might interpret as antagonistic. Again, this is in part because many are managers at least some of the time. In 2014, performers founded APAC in hopes of bringing performers together for policy advocacy, education, and support. After talking about the limited possibilities of organizing around standardized rates, jessica drake, a founding member, explained the group's different focus: "What we do instead is just try to give performers sort of a starting point and a soundboard for their questions, their ideas and things like that, and just kind of educate them as to what maybe would be a good business practice."[122] Also a founding member, Chanel Preston explained that APAC hoped to avoid being perceived as "negative or taking something away from someone. Education isn't gonna take anything away. It might take away business from a slimy agent that wants to get naïve girls in the industry, but who cares about them. So, the first things we do, we want it to be supported by everyone. We don't want to be coming out and be like, 'By the way, we're demanding!'"[123] The strategy has been successful, and APAC now stands as the longest-running performer organization in porn's history. It has found significant support from management and the FSC, which has collaborated with APAC in working to defeat mandatory condom legislation in California and on STI-testing protocols.

APAC's focus on policy collaboration with management, education, and recommending (rather than demanding) best practices also reflects its initial composition—a coalition of performers and performer-director-producers. When I asked current members why APAC did not call itself a union, many explained that the organization's then president, a powerful producer, director, and performer, had told members that forming as a union would "bankrupt the industry. The companies we work for would have to pay back taxes indefinitely," since it would have involved a claim for employee, rather than independent contractor, status.[124] Another member elaborated this concern: "I think we have to be labeled as employees to unionize and then that would be a really big deal for producers, because they would be required to give us health insurance, pay for testing, so that would not be good right now. So we're just an organization. A 501(c) nonprofit organization, and that's best for us."[125] Regardless of whether a successful unionizing drive would indeed bankrupt the industry, this threat was effective, and most members agreed to focus on education, working with management on best practices, and serving as a collective voice for performers in policy advocacy. Others left the organization, and some stayed in hopes of shifting its focus.

While most APAC members support its educational programming and lobbying against unwanted occupational health policy, there remain debates within the organization about its ideal stance vis-à-vis management. Unsurprisingly, members who also hold established managerial roles—not just producing their own content but regularly hiring others to perform for studio-funded projects—tend to be most supportive of organizing that benefits "everyone," while workers who only or predominantly perform tend to support more militant strategies. Meanwhile, the FSC is publicly invested in a narrative that no class conflict exists between workers and managers or between a trade organization and a worker group. I interviewed then FSC CEO Diane Duke around the time of APAC's founding, and she was proud to tell me about the FSC's support, which consisted of providing an initial meeting space, legal counsel, and evidently, a stamp of approval that helped to spare APAC organizers the management retribution previous organizers have encountered. I asked about this. "We're providing as much support for them as we can," she explained. "It's not something we would oppose. . . . The industry is extremely supportive of its performers."[126] "Whenever I lobby," she went on, "I talk about the conversations I have with performers, but I'm seen as the employer because I represent a lot of the studios."

Performer-organizers confronted similar dynamics when they founded the BIPOC Adult Industry Collective to address porn industry racism.[127] The FSC shared the collective's press release in a show of alliship,[128] but the trade group's capacity to lend material support will be limited by its position as a representative of the very employers who profit from racist norms. Indeed, as a trade group, the FSC's express purpose is to represent studios and producers. After significant leadership changes in the late 2010s, the FSC worked to more fully integrate performer voices.[129] It remains fundamentally constrained by its location as an employer-funded organization.

Interviewees who identify more strongly as performers than as management were distrustful of the FSC's capacity to represent their interests. Stoya explained, "I think the FSC is very good at what they they're supposed to do, which is protect producers' interests and defend adult content under the First Amendment. And they need to keep their fingers out of performers' business."[130] Another founding APAC member explained her position: "[The FSC is] a trade organization and they do not represent our best interest. They are not fighting for us."[131] This is why, she went on, it is so important that APAC exists as a separate entity. To the threat that forming as a union would "bankrupt the industry," she said, "To me, that's a huge bargaining chip." Later, members were angry when, after a performer accused her costar and a director of on-set assault, the FSC's own attorney represented the director in a defamation countersuit against the aggrieved performer.[132] For some, this confirmed the suspicion that the organization's loyalties are with managers, not performers. But sex work stigma, as it is played out both in the mainstream labor left and in state policy, means that managers and their organizations are often the only allies workers have. Workers take support where they can get it.

The tricky class alliances sex work stigma engenders come together with broader barriers to organizing among the precarious. Traditional forms of organizing do not hold for precarious workers, writes Isabell Lorey, because "their interests are so disparate."[133] But, she cautions, "this should by no means be understood solely as a lack, since it also holds out the opportunity to invent new and appropriate forms of political agency."[134] Porn work's location at the intersection of sex and work heightens these tensions. Workers' interests are so disparate, in fact, that some do not identify as workers at all. And for many of those who do, appeals for the kind of uniform policy demands typical of collective organizing are profoundly out of sync with desires for sexual autonomy and freedom from surveillance. As we return to the state, we are left with the task of envisioning policy demands that take privacy seriously without leaving it open to appropriation by capital. This would, to borrow Lorey's language, require some work of invention, and it would mean reimagining political subjectivity.

WHAT TO DO WITH THE STATE?

No regulatory apparatus can fully protect workers' autonomy when one must work to live and "if you don't want to do it, they'll find someone who will."[135] DIY entrepreneurship is a kind of resistance to these rules, but freedom from a direct boss does not equal freedom from the market—there are still bills to pay. Only a radical refusal of these terms would mean full freedom from these constraints, but policy for the meantime can support working people's well-being *now*. The central question in imagining what this would look like is, as Danny Wylde put it, "How can people do this for a living legally and still be okay in the end?"[136] Workers say that autonomy—worker self-governance but also individual privacy—is crucial to that okay-ness. As we have seen, the version of privacy we have now risks serving capital even as it also partially answers workers' demands.

We need instead privacy that protects workers' autonomy as sexual subjects without enabling their exploitation as workers. This calls for a resolutely anti-capitalist sex work exceptionalism—"eroticism in the public interest," as feminist theorist Nick Mitchell suggested I call it.[137] Workers' calls for occupational health policy that protects them from both state and employer control—the ability to choose safer sex methods, for example, and have that choice vigorously guarded—are one example of what this might look like. This represents a radical rethinking of what occupational health policy is imagined to do. If the state has sometimes (compelled by organized pressure from below) protected workers from capital's worst harms, this has often come with forms of regimentation many porn workers find untenable. Porn workers want protection without standardization, and there is neither an existing model for this nor a good reason not to demand it.

Nor is there a reason to maintain that being a worker legible to (and observable by) the state is a precondition of social citizenship. Concerted decisions, not historical inevitability, tied these things together and thus manufactured precarity for those excluded. While movements among domestic and other care workers have typically sought to counter such exclusions by making a case for their labors as *work*, sex workers have good reason to be wary of this strategy. Among them is that bids for care work's legibility often rest on arguing for its status as a "public good," a normalizing move that is incompatible with the ways creative sexual expression can be usefully offensive to the "public" and disruptive to the normal.[138] The tying of social citizenship to work status is not inexorable, and undoing it makes it possible to support those currently excluded without reinstantiating the idea that security should be contingent on employment in the first place. These priorities echo Kathi Weeks's call for politics that contest work's "misrecognition and devaluation on the one hand, and its metaphysics and moralism on the other."[139]

This represents a political rejection of the normalizing force of "work" that not all readers will endorse. But it is also a practical push for policy that fits the world of work as it is, not as those nostalgic for the Fordist welfare state wish it to be. While recent moves to expand the definition of employee status[140] will undoubtedly help win some workers protection, they also represent a backward-looking attempt to bring a few more workers into a broken category (and one that, again, some workers do not want).

A politics for the meantime is more interested in policies that give people what they need regardless of their work status. A French performer-director seemed to find the question of whether studios or performers should cover the costs of work-related injury rather beside the point: "I don't think it has to be a work-related injury. If you sprain an ankle on set or whatever, you should have health insurance in America. It doesn't matter where it happens."[141] To the question of who should cover STI-testing costs, Tara Holiday ventured, "Maybe the state should pay. It's for the state's convenience that we're all [testing]."[142] It is a radical move to insist that community well-being is for the state and thus its financial responsibility. This idea applies beyond the realm of health, and it is in line with most porn workers' demands to say that social welfare should be totally decoupled from regulatory oversight. Without the forms of control typical of the U.S. welfare state, policies based on the idea that the state should pay could provide privacy that builds working-class power rather than undermines it. They could do this, too, without (I think, vainly) trying to redraw boundaries between employment and contracting, work and nonwork.

A regulatory system premised on artificial boundaries between private life and public work does an especially poor job of making sense of subjects who are sometimes workers, sometimes contractors, sometimes bosses, and also sometimes (or at the very same time) sexual subjects. But these failures are not limited to porn. Meting out protections according to boundaries between work and nonwork (or, more narrowly, employment and contracting) will not hold in a moment in which life is "put to work" and those boundaries blur for more and more of us.[143] Organizers, scholars, and policy makers of straight work are well served to pay attention to how porn workers fashion policy demands. Etsy-style craft producers, YouTube celebrities, and Uber drivers, for instance, do not share sex workers' gendered and racialized history of state violence, but they do share labors in which workers both feel the harms of state neglect *and* might reject greater state control over personal lives that have entered the market.

With a long history of navigating that double bind, sex workers are experts at imaging what security without control might look like. They are also skilled at building community in ways that keep one another safe in the meantime. The "public-private" divide is "gasping for air," as theorist Paolo Virno puts it.[144] For many, it never existed. Certainly, it cannot be rehabilitated now. Porn workers suggest that this is not something to mourn. The divide between work and life was not built for working people, and it cannot be neatly refashioned to serve us. "Maybe the state should pay."[145]

Epilogue

Fuck Jobs

This book closes where it began, returning to the question of what it means to call porn "work." "There's a part of the work aspect that's distasteful to me," Conner Habib said. "I don't like the idea of jobs. The most obscene thing is 'working for a living.'"[1] He went on:

> I'm tired of hearing people, especially feminists, saying "it's just a job," just like any other job. There's a difference. . . . I get to have and give pleasure every day for my job. Is that not in some ways a great potential to sidestep "I get to give and experience misery"? That makes it less of a job in some ways. And I know we're not supposed to say that because we're at this moment where we're trying to prove to people that this is a job. But then let's take one step beyond that and say, "Okay, fuck jobs."

Laughing, he added, "That should be your title." I agreed—it is a great title—but worried that leading with "Fuck Jobs" would make it harder for me to get one. Like porn workers, academics make compromises in the service of making a living. But "fuck jobs" is very much the spirit of this book. It gestures both to the irretrievable "problem with work," as Kathi Weeks puts it, and to workers' remarkable strategies for living "within and against" work.[2] These two things—the fact that work is a problem and the fact that workers are endlessly creative in resisting it—are the foundation of *Porn Work*'s politics.

To call something "work" is, from an antiwork position, not to bid for respectability or repudiate pleasure. It is, instead, to refuse that pleasure be appropriated and bled dry as yet another site of extraction. There is something disruptive about getting paid to give and receive pleasure. It is an exchange that beckons a postwork utopia in which guaranteed annual incomes replace the compulsion to work and pleasure seeking takes the place of drudgery. We are not there yet. Instead, ours is a moment in which employers peddle the language of pleasure at work even in the most implausible contexts. And yet, we know that pleasure sometimes matters to workers, too. Habib's incitement to "fuck jobs" reminds us not to let bosses set the terms here.

The narrative of porn as an escape from work operates on multiple registers. First and most important from an ethnographic perspective, it makes the day-to-day experience of working for a living (an obscene thing, to be sure) less crushing. Loving porn work also rejects stigmas that assign misery to monetized sex, at once revising fundamental assumptions about sex workers' abjection and reminding us that straight work trades in misery. Marking porn as a departure from work can, as we have seen, provide some protections from an abusive state. And it can give clues to what life lived otherwise might look like. But the idea of porn as a fun departure from the daily grind can also obscure that porn work shares many of the tediums, vulnerabilities, and frustrations associated with straight work. Contesting this matters for sex worker organizing, including the demand for policies that ensure sex workers' access to labor protections and freedom from violence and harassment.[3] It matters, as I have claimed throughout this book, for harnessing porn workers' insights about surviving late capitalism. And it matters, as Ela Darling reminded us at the beginning of this book, for highlighting that this is how people pay their rent. This is why Habib amended his critique of the language of "work" with "I know we're not supposed to say that."

But sometimes the things we are not supposed to say are the ones that most need saying, and there is real danger that calling porn work "work" will legitimize it in ways no work should be legitimized. We see this when managers talk about porn as a business "like any other" by way of resisting state oversight and borrowing HR techniques and corporate restructuring tools from mainstream. It is also evident when scholars and other commentators acknowledge porn as a business but fail to problematize business as such. Here, it matters not only that we call porn "work" but also that we are clear about what "work" means: exploitation but also struggle. This means marking porn as work while also taking "one step beyond that."

Like Habib, many porn performers define straight work as misery dealing, and interviewees framed their career choices as ways of resisting what straight work has to offer—tedium, fatigue, inflexible hours, low wages, stress. At the same time, they make clear that the problems of porn work in many ways mirror those of straight jobs. Porn is "a job . . . a gig."[4] I have sought not to resolve that tension, or to suggest that it arises from workers' misunderstanding their own conditions, but rather to theorize what it tells us about work under and against late capitalism—this is a system rife with contradiction, contradiction that workers harness in creative and uneven ways. We are left with the ongoing task of forging a politics that can make work better now and obsolete in the future. What that future might look like is a question that has long concerned left critics, and I do not pretend to offer a definitive answer here. Leftists do a lot of guessing about whether sex work will exist in the future, and I think the better answer is that we will not know until we get there.

This book makes a claim for how we might tell stories about what work looks like now with an eye for that which is "one step beyond." How we talk about the problems of work—as exceptional or mundane, impermeable or porous—shapes the politics that emerge from these stories. How we talk about struggle shapes these politics, too, and porn work is only one site in which an invigorated commitment to dialectical thinking reveals new possibilities. Workers' strategies for navigating, resisting, and reimagining porn work give vital clues about surviving this moment of profound capitalist crisis. In laying bare those pressure points, porn work reimagines porn, and work. "Okay, fuck jobs."[5]

Acknowledgments

Before I went to graduate school, visited a porn set, or read theory, I was interested in workers' crafty survival strategies because I depended on them. Thanks to the women who taught me to charm my way to rent money and that tooth-numbing cream makes your feet hurt less after a shift in heels. Sex workers, especially, know that none of this is built for working people, and they are really good at figuring out how to make use of it anyway. Thank you for inspiring me to write this book and, later, for the time, ideas, and community that made it possible.

I'm deeply grateful to the interviewees who gave their time and expertise to this project. They took me into their homes, entrusted me with their stories, invited me to watch them work, and connected me with friends and colleagues. Their interventions taught me about porn work and also shaped my politics in ways that will outlive this book. Everything I know about class, pleasure, the state, and solidarity bears the marks of our conversations. As public thinkers on their own terms (and often with a much wider reach), interviewees knew very well that they did not need my help in conveying their ideas. They were also busy making a living, organizing, and helping each other get by. It was out of tremendous generosity that you found time for me. I hope what follows does your ideas justice. Special thanks to Ela Darling, Conner Habib, Maxine Holloway, Jiz Lee, Lorelei Lee, Ian O'Brien, Chanel Preston, Siouxsie Q, Sovereign Syre, and the members of the Adult Performer Advocacy Committee for conversation, collaboration, and inspiration throughout the years. Conner Habib turned my ideas inside out when we first interviewed and never stopped. When academia's own abusive conditions were crushing my spirit, he helped put my head back on straight. Any errors (including, Conner might say, that I'm still a Marxist) are of course my own.

Feminist mentorship has sustained me throughout the process of writing this book. Eileen Boris's interventions on home and work (things she likes to remind us are the same) radically shifted my thinking, and our continued conversations have shaped this project in more ways than I can count. She has supported this project from the start with a kind of generosity that you only see from those rare radical academics who actually believe in their politics. Mireille Miller-Young's groundbreaking work on porn labor and commitment to interviewees as "critical knowledge producers" inspire my thinking and remind me that this work has real stakes. A fierce advocate throughout this process, she pushed me to take risks and helped me land on my feet when I did. Constance Penley—*the* porn professor—has been unsparing with her time, connections, and ideas. I have left every conversation newly confident that there's a reason to keep writing. Leila Rupp's generosity of spirit, unflagging support, and bone-dry wit have been sustaining. Her talent for sympathetic reading has changed the way I think and write, not least because she is so good at divining what one is trying to say and helping them say it. Thanks to all of you, too, for bearing with four years of recommendation writing as I tried to score health insurance and steady rent money.

It is a tremendous privilege to pay one's bills writing and teaching about hacking capitalism. I still can't believe I get to do it. Alice Echols gave me a place to land and mentorship that sustained me during the most precarious years of my academic career. Treating me as a colleague with ideas rather than contingent labor to be bled dry, she fought for working conditions that gave me time to think and write. Thanks to Sarah Banet-Weiser, Chris Freeman, C. J. Giovingo, Edwin Hill, Caroline Muglia, Jessica Ng, Rhacel Salazar Parreñas, and Karen Tongson for their support during my time at USC. To my colleagues at the Department of Women, Gender, and Sexuality Studies at Washington University in St. Louis, thank you for taking a chance on me. Cynthia Barounis, Barbara Baumgartner, Rachel Brown, Adrienne Davis, Mary Ann Dzuback, René Esparza, Andrea Friedman, Rebecca Lester, Jeffrey McCune, Stephen McIsaac, Shanti Parikh, Anca Parvulescu, Trevor Sangrey, and Rebecca Wanzo welcomed me and helped me think through the final stages of this project. Donna Kepley went out of her way to facilitate my transition. Thanks to interlocutors at Washington University's Women, Gender, and Sexuality Studies Colloquium and Ethnographic Theory Workshop for thoughtful feedback.

Thanks especially to Rachel, Shanti, Trevor, and Rebecca for comments on this book's introduction and first chapter. I feel incredibly lucky to work among such smart, generous thinkers.

I'm grateful to the teachers and interlocutors who have informed this project at its many stages. Sinan Antoon, Maurizia Boscagli, Lauren Kaminsky, Nelson Lichtenstein, Daniel Moshenberg, Jennifer Nash, Todd Ramlow, Rachel Riedner, and France Winddance Twine taught courses that shaped my thinking early on. Thanks to Audrey Chu, David Delgado, Nova Garcia, Rebecca Hu, Shannon Lam, Valerie Lopez, Kalev Rudolph, and Ailee Yanagishita for making teaching such a pleasure. Thomas Adams, Richard Anderson, Mary Francis Berry, Cynthia Blair, Jennifer Brier, Brenda Cossman, Deborah Dinner, Erik Gelman, Anne Gray Fischer, Rosemary Hennessy, Nate Holdren, Alice Kessler-Harris, Premilla Nadasen, Annelise Orleck, Gayle Rubin, Matt Stahl, Jayne Swift, Katherine Turk, Ken Wissoker, and the participants at the Newberry Library Seminar in Labor History gave generous feedback at various points in the process. Thanks to Christopher Baum, Brooke Beloso, Thad Blanchette, Denise Brennan, Vanessa Carlisle, Mindy Chateauvert, Lynn Comella, Emily Coombes, Kate D'Adamo, Susan Dewey, Sonja Dolinsek, Finley Freibert, Melissa Gira Grant, Patrick Grzanka, Carol Leigh, Samantha Majic, Laura Helen Marks, Laura McTighe, Greg Mitchell, Jennifer Nash, Becki Ross, Cris Sardina, Zahra Zsuzsanna Stardust, Shira Tarrant, Georgina Voss, and Valerie Webber for their community and example. Neda Atanasoski, Nick Mitchell, Lynn Sacco, Kyla Wazana Tompkins, and Kathi Weeks advocated for this project, and me, at crucial moments.

Parts of chapters 2 and 3 appeared in the journals *Signs* and *Porn Studies*, respectively, and previous publications in *Feminist Studies*, *Queer Sex Work*, and *WSQ* helped develop my thinking. Thanks to Meena Alexander, Feona Attwood, Nancy Fischer, Mary Laing, Jiz Lee, Rosalind Petchesky, Katy Pilcher, Steven Seidman, Clarissa Smith, Nicola Smith, Rebecca Sullivan, Ashwini Tambe, Suzanna Danuta Walters, Valerie Webber, and the anonymous reviewers who gave feedback and editorial support on those pieces. Jessie Kindig's feedback on an earlier draft of the introduction gave me the confidence to frame this story on its own terms.

Brandon Proia, my editor at University of North Carolina Press, understood what I was trying to do with this book from the start and gave comradely, smart edits that helped me get there. His reputation for supporting left scholarship that doesn't conceal its politics convinced me to publish with UNC Press, and I'm grateful to have found a home for the book that let me say what I meant. Thanks to Mary Caviness, Cate

Hodorowicz, Dylan White, and Iza Wojciechowska for careful support through the production process. I'm grateful to UNC Press's anonymous reviewers for generous feedback and for distilling what was innovative about the book when I was in too deep to see it. I keep the kind things you said in a folder and return to them when my confidence wavers.

Thanks to the Mellon Foundation/American Council of Learned Societies; Washington University Center for the Humanities; and UCSB's Dean's Fellowship, Humanities and Social Sciences Research Grant, and Affiliates Fellowship for funding research travel and time to write. Any views, findings, conclusions, or recommendations expressed in this publication do not necessarily reflect those of these organizations. UAW Local 2865 fought for contracts that gave us the security necessary to choose projects independent of institutional approval. Lastly on the subject of money: I conducted research for this book on a contingent scholar's shoestring budget, and interviewees gave me their time for free. The irony of asking workers for their free time to do a study on labor is not lost on me. I'm indebted to all the porn workers who were willing to sit with this contradiction, especially as we both know exactly how much an hour is worth.

I'm grateful to my friends and family for their unwavering support. Thanks to Vanessa Carlisle, Mindy Chateauvert, Sasha Coles, Conner Habib, Nik Haug, Heidi James, Lily Langerud, Kate Levin, Beatrix McBride, Kurt Newman, John Richmond, Leila Roberts, Caitlin Smith, Samir Sonti, Annika Speer, David Stein, Cody Stephens, Annamaria Sundbye, Carly Thomsen, Theresa Wiesner, the UCSB Marxist crew, and our Shanty folks for making me take breaks from work and to Nettie Bachman, Herb Berg, Stephen Kulis, Margaret Mahoney, Flavio Marsiglia, Nancy and Ken Smemo, Arlene and Michael Spiegler, Rochelle Trochtenberg, Maria Velasquez, and Trinity Williams for bringing me home. Kit Smemo's love, support, and confidence have sustained me and shaped this book at every turn. Everything, even the bourgeois family, is better when you're around. Kit has been present always with in-house edits and vital perspective, reminding me of this book's stakes for political economy and pointing to those moments in which porn work looks a lot like Progressive Era craft labor. Thanks to Gus for snuggles and for embodying postwork politics. Finally, thanks to Margi Waller for fierce encouragement, perspective, keen edits, and a magical writing outpost in the redwoods. Thirty years of watching her meet people where they are was my first and best training in organizing and ethnography. This book's preoccupation with creative ways of struggling, breaking rules, and getting by comes straight from her.

Acknowledgments

Appendix

Research Methods

This book is grounded in interviews and fieldwork I conducted between 2012 and 2019.

I interviewed eighty-one porn performers, managers, and crew members and conducted nonparticipatory observation on set and at industry events. Directors of gonzo, mainstream, feminist, and trade productions invited me to observe their sets. There, I saw the production process and made connections with performers, some of whom would later agree to be interviewed for the project. Industry events included annual meetings at the Adult Entertainment Expo and XBIZ and trade meetings I attended on invitation from the Free Speech Coalition. With the help of industry publicists, and with press credentials made possible by my nonacademic writing, I was able to attend industry-only meetings.

Over time, I became involved beyond the role of observer. The Adult Performer Advocacy Committee said it needed hard data, so I worked with Chanel Preston and Conner Habib, then the organization's president and vice president, respectively, to develop the first large-scale survey of industry workers. Together we designed questions aiming to better understand workers' experiences around income inequality, consent, health practices, and stigma. Later, I joined the Performer Availability Screening Services advisory board, the group of performers, management, and experts that advises on industry sexually transmitted infection testing policy. These engagements do not appear directly in this book—it was important to be of service in ways that were not focused on gathering data—but alongside other collaborations and friendships, they helped shape my understanding of what is at stake in this project.

I conducted interviews between 2012 and 2015. They lasted between forty-five minutes and two hours. I interviewed workers and managers predominantly in Los Angeles, the San Fernando Valley, and San Francisco, where most adult films are produced, as well as those who live in Las Vegas and Miami (also popular filming locations) and throughout the country. Interviewees included fifty-nine current or retired performers, most of whom also held other roles in the porn industry, working as managers, crew, or in PR. Twenty-two interviewees had worked only in nonperforming roles as agents, producers, directors, screenwriters, photographers, crew members, and publicists. Interviewees ranged in age from twenty-one to seventy. Their years active in the industry ranged from 1973 to the present, with most currently working in the industry. Interviewees included those who were struggling to get by and others who had just paid cash for mansions in the valley. Most experienced something in the middle.

Interviewees identified as Black, white, Latino, Middle Eastern, Asian, and mixed race. As in the U.S. racial economy more broadly, such identities can be fluid in the industry. One mixed-race interviewee identified as Black for some productions and Asian for others, for example. Interviewees' gender identities include cis female, male, trans, and genderqueer. Informed by queer theoretical analyses of identity, I come to this project understanding that points of identity matter to people at different times. In the text, I foreground those identities, if any, that workers mark as most salient in the stories they tell. More often than not, these are the identities that determine working conditions. When I include identity markers, I mean to signal workers' workplace identities and do so using standard industry terms. When I refer to someone as a "gay" performer, for example, I mean the industry sector in which they work rather than their off-screen sexual identity.

I located interviewees primarily through referrals. Porn workers are often regarded as a "difficult-to-access population."[1] This was not my experience. If a population seems difficult to access, this may be because we are asking the wrong questions or asking them in the wrong way. Porn workers and managers were eager to share insights about their industry. This is not to say that my research process was easy or seamless. It took years to establish the connections that made possible layered interviews with a broad group of workers and managers. Many porn workers and managers have had countless negative interactions with academic and journalistic interviewers, and it was my job to demonstrate that I would not re-create those dynamics.

I came to the research process with some connections to the community because of my previous involvement in sex worker organizing. Some workers I knew from the world of organizing vouched for me to people in the porn community. This background also allowed me to enter the research encounter with a base knowledge of the frustrations sex workers often experience when dealing with researchers and journalists and an understanding of how I might avoid reproducing them. I also had a great deal of help. I was fortunate to have the support of Mireille Miller-Young and Constance Penley, two mentors who have together spent decades building reputations in the porn worker community. The stamp of approval these connections provided gave potential interviewees a sense of who I might be. As Juba Kalamka put it when I asked if he had any questions for me before our interview began, "No, you're with Mireille so you're all good."[2]

Interviewees were generous in helping me connect with others who might be interested in speaking with me. Some did this by passing my information on to friends and colleagues. Porn worker communities are tight-knit, and word spreads quickly. "Your name has come up at a couple of APAC [Adult Performer Advocacy Committee] meetings," jessica drake told me. "That's how I knew you were good and okay to talk to."[3] Others posted on social media. After our interview, director and then widely read industry blogger Mike South published a blog post encouraging people to contact me. South is a controversial figure in the industry, and about half of the flood of respondents who wrote to me after the post said they did so to make sure I heard a different perspective.

After our interview, Dominic Ace, an industry publicist, asked me to work the 2014 Adult Entertainment Expo as the interviewer for his press circuit during the three-day event. I did not include information from these interviews in this book—most were rather short, designed for the particular flows of the event and intended for a web series made for fans. But the experience made me visible in a way not typically accessible to academic interviewers and accelerated the process of making my face and name recognizable. Later, a director organizing an awards ceremony asked me to seat guests and work the greenroom. I also did not solicit interviews here, but it was another experience that helped to nurture the community connections I had been building.

In these moments, working for free facilitated the process of connecting with interviewees. I struggled with the decision to take these unpaid gigs for the same reasons I critique "exposure" as free labor in the porn context—accepting exposure (or, in my case, community visibility and potential connections) as pay undermines other workers' ability to demand payment. No one would have been paid for these labors under these circumstances. "If you don't want to do it, they'll find someone that will" applies here, too, and any number of those hoping for industry connections—fans, aspiring actors, the curious—would have happily accepted. But this is not the point. In taking these gigs, I occupied the position of scab, a class position Yasmin Nair incisively critiques in the figure of academics experimenting with journalistic writing for little or no pay (a sin I have also committed).[4] There is something rather perverse about being party to a system that devalues work in order to write about work. I note this to make clear that I—and indeed all workers, especially academics—am implicated in the same problematics and compromises I write about in the porn work context.

I posed interview questions about wage and hour issues, workplace health, emotional labor, and work processes, making clear that interviewees were free to skip over anything they would rather not discuss. Interviewees were overwhelmingly eager to talk about these nuts-and-bolts realities of their jobs, and many told me they enjoyed the reprieve from the questions they often encounter. I made a habit of apologizing before asking about wages with a joke about how I knew this was not generally understood as a polite question, and workers overwhelmingly said that they were happy to discuss money off the record. Juba Kalamka, who is also a musician, said he was glad I asked and talked about his frustration with most music industry interviews in which "none of the performers talk about the reality of the working artist."[5] Stoya volunteered detailed information about her rates and said "that's a thing that workers need to start getting comfortable talking about."[6] I also asked workers what they enjoyed about their jobs, and on this question some hesitated because this is not a query they often receive outside of interviews intended for fans in which the ideal answer is something like "All the double anal!" When I posed this question to Conner Habib, he replied, "It's just a weird thing to say because I'm so used to telling people, 'Oh, I love my job,' because they think porn stars hate it. But asking the specifics of it, it's funny."[7]

Equally important were the questions I did not ask. They included anything about performers' childhoods, porn's social effects, performers' medical information (including sexually transmitted infection status and history), or their off-camera interpersonal and sexual lives. Performers are whole people, and I appreciate those studies that look at other aspects of sex workers' lives. I recognize, too, that the ethnographic tradition typically involves more space for thick descriptions and more holistic portraits of subjects. At the same time, I am wary of a research encounter that in any way reproduces the perception by fans and in marketing that any part of a performer's life is up for grabs or that feeds consumer "interest in the interiority, multifacetedness, and behind-the-scenes lives of porn performers."[8] I did not want to produce a version of behind-the-scenes footage. The reader will not find rich descriptions of the set or the home, and this book does not offer a sketch of workers' lives outside work and organizing. Some interviewees did volunteer this information, and I include it where they identify it as relevant to their analysis of working life.

Even as I expressly introduced my project as focused on work and excluded any questions about representation, the discursive landscape is so overdetermined in favor of representational analyses that these seeped into interviewees' responses. Interviewees are so accustomed to being asked about porn as a product that they often offered answers to the questions I explicitly did not ask. Thus, after Dominic Ace asked me what I was interested in writing about and I told him "porn as a workplace, how workers experience their jobs, how the work is organized, things like that," he replied, "Can porn affect relationships? Absolutely. Can drinking too much affect relationships? Absolutely. . . . There's a hundred different ways of looking at the effects of porn on people, on girls." Others (mostly men in management) volunteered their own understandings of whether the trope of porn performers as childhood abuse survivors is supported by evidence and went out of their way to explain that they do not condone recreational drug use on set, even as I never asked about these things.

Both before and after interviews, I asked workers whether they would like to remain anonymous in some or all quotes. The vast majority wanted to be on the record under their stage names. Later, when I transcribed interviews and particularly controversial topics (especially those that might risk lost work in the future) came up, I contacted workers again to ensure that they still wanted to use their stage names in connection with quotes. Again, most did. Workers want their stories heard, and most wanted their names attached to their ideas.[9] Not the least of reasons why performers wanted attribution is that they are, as we have seen, constantly self-marketing. But they also know that few people buy and read academic books. Overwhelmingly, workers agreed to give me their time to be kind, not because they thought an academic book would radically change their industry. I do not maintain those illusions either. It is a small, imperfect acknowledgment of the collective work of thinking these ideas through (work that benefits me more than any other person who gave their ideas to this project) that I direct all author royalties to sex worker organizers.

In his porn work memoir, Zak Smith explains that he changed the names of characters based on people in his life "not so much to disguise people . . . as to remind readers—and myself—that there is probably more to them than I managed to see or record."[10] This is a crucial point, even as I have attributed quotes directly when interviewees wanted them to be. My hope is that readers can both honor interviewees' analyses as their own *and* recognize that quotes from one interview can never tell a person's whole story. A lot can change in the years it takes to write a book. My own ideas certainly have.

Notes

INTRODUCTION

1. Dominic Ace, interview by author, Reseda, Calif., November 8, 2013.

2. Conner Habib, interview by author, Los Angeles, February 27, 2014.

3. Ela Darling, interview by author, Los Angeles, May 7, 2014.

4. Conner Habib, email to author, January 1, 2019.

5. Interviewees' experiences included work in gay, straight, and feminist/queer productions as well as in the full range of production styles and budgets (i.e., low-to-mid-budget scenes focusing primarily or entirely on sex, mainstream features [big-budget, multiscene films with dialogue], feminist productions [typically low budget with explicit social justice commitments], and trade productions). Many workers take gigs in more than one sector of the industry. I use standard industry terms throughout this book. As with so many discourses of sexuality, straight porn with cis partners is not typically named as such but is simply "mainstream." "Gay" refers to productions involving cis men and is commonly regarded as a discrete industry, while "girl-girl" refers to scenes featuring two or more women performers and is included in the mainstream heterosexual industry. Scenes with trans women and cis partners are typically assigned to the trans porn subgenre, while trans men generally find work in queer or feminist productions. "Queer" and "feminist" porn share key players and production practices, and have similar representational norms.

6. Quoted in Isabell Lorey, *State of Insecurity: Government of the Precarious*, trans. Allen Derieg (London: Verso, 2015), 97.

7. Precarias a la Deriva, "Adrift through the Circuits of Feminized Precarious Work," *Feminist Review*, no. 77 (April 2004): 157.

8. Melinda Chateauvert, *Sex Workers Unite: A History of the Movement from Stonewall to Slutwalk* (Boston: Beacon, 2013), 4.

9. See Gregor Gall, *An Agency of Their Own: Sex Worker Union Organizing* (Winchester, UK: Zero Books, 2012), 28.

10. Silvia Federici, *Caliban and the Witch: Women, the Body and Primitive Accumulation* (New York: Autonomedia, 2003), 49.

11. Thus, John Holloway urges us to think about social identity in terms of verbs rather than nouns. John Holloway, "We Are the Fragility of the System," interview by Fiona Jeffries, in *We Have Nothing to Lose but Our Fear: Activism and Resistance in Dangerous Times,* by Fiona Jeffries (London: Zed Books, 2015), 105.

12. See Dennis Mumby, "Theorizing Resistance in Organization Studies: A Dialectical Approach," *Management Communication Quarterly* 19, no. 1 (2005): 39.

13. Margaret Waller, "Resilience in Ecosystemic Context: Evolution of the Concept," *American Journal of Orthopsychiatry* 71, no. 3 (2001): 295.

14. Precarias a la Deriva, "Adrift through the Circuits," 157.

15. Shira Tarrant, *The Pornography Industry: What Everyone Needs to Know* (New York: Oxford University Press, 2016), 31.

16. See Sylvère Lotringer and Christian Marazzi, eds., *Autonomia: Post-political Politics,* Intervention Series 1 (Los Angeles: Semiotext(e), 2007).

17. Ursula Huws, "Expression and Expropriation: The Dialectics of Autonomy and Control in Creative Labor," *Ephemera: Theory & Politics in Organization* 10, no. 3/4 (2010): 504.

18. Franco Berardi, "What Is the Meaning of Autonomy Today?," *European Institute for Progressive Cultural Policies,* March 2003, https://transversal.at /transversal/1203/berardi-aka-bifo/en.

19. That is, conditions like those one might associate with factory labor, in which workers feel totally disconnected from the products they produce.

20. Anonymous performer, interview by author, Woodland Hills, Calif., May 10, 2014.

21. Mariarosa Dalla Costa, *Women and the Subversion of the Community: A Mariarosa Dalla Costa Reader,* ed. Camille Barbagallo (Oakland, Calif.: PM Press, 2019), 33.

22. Scott describes infrapolitics as the subtle, sometimes hidden forms of protest that are not immediately recognizable as the stuff of politics. James Scott, *Domination and the Arts of Resistance: Hidden Transcripts* (New Haven, Conn.: Yale University Press, 1990).

23. John Holloway, *Crack Capitalism* (London: Pluto, 2010).

24. L. H. Horton-Stallings, *Funk the Erotic: Transaesthetics and Black Sexual Cultures* (Urbana: University of Illinois Press, 2015).

25. Roderick Ferguson, *Aberrations in Black: Toward a Queer of Color Critique,* Critical American Studies (Minneapolis: University of Minnesota Press, 2004), 1; Sara Ahmed, *The Promise of Happiness* (Durham, N.C.: Duke University Press, 2010).

26. Vanessa Carlisle, "Sex Worker Organizing at the Front Lines in Fascist Times" (roundtable discussion, National Women's Studies Association, San Francisco, November 16, 2019).

27. Annelise Orleck, *We Are All Fast Food Workers Now: The Global Uprising against Poverty Wages* (Boston: Beacon, 2018), 8.

28. Cathy Cohen, "Punks, Bulldaggers, and Welfare Queens: The Radical Potential of Queer Politics?," *GLQ* 3, no. 4 (1997): 437–65.

29. Hacking//Hustling (@hackinghustling), photo, Twitter, July 8, 2019, https://twitter.com/hackinghustling/status/1148302287946878981?s=20.

30. Samantha Grace, interview by author, Los Angeles, November 2, 2013.

31. Kathi Weeks, *The Problem with Work: Feminism, Marxism, Antiwork Politics, and Postwork Imaginaries* (Durham, N.C.: Duke University Press, 2011).

32. Harry Cleaver, *Reading Capital Politically* (Edinburgh, UK: AK Press, 2000), 17.

33. Michael Hardt and Antonio Negri, *Assembly* (New York: Oxford University Press, 2017), 43.

34. Hardt and Negri, 43.

35. In thinking about the limits of reform, I am inspired by the sometimes overlapping communities of anti-capitalists, radical queers, Black feminists, and prison abolitionists who aim to dismantle dominant institutions while also supporting those currently caught up in their dragnet. See Angela Davis, *Are Prisons Obsolete?* (New York: Seven Stories, 2003); Dean Spade, *Normal Life: Administrative Violence, Critical Trans Politics, and the Limits of Law* (Durham, N.C.: Duke University Press, 2015).; and Weeks, *Problem with Work.*

36. Richie Calhoun, interview by author, Los Angeles, October 15, 2013.

37. Lisa Duggan and José Esteban Muñoz, "Hope and Hopelessness: A Dialogue," *Women & Performance* 19, no. 2 (July 2009): 278.

38. For the same reason, Mireille Miller-Young describes income streams outside of waged porn performance as central to the economic survival of many Black women performers, whose porn work is systematically devalued and hyperexploited. Mireille Miller-Young, *A Taste for Brown Sugar: Black Women in Porn* (Durham, N.C.: Duke University Press, 2014), 217.

39. Mr. Marcus, interview by author, Balboa Park, Calif., October 29, 2013.

40. Herschel Savage, interview by author, Los Angeles, April 5, 2013.

41. Hardt and Negri, *Assembly.*

42. J. K. Gibson-Graham, *The End of Capitalism (As We Knew It): A Feminist Critique of Political Economy* (Minneapolis: University of Minnesota Press, 2006). See also debates regarding E. P. Thompson's articulation of class as "a relationship and not a thing." While I am sympathetic to critiques suggesting that Thompson's empiricism leads him to falsely evacuate class of its mechanical relationship to production processes, my approach here follows from his insistence that class is dynamic, rather than static, and that historical subjects are active in constituting their own class perspectives. E. P. Thompson, *The Making of the English Working Class* (London: Penguin Books, 1963), 11. See also Ellen Meiksins Wood, "The Politics of Theory and the Concept of Class: E. P. Thompson and His Critics," *Studies in Political Economy* 9, no. 1 (1982): 45–75. For an overview of core Marxist perspectives on class composition, see Erik Olin Wright, "Varieties of Marxist Conceptions of Class Structure," *Politics & Society* 9, no. 3 (1980): 325–70.

43. See Ruth Rosen, *The Lost Sisterhood: Prostitution in America, 1900–1918* (Baltimore: Johns Hopkins University Press, 1982), 88.

44. Mao Tsetung, *Selected Readings from the Works of Mao Tsetung* (Peking, China: Foreign Languages Press, 1971), 66.

45. Joanna Angel, interview by author, by phone, January 23, 2014.

46. Anonymous performer interview, May 10, 2014.

47. For in-depth histories of porn, see Peter Alilunas, *Smutty Little Movies: The Creation and Regulation of Adult Video* (Oakland: University of California Press, 2016); Carolyn Bronstein, *Battling Pornography: The American Feminist Antipornography Movement, 1976–1986* (Cambridge: Cambridge University Press,

2011); Jeffrey Escoffier, *Bigger Than Life: The History of Gay Porn Cinema from Beefcake to Hardcore* (Philadelphia: Running Press, 2009); Elena Gorfinkel, *Lewd Looks: American Sexploitation Cinema in the 1960s* (Minneapolis: University of Minnesota Press, 2017); Miller-Young, *Taste for Brown Sugar*; and Linda Williams, *Hard Core: Power, Pleasure, and the "Frenzy of the Visible"* (Berkeley: University of California Press, 1999).

48. On stag, see Miller-Young, *Taste for Brown Sugar*. On sexploitation, see Gorfinkel, *Lewd Looks*.

49. Interviewees who worked during this period reported flat (i.e., equal among all performers) day rates averaging $100 (approximately $500 in today's dollars) for full-length films and fifty to seventy dollars for individual scenes.

50. On organized crime during the period, see Vincent Barnett, "'The Most Profitable Film Ever Made': Deep Throat (1972), Organized Crime, and the $600 Million Gross," *Porn Studies* 5, no. 2 (2018): 131–51.

51. Carter Stevens, interview by author, Skype, November 1, 2013. With a major economic recession under way, there was, of course, "no money" in a lot of jobs.

52. See Tarrant, *Pornography Industry*, 23.

53. See Alilunas, *Smutty Little Movies*, 127.

54. An early model here was Candida Royalle; see Williams, *Hard Core*, 249.

55. For stories of Golden Age production communities, see the remarkable *Rialto Report* oral history podcast. Rialto Report (website), accessed July 14, 2016, https://www.therialtoreport.com.

56. Escoffier, *Bigger Than Life*.

57. See Chuck Kleinhans, "The Change from Film to Video Pornography: Implications for Analysis," in *Pornography: Film and Video Culture*, ed. Peter Lehman (New Brunswick, N.J.: Rutgers University Press, 2006), 154–67.

58. Alilunas, *Smutty Little Movies*, 11.

59. Miller-Young, *Taste for Brown Sugar*, 105.

60. Miller-Young, 140.

61. Katrien Jacobs, *Netporn: DIY Web Culture and Sexual Politics* (Lanham, Md.: Rowman and Littlefield, 2007), 12.

62. Tarrant, *Pornography Industry*.

63. See Malcolm Harris, *Kids These Days: Human Capital and the Making of Millennials* (New York: Little, Brown, 2017).

64. VJ, interview by author, by phone, November 18, 2013.

65. Christopher Daniels, interview by author, Los Angeles, April 9, 2014.

66. Rebecca Sullivan and Alan McKee, *Pornography: Structures, Agency and Performance* (Malden, Mass.: Polity, 2015), 22.

67. Dave Pounder, interview by author, by phone, April 8, 2014.

68. Ace interview.

69. Sullivan and McKee, *Pornography*, 72.

70. See Katrien Jacobs, Marije Janssen, and Matteo Pasquinelli, eds., *C'lickme: A Netporn Studies Reader* (Amsterdam, Netherlands: Institute of Network Cultures, 2007).

71. See Feona Attwood, "'Younger, Paler, and Decidedly Less Straight': The New Porn Professionals," in *Porn.Com: Making Sense of Online Pornography*, ed. Feona Attwood, Digital Formations (New York: Peter Lang, 2010), 88–104; Jacobs, Janssen, and Pasquinelli, *C'lickme*; and Sullivan and McKee, *Pornography*, 57.

72. Lux Alptraum, "What's Really Happening with VR Porn," *Refinery 29*, May 20, 2016, https://www.refinery29.com/en-us/2016/05/109121/vr-porn-ela-darling-vrtube-interview.

73. Brooke Meredith Beloso, "Sex, Work, and the Feminist Erasure of Class," *Signs* 38, no. 1 (2012): 47–70.

74. Yasmin Nair, "Bright Life, Big Sex: The Susie Bright Interview," *Yasmin Nair* (blog), April 8, 2011, https://yasminnair.com/bright-life-big-sex-the-susie-bright-interview.

75. See Leopoldina Fortunati, *The Arcane of Reproduction: Housework, Prostitution, Labor and Capital*, trans. Hilary Creek (Brooklyn, N.Y.: Autonomedia, 1981).

76. Heather Berg, "Labouring Porn Studies," *Porn Studies* 1, no. 1–2 (2014): 75–79. I use the term "anti-sex-worker feminists" to honor how the subjects of this book view this community of thinkers—not as critics of sex industries but as antagonists against them as workers.

77. Catharine MacKinnon, "Not a Moral Issue," *Yale Law & Policy Review* 2, no. 2 (1984): 328. Where they make a claim for how porn texts impact workers, anti-sex-worker feminists collapse the process of making porn with the finished product. Thus, Gail Dines and Robert Jensen celebrate antiporn feminists' focus on the "meaning of the pornographic text in the context of the lives of the women who are used in the making." Gail Dines, "Feminist Debates on Pornography," with Robert Jensen, in *International Encyclopedia of Communication*, ed. Wolfgang Donsbach (Oxford, UK: Wiley-Blackwell, 2008), 8:3807–11.

78. Melissa Gira Grant, *Playing the Whore: The Work of Sex Work* (London: Verso, 2014), 88.

79. This is per Gail Dines writing on the context of occupational health; Gail Dines, "LA County's Measure B Is a Major Win for Safe Sex in Adult Entertainment," *Guardian*, November 12, 2012, http://www.theguardian.com/commentisfree/2012/nov/12/la-county-measureb-safe-sex.

80. Nina Ha®tley, interview by author, Los Angeles, February 17, 2012.

81. See Lisa Duggan and Nan D. Hunter, *Sex Wars: Sexual Dissent and Political Culture* (New York: Routledge, 2006); Laura Kipnis, *Bound and Gagged: Pornography and the Politics of Fantasy in America* (Durham, N.C.: Duke University Press, 1999); Jennifer Nash, *The Black Body in Ecstasy: Reading Race, Reading Pornography*, Next Wave (Durham, N.C.: Duke University Press, 2014); Gayle Rubin, "Misguided, Dangerous, and Wrong: An Analysis of Antipornography Politics," in *Deviations: A Gayle Rubin Reader* (Durham, N.C.: Duke University Press, 2012), 254–75; and Carole Vance, ed., *Pleasure and Danger: Exploring Female Sexuality* (London: Pandora, 1992).

82. Alice Echols, "Cultural Feminism: Feminist Capitalism and the Antipornography Movement," *Social Text*, no. 7 (1983): 53.

83. Strub, *Perversion for Profit: The Politics of Pornography and the Rise of the New Right* (New York: Columbia University Press, 2019), 215.

84. "Women in the sex industry do not perform work as it is typically understood. Most radical feminists are anti-capitalist and supportive of labour organizing, but see pornography as a practice central to the subordination of women and as a form of violence." Dines and Jensen, "Pornography."

85. Kipnis, *Bound and Gagged*, xi.

86. For a prototypical example of how nominally feminist political economy can be weaponized against workers, see Sheila Jeffreys, *The Industrial Vagina: The Political Economy of the Global Sex Trade* (London: Routledge, 2009). For an in-depth anti-capitalist feminist critique of anti-sex-worker thought, see Prabha Kotiswaran, *Dangerous Sex, Invisible Labor: Sex Work and the Law in India* (Princeton, N.J.: Princeton University Press, 2011), esp. 186. See also Berg, "Labouring Porn Studies," 77; and Kate Hardy, "Equal to Any Other, but Not the Same as Any Other: The Politics of Sexual Labour, the Body, and Intercorporeality," in *Body/Sex/Work: Intimate, Embodied and Sexualized Labour*, ed. Carol Wolkowitz, Rachel Lara Cohen, Teela Sanders, and Kate Hardy (Hampshire, UK: Palgrave Macmillan, 2013), 56.

87. See Carolyn Bronstein and Whitney Strub, *Porno Chic and the Sex Wars: American Sexual Representation in the 1970s* (Amherst: University of Massachusetts Press, 2016); *The Feminist Porn Book: The Politics of Producing Pleasure*, ed. Tristan Taormino, Constance Penley, Celine Parreñas Shimizu, and Mireille Miller-Young (New York: Feminist Press, 2013); and Williams, *Hard Core*.

88. Constance Penley, "A Feminist Teaching Pornography? That's Like Scopes Teaching Evolution!," in Taormino et al., *Feminist Porn Book*, 187. Taking up these questions, scholars have critiqued antipornography feminist positions, arguing that they flatten the diverse body of pornographic representation, support censorship, constitute dangerous alliances with the repressive state, lack evidence, rely on gender essentialism and fundamentally conservative normative judgments about appropriate sexuality, betray palpable disdain for the working-class aesthetics in which porn often trades, and ignore that pornographic texts can be read in a variety of different ways.

89. Penley.

90. Linda Williams, ed., *Porn Studies* (Durham, N.C.: Duke University Press, 2004).

91. Heather Berg, "Sex, Work, Queerly: Identity, Authenticity, and Labored Performance," in *Queer Sex Work*, ed. Mary Laing, Katy Pilcher, and Nicola Smith (London: Taylor and Francis, 2015), 23–32; Helen Hester, "After the Image: Labour in Pornography," in Laing, Pilcher, and Smith, *Queer Sex Work*, 32–42.

92. See Taormino et al., *Feminist Porn Book*.

93. Hester, "After the Image," 38.

94. Sociologist Sharon Abbott investigates workers' diverse motivations for entering the industry and career trajectories therein. Sharon Abbott, "Motivations for Pursuing a Career in Pornography," in *Sex for Sale: Prostitution, Pornography, and the Sex Industry*, ed. Ron Weitzer (London: Routledge, 2009); Sharon Abbott, "Doing Porn," in *Deviance: The Interactionist Perspective* (New York: Routledge, 1996), 309–15. Media scholar Feona Attwood investigates the "new porn professionalism" in view of larger trends in creative labor. Attwood, *Porn. Com.* Gender studies scholar Ariane Cruz explores porn workers' confrontations with racialized porn in the BDSM context. Ariane Cruz, *The Color of Kink: Black Women, BDSM, and Pornography* (New York: New York University Press, 2016). Jeffrey Escoffier's history of gay porn explores wages, ongoing conflict surrounding safer sex, and performers' branding labors. Escoffier, *Bigger Than Life.* Media scholar Elena Gorfinkel explores the labor of sexploitation performance.

Elena Gorfinkel, "The Body's Failed Labor: Performance Work in Sexploitation Cinema," *Framework* 53, no. 1 (2012): 79–98. Sex work scholar Mireille Miller-Young's exploration of Black women's porn labor foregrounds workers' creative strategies for moving within and against racial capitalism. Miller-Young, *Taste for Brown Sugar*, 9. Media scholar Darshana Mini explores labor and performance in Indian soft-core. "The Rise of Soft Porn in Malayalam Cinema and the Precarious Stardom of Shakeela," *Feminist Media Histories* 5, no. 2 (2019): 49–82. Media scholar Jennifer Moorman explores women-led production. Jennifer Moorman, "'The Hardest of Hardcore': Locating Feminist Possibilities in Women's Extreme Pornography," *Signs* 42, no. 3 (2017): 693–716. Media scholar Susanna Paasonen explores labored performance at the point of consumption. Susanna Paasonen, *Carnal Resonance: Affect and Online Pornography* (Cambridge, Mass.: MIT Press, 2011). Sociologist Akiko Takeyama advances a critique of individualized consent in the Japanese porn production context. Akiko Takeyama, "Possessive Individualism in the Age of Postfeminism and Neoliberalism: Self-Ownership, Consent, and Contractual Abuses in Japan's Adult Video Industry," in *Feminist and Queer Theory: An International and Transnational Reader,* ed. Ayu Saraswati and Barbara Shaw (Oxford: Oxford University press, 2020). Sociologist Chauntelle Tibbals explores women's behind-the-scenes office work in the industry and debates surrounding condom regulation. Chauntelle Tibbals, "'Anything That Forces Itself into My Vagina Is by Definition Raping Me . . .': Adult Performers and Occupational Safety and Health," *Stanford Law and Policy Review* 23, no. 1 (2012): 231–52. Chauntelle Tibbals, "Sex Work, Office Work: Women Working behind the Scenes in the U.S. Adult Film Industry," *Gender, Work & Organization* 20, no. 1 (January 2013): 20–35. Writing on the French context, gender studies scholar Mathieu Trachman points to porn work's commonalities with other jobs that demand both interpersonal and creative labor. Mathieu Trachman, "The Market for Actresses: Gender, Reputation, and Intermediation in French Pornography," in *Brokerage and Production in the American and French Entertainment Industries: Invisible Hands in Cultural Markets,* ed. Violaine Roussel and Denise Bielby (London: Lexington Books, 2015). Gender and cultural studies scholar Zahra Stardust writes on regulation and resistive performance in the Australian queer porn industry. Zahra Zsuzsanna Stardust, "Alternative Pornographies, Regulatory Fantasies and Resistance Politics" (PhD diss., University of New South Wales, 2019). Public health scholar Valerie Webber explores regulation and performer self-organization. Valerie Webber, "Public Health versus Performer Privates: Measure B's Failure to Fix Subjects," *Porn Studies* 2, no. 4 (2015): 299–313. See also Rebecca Sullivan and Jiz Lee, eds., "Porn and Labour: The Labour of Porn Studies," special issue, *Porn Studies* 3, no. 2 (2016).

95. Georgina Voss, "'Treating It as a Normal Business': Researching the Pornography Industry," *Sexualities* 15, no. 3–4 (2012): 391–410. Gender studies scholar Lynn Comella explores key shifts in the organization of the porn industry and the methods of porn studies inquiry. Lynn Comella, "Studying Porn Cultures," *Porn Studies* 1, no. 1–2 (2014): 64–70. Business scholar David Kopp explores the human resources context. David Kopp, *Human Resources Management in the Pornography Industry* (New York: Palgrave Macmillan, 2020). Technology scholar Georgina Voss uses the framework of "dirty work" to link work in the porn industry

to other stigmatized jobs. Georgina Voss, *Stigma and the Shaping of the Pornography Industry* (London: Routledge, 2015). Cultural studies scholars Rebecca Sullivan and Alan McKee situate porn performance alongside other creative labors. Sullivan and McKee, *Pornography*. Gender studies scholar Shira Tarrant explores monopoly and globalization in porn's political economy. See Tarrant, *Pornography Industry*.

96. Lynn Comella, "From Text to Context: Feminist Porn and the Making of a Market," in Taormino et al., *Feminist Porn Book*, 92.

97. Eleanor Wilkinson, "The Diverse Economies of Online Pornography: From Paranoid Readings to Post-capitalist Futures," *Sexualities* 20, no. 8 (December 2017): 992.

98. Smith and Attwood, "Anti/Pro/Critical Porn Studies," *Porn Studies* 1, no. 1–2 (2014): 13.

99. Quoted in Wendy Goldman, *Women, the State and Revolution: Soviet Family Policy and Social Life, 1917–1936* (Cambridge: Cambridge University Press, 1995), 119.

100. While Marx himself famously unexceptionalized prostitution through the suggestion that "prostitution is only a specific expression of the general prostitution of the labourer," Marxists (enabled by Marx's disengagement with reproductive work) have overwhelmingly chosen to frame sex work as a limit case for capital's harms rather than one site of the wage relation. Karl Marx, *Economic and Philosophic Manuscripts of 1844* (Blacksburg, Va.: Wilder, 1844), 44. Prostitution as limit case persists even in heterodox work that otherwise escapes the limitations of productivism. Franco "Bifo" Berardi, for example, offers crucial insights about alienation and affective labor but also locates sex work not with other kinds of work but alongside only the most spectacular harms. That "torture, homicide, child exploitation, the drive to prostitution, and production of instruments of mass destruction have become irreplaceable techniques of economic competition" is taken as evidence for our truly dark times. Franco Berardi, *After the Future*, ed. Gary Genosko and Nicholas Thoburn (Baltimore, Md.: AK Press, 2011), 80.

101. Fortunati, *Arcane of Reproduction*, 99.

102. Lorelei Lee, "Cash/Consent: The War on Sex Work," *n+1*, Fall 2019, https://nplusonemag.com/issue-35/essays/cashconsent.

103. Grant, *Playing the Whore*, 39.

104. Gayle Rubin, "Thinking Sex: Notes for a Radical Theory of the Politics of Sexuality," in Vance, *Pleasure and Danger*, 267–93.

105. For a comprehensive review, see Susan Dewey, "The Feminized Labor of Sex Work: Two Decades of Feminist Historical and Ethnographic Research," *Labor* 9, no. 2 (2012): 113–32.

106. Clare Hemmings, *Why Stories Matter: The Political Grammar of Feminist Theory* (Durham, N.C.: Duke University Press, 2011), 206.

107. See Elizabeth Bernstein, *Temporarily Yours: Intimacy, Authenticity, and the Commerce of Sex* (Chicago: University of Chicago Press, 2007); Denise Brennan, *What's Love Got to Do with It? Transnational Desires and Sex Tourism in the Dominican Republic* (Durham, N.C.: Duke University Press, 2004); Susan Dewey, *Neon Wasteland: On Love, Motherhood, and Sex Work in a Rust Belt Town* (Berkeley: University of California Press, 2011); Kimberly Kay Hoang, *Dealing in Desire: Asian Ascendancy, Western Decline, and the Hidden Currencies of Global Sex*

Work (Oakland: University of California Press, 2015); Gregory Mitchell, *Tourist Attractions: Performing Race and Masculinity in Brazil's Sexual Economy* (Chicago: University of Chicago Press, 2015); Teela Sanders and Kate Hardy, "Sex Work: The Ultimate Precarious Labour?," *Criminal Justice Matters* 93, no. 1 (2013): 16–17; Svati Pragna Shah, *Street Corner Secrets: Sex, Work, and Migration in the City of Mumbai*, Next Wave (Durham, N.C.: Duke University Press, 2014); and Nicola Smith, "Body Issues: The Political Economy of Male Sex Work," *Sexualities* 15, no. 5–6 (2012): 586–603.

108. See Laura María Agustín, *Sex at the Margins: Migration, Labour Markets and the Rescue Industry* (London: Zed Books, 2007); Paul Amar, *The Security Archipelago: Human-Security States, Sexuality Politics, and the End of Neoliberalism* (Durham, N.C.: Duke University Press, 2013); Susan Dewey and Tonia St. Germain, *Women of the Street: How the Criminal Justice–Social Services Alliance Fails Women in Prostitution* (New York: New York University Press, 2016); Patty Kelly, *Lydia's Open Door: Inside Mexico's Most Modern Brothel* (Berkeley: University of California Press, 2008); Kamala Kempadoo, Jyoti Sanghera, and Bandana Pattanaik, eds., *Trafficking and Prostitution Reconsidered: New Perspectives on Migration, Sex Work, and Human Rights* (Boulder, Colo.: Paradigm, 2005); Kotiswaran, *Dangerous Sex, Invisible Labor*; and Rhacel Salazar Parreñas, *Illicit Flirtations: Labor, Migration, and Sex Trafficking in Tokyo* (Stanford, Calif.: Stanford University Press, 2011).

109. See Bernstein, *Temporarily Yours*; Amalia Lucia Cabezas, *Economies of Desire: Sex and Tourism in Cuba and the Dominican Republic* (Philadelphia: Temple University Press, 2009); and Danielle Egan, *Dancing for Dollars and Paying for Love: The Relationships between Exotic Dancers and Their Regulars* (New York: Palgrave Macmillan, 2006).

110. Gall, *Agency of Their Own*; Chateauvert, *Sex Workers Unite*; Chi Mgbako, *To Live Freely in This World: Sex Worker Activism in Africa* (New York: New York University Press, 2016).

111. Katie Cruz, "Beyond Liberalism: Marxist Feminism, Migrant Sex Work, and Labour Unfreedom," *Feminist Legal Studies* 26 (2018): 65–92; Grant, *Playing the Whore*; Hardy, "Equal to Any Other"; Molly Smith and Juno Mac, *Revolting Prostitutes: The Fight for Sex Workers' Rights* (London: Verso, 2018); suprihmbé, *Heauxthots: On Terminology and Other [Un]Important Things* (Chicago: Bbydoll Press, 2019); Weeks, *Problem with Work*, 67–68.

112. Hardy, "Equal to Any Other," 56.

113. Cynthia M. Blair, *I've Got to Make My Livin': Black Women's Sex Work in Turn-of-the-Century Chicago* (Chicago: University of Chicago Press, 2018); LaShawn Harris, *Sex Workers, Psychics, and Numbers Runners: Black Women in New York City's Underground Economy* (Urbana: University of Illinois Press, 2016).

114. Horton-Stallings, *Funk the Erotic*, 20. See also Blair, *I've Got to Make*; Miller-Young, *Taste for Brown Sugar*; and LaShawn Harris, *Sex Workers*.

115. Suprihmbé, *Heauxthots*.

116. Smith and Mac, *Revolting Prostitutes*, 13.

117. I lay out a similar argument in Heather Berg, "Working for Love, Loving for Work: Discourses of Labor in Feminist Sex-Work Activism," *Feminist Studies* 40, no. 3 (2014): 693–721.

118. Audacia Ray, "Why the Sex Positive Movement Is Bad for Sex Workers' Rights," *Audacia Ray* (blog), March 31, 2012, https://audaciaray.tumblr.com/post/20228032642/why-the-sex-positive-movement-is-bad-for-sex.

119. A methodological appendix in this volume offers more detail about the composition of my interviews and fieldwork.

120. Stuart Hall, "The Problem of Ideology: Marxism without Guarantees," in *Stuart Hall: Critical Dialogues in Cultural Studies* (London: Routledge, 1996), 31.

121. Lily Cade, interview by author, Pasadena, Calif., November 10, 2013.

122. Mike South, "A PhD Candidate at UC Santa Barbara Would Like to Interview to You," *Mike South* (blog), October 30, 2013, http://www.mikesouth.com/mike-south-commentary/a-phd-candidate-at-uc-santa-barbara-would-like-to-interview-to-you-8678.

123. Stoya, interview by author, Woodland Hills, Calif., May 7, 2014.

124. Raylene, interview by author, Northridge, Calif., October 29, 2013.

125. Tara Holiday, interview by author, by phone, February 22, 2014.

126. Jasbir Puar, ed., "Precarity Talk: A Virtual Roundtable with Lauren Berlant, Judith Butler, Bonja Cvejic, Isabell Lorey, Jasbir Puar, and Ana Vujanovic," *TDR* 56, no. 4 (2012): 166. See also Lorey, *State of Insecurity*, 63.

127. Nina Power, *One Dimensional Woman* (Winchester, UK: Zero Books, 2009), 23.

128. Ha®tley interview.

129. Cristina Morini and Andrea Fumagalli, "Life Put to Work: Towards a Life Theory of Value," *Ephemera: Theory & Politics in Organization* 10, no. 3 (2010).

CHAPTER I

1. Devlyn Red, interview by author, Granada Hills, Calif., February 21, 2014.

2. Dick Chibbles, interview by author, Granada Hills, Calif., February 21, 2014.

3. Nina Ha®tley, interview by author, Los Angeles, February 17, 2012.

4. On "invisible labor" in straight work, see Marion G. Crain, Winifred Poster, and Miriam A. Cherry, eds., *Invisible Labor: Hidden Work in the Contemporary World* (Oakland: University of California Press, 2016).

5. Conner Habib, interview by author, Los Angeles, February 27, 2014.

6. Laura Helen Marks details the "semantic drift" at work in discussions of the gonzo genre. I use "gonzo" generally as many interviewees did and, in the interests of brevity, to signal sex-focused scenes with little plot or dialogue. Laura Helen Marks, "Porn Drift: Semantic Discord in the World of Gonzo," *JCMS* 58, no. 1 (2018): 164.

7. Chanel Preston, interview by author, Los Angeles, November 13, 2013.

8. Lily Cade, interview by author, Pasadena, Calif., November 11, 2013.

9. Charity Bangs, interview by author, by phone, November 7, 2013.

10. Siri, interview by author, Los Angeles, February 27, 2014.

11. Jacky St. James, interview by author, Northridge, Calif., November 4, 2013.

12. Ana Foxxx, interview by author, Los Angeles, January 24, 2014.

13. Mireille Miller-Young, *A Taste for Brown Sugar: Black Women in Pornography* (Durham, N.C.: Duke University Press, 2014).

14. Raylene, interview by author, Northridge, Calif., October 29, 2013.

15. Ariane Cruz, *The Color of Kink: Black Women, BDSM, and Pornography* (New York: New York University Press, 2016), 152, 154.

16. On Asian erasure in porn, see Celine Parreñas Shimizu, *Straitjacket Sexualities: Unbinding Asian American Manhoods in the Movies* (Stanford, Calif.: Stanford University Press, 2012); and Linda Williams and Richard Fung, "Interracial Joysticks: Pornography's Web of Racist Attractions," in *Pornography: Film and Culture*, ed. Peter Lehman (New Brunswick, N.J.: Rutgers University Press, 2006). On the Black/non-Black binary in the fashion industry, see Ashley Mears, *Pricing Beauty: The Making of a Fashion Model.* (Berkeley, Calif.: University of California Press, 2011), 194. Here, porn looks a lot like the fashion industry, where whiteness can flex to make space for Asian and Latino workers only because Blackness operates as an outside. On the ways the term "people of color" can erase anti-Blackness, see Jared Sexton, "People-of-Color-Blindness," *Social Text* 28, no. 2 (2010): 31–56.

17. Wolf Hudson, interview by author, Los Angeles, November 14, 2013.

18. BIPOC Adult Industry Collective, accessed June 15, 2020, https://www.bipoc-collective.org.

19. Christopher Daniels, interview by author, Los Angeles, April 9, 2014.

20. Herschel Savage, interview by author, Los Angeles, March 5, 2013.

21. Chi Chi LaRue, interview by author, Los Angeles, April 10, 2014.

22. jessica drake, interview by author, by phone, February 25, 2014.

23. "Talent Interview Form & Checklist," November 1, 2013, in author's possession.

24. Queer and feminist productions tend to have rigorous, but less standardized, consent practices. Screen partners are encouraged to discuss what will be done on camera informally.

25. "Limits Check List" from Kink.com, March 17, 2014, in author's possession. Kink.com's internal policies were more stringent than those of other BDSM productions in part because, as the most high-profile in the business, the company was particularly vulnerable to ridicule and legal liability. But Kink.com and other BDSM productions are also often connected to kink communities and remain invested in their politics of consent. On recreational kink and consent, see Margot Weiss, *Techniques of Pleasure: BDSM and the Circuits of Sexuality* (Durham, N.C.: Duke University Press, 2011).

26. Siri interview.

27. Matt Frackas, interview by author, by phone, December 12, 2013.

28. drake interview.

29. As media scholar Jennifer Moorman details, such negotiations may be made explicit not just behind the scenes but also on film. Indeed, this is part of the transformative potential of what Moorman calls "extreme" porn, especially when women themselves create it. Jennifer Moorman, "'The Hardest of Hardcore': Locating Feminist Possibilities in Women's Extreme Pornography," *Signs* 42, no. 3 (2017): 699.

30. Lorelei Lee, "Cum Guzzling Anal Nurse Whore: A Feminist Porn Star Manifesta," in *The Feminist Porn Book: The Politics of Producing Pleasure*, ed. Tristan Taormino, Constance Penley, Celine Parreñas Shimizu, and Mireille Miller-Young (New York: Feminist Press, 2013), 209.

31. Nicolas DiDomizio, "More Adult Performers Have Accused James Deen of Abuse on Set," *Mic*, December 4, 2015, https://mic.com/articles/129700/more-adult-performers-have-accused-james-deen-of-abuse-on-set#.y6oSyDv27.

32. Tracy Clark-Flory, "Porn Actors Leigh Raven and Riley Nixon Allege Abuse, Violence, and Boundary Violation on Set," *Jezebel*, March 11, 2018, https://jezebel.com/porn-actors-leigh-raven-and-riley-nixon-allege-abuse-v-1823677195.

33. Most straight productions and some gay and trans ones require performers to confirm negative results on an STI panel within two weeks before working. The standard panel includes the most sophisticated (able to detect an infection with the shortest possible lag time) HIV test available as well as tests for hepatitis B and C, chlamydia, gonorrhea, trichomoniasis, and syphilis. The straight mainstream industry insists that its policy of relying on testing in lieu of barrier methods works. From the perspective of HIV prevention, this is true—there have been no documented on-set transmissions since 2004.

34. When taken daily, PrEP is 90 percent effective at reducing the chance that an HIV-negative person will seroconvert as a result of sex with someone with a transmittable HIV infection. HIV treatment can bring an affected person's viral load to zero. Reducing a viral load to zero negates the risk of transmitting HIV.

35. The law requires producers to maintain 2257 records that include performers' legal names and copies of their photo identifications, requirements that workers say present serious privacy concerns. Here as elsewhere, ostensibly protective regulation actually makes workers more vulnerable.

36. Makeup artists make an average of $150 per performer and provide their own supplies. Some work exclusively in this position; it is also a popular income source for women performers who retire or find filming opportunities dwindling.

37. Ha®tley interview.

38. Alex Linko, interview by author, Los Angeles, November 9, 2013.

39. On the strains of crew labor in soft-core production, see Vicki Mayer, *Below the Line: Producers and Production Studies in the New Television Economy* (Durham, N.C.: Duke University Press, 2011), 74.

40. Dominic Ace, interview by author, Reseda, Calif., November 8, 2013.

41. Such a distinction is a mainstay of antiporn feminist argument and conservatively reinforces the idea that such a thing as "real" sex exists and can be identified as such, presumably because it features the sorts of sexual activity with which one feels politically comfortable. This distinction also suggests that sex off-camera or unpaid is not also labored, a premise Marxist feminists have helpfully deconstructed. On "the real" in porn, see Julie Levin Russo, "'The Real Thing': Reframing Queer Pornography for Virtual Spaces," in *C'lickme: A Netporn Studies Reader*, ed. Katrien Jacobs, Marije Janssen, and Matteo Pasquinelli (Amsterdam, Netherlands: Institute of Network Cultures, 2007), 239–51. On sex as work, see Silvia Federici, "Why Sexuality Is Work," in *Revolution at Point Zero: Housework, Reproduction, and Feminist Struggle* (Oakland, Calif.: PM Press, 1975). For a discussion of how unpaid, off-screen sex increasingly requires work-like effort, see Feona Attwood, *Sex Media* (Malden, Mass.: Polity, 2018), 1981, Kindle.

42. Prince Yahshua, interview by author, Canoga Park, Calif., February 28, 2014.

43. On emotional labor in straight work, see Arlie Russell Hochschild, *The Managed Heart: Commercialization of Human Feeling* (Berkeley: University of California, 2003).

44. Kay Parker, interview by author, Woodland Hills, Calif., November 13, 2013.

45. Venus Lux, interview by author, by phone, June 30, 2014.

46. Eileen Boris and Rhacel Salazar Parreñas, eds., *Intimate Labors: Cultures, Technologies, and the Politics of Care* (Stanford, Calif.: Stanford Social Sciences, 2010).

47. Raylene interview.

48. Cade interview.

49. Daniels interview.

50. Ela Darling, interview by author, Los Angeles, May 7, 2014.

51. Attwood, *Sex Media*.

52. Attwood.

53. Charlotte Shane, "'Getting Away' with Hating It: Consent in the Context of Sex Work," *Tits and Sass* (blog), March 21, 2013, http://titsandsass.com /getting-away-with-hating-it-consent-in-the-context-of-sex-work.

54. See "On Sexuality as Work," in *The New York Wages for Housework Committee 1972–1977: History, Theory and Documents*, ed. Silvia Federici and Arlen Austin (Brooklyn: Autonomedia, 2017), 144–45.

55. See Boris and Parreñas, *Intimate Labors*.

56. Daniels interview.

57. Raylene interview.

58. Darling interview.

59. Preston interivew.

60. Tanya Tate, interview by author, by phone, February 4, 2014.

61. Linko interview.

62. LaRue interview.

63. In this position, the receptive partner is on top, facing away from the other partner.

64. Red interview.

65. Chibbles interview.

66. "Phantom length" describes a camera-friendly shot in which a performer's penis fully exits the other partner with each thrust.

67. Daniels interview.

68. Darling interview.

69. Anonymous director, interview by author, Northridge, Calif., November 4, 2013.

70. Rosemary Hennessy, "The Value of a Second Skin," in *Intersections in Feminist and Queer Theory: Sexualities, Cultures and Identities*, ed. Diane Richardson, Janice McLaughlin, and Mark Casey (Basingstoke, UK: Palgrave Macmillan, 2006), 125.

71. Dave Pounder, interview by author, by phone, April 8, 2014.

72. Mr. Marcus, interview by author, Balboa Park, Calif., October 29, 2013.

73. For a discussion of "hypersexuality" in historical context, see Miller-Young, *Taste for Brown Sugar*.

74. Marcus interview.

75. Lexington Steele, interview by author, by phone, January 20, 2014.

76. Cedric Robinson, *Black Marxism: The Making of the Black Radical Tradition* (Chapel Hill: University of North Carolina Press, 2000).

77. Peter Ackworth, interview by author, San Francisco, March 17, 2014.

78. Foxxx interview.

79. See Bruce Nelson, *Divided We Stand: American Workers and the Struggle for Black Equality*, Politics and Society in Twentieth-Century America (Princeton, N.J.: Princeton University Press, 2002); and David Roediger, *The Wages of Whiteness: Race and the Making of the American Working Class* (London: Verso, 1999).

80. Amia Srinivasan, "Does Anyone Have the Right to Sex?," *London Review of Books*, March 22, 2018, 5–10.

81. April Flores, interview by author, Los Angeles, February 22, 2014.

82. Habib interview.

83. Jake Rosenfeld, "Don't Ask or Tell: Pay Secrecy Policies in U.S. Workplaces," *Social Science Research* 65 (2017): 1–16.

84. Anonymous performer, interview by author, Northridge, Calif., October 29, 2013.

85. Foxxx interview.

86. Yahshua interview.

87. Sinnamon Love, interview by author, by phone, January 13, 2014.

88. Foxxx interview.

89. Bangs interview.

90. Maxine Holloway, interview by author, San Francisco, March 19, 2014.

91. Fifi and Edwin, interview by author, Skype, November 1, 2013.

92. Aya Gruber, "Consent Confusion," *Cardozo Law Review* 38, no. 415 (2016): 425.

93. For a discussion of the escorting context, see Shane, "'Getting Away.'"

94. Richie Calhoun, interview by author, Los Angeles, October 15, 2013.

95. Siouxsie Q, "Authentically Yours: Feminist Porn Gets Political," *SF Weekly*, April 16, 2014, http://www.sfweekly.com/2014-04-16/culture/whore-next-door-feminist-porn-authenticity.

96. Suprihmbé, "Defined/Definers: My Thoughts on Common Terminology around Erotic Labor & Trafficking," Patreon, February 23, 2019, https://www.patreon.com/posts/24904015.

97. Holloway interview.

98. Karl Marx, *Capital: A Critique of Political Economy*, trans. Ben Fowkes (1867; repr., New York, N.Y: Penguin Books in association with New Left Review, 1976), 1:900.

99. Jolene Parton (@jolenestarshine), Twitter, January 31, 2015, 7:44 P.M., https://twitter.com/jolenestarshine/status/561686375552925696.

100. Chi Mgbako, *To Live Freely in This World: Sex Worker Activism in Africa* (New York: New York University Press, 2016), 57.

CHAPTER 2

1. Sovereign Syre, "The Porn Performer as Quantum Mechanic," video, 2:48, April 28, 2013, https://www.youtube.com/watch?v=g5DIcZnoQsA.

2. Miya Tokumitsu, *Do What You Love: And Other Lies about Success and Happiness* (New York: Regan Arts, 2015).

3. Nicholas Ridout and Rebecca Schneider, "Precarity and Performance: An Introduction," *TDR* 56, no. 4 (2012): 7.

4. Sarah Banet-Weiser, *Authentic TM: Politics and Ambivalence in a Brand Culture* (New York: New York University Press, 2012).

5. Richard Peterson, "In Search of Authenticity," *Journal of Management Studies* 42, no. 5 (2005): 108.

6. Brooke Erin Duffy, *(Not) Getting Paid to Do What You Love: Gender, Social Media, and Aspirational Work* (New Haven, Conn.: Yale University Press, 2017), 135.

7. Susanna Paasonen, *Carnal Resonance: Affect and Online Pornography* (Cambridge, Mass.: MIT Press, 2011), 80.

8. Paasonen, 81.

9. Helen Hester, *Beyond Explicit: Pornography and the Displacement of Sex* (Albany, N.Y.: SUNY Press, 2015), 138.

10. Film theorist Linda Williams identifies, for example, authentic evidence of (male) orgasm as central to porn's visual culture since its inception. Linda Williams, *Hard Core: Power, Pleasure, and the "Frenzy of the Visible"* (Berkeley: University of California Press, 1999), 100. See also Florian Cramer, "Sodom Blogging: Alternative Porn and Aesthetic Sensibility," in *C'lickme: A Netporn Studies Reader*, ed. Katrien Jacobs, Marije Janssen, and Matteo Pasquinelli (Amsterdam, Netherlands: Institute of Network Cultures, 2007), 171–76; Julia Levin Russo, "'The Real Thing': Reframing Queer Pornography for Virtual Spaces," in Jacobs, Janssen, and Pasquinelli, *C'lickme*, 239–51; and Paasonen, *Carnal Resonance*.

11. Paasonen, *Carnal Resonance*, 72.

12. Paasonen, 80.

13. Melissa Gira Grant, "For the Love of Kink," *Dissent*, Spring 2014.

14. Chuck Kleinhanz, "'Creative Industries,' Neoliberal Fantasies, and the Cold, Hard Facts of Global Recession: Some Basic Lessons," *Jump Cut*, no. 53 (2011), https://www.ejumpcut.org/archive/jc53.2011/kleinhans-creatIndus.

15. "A Primer on Scene Direction & Production" (Adult Entertainment Expo, Las Vegas, Nev., January 24, 2015).

16. Alt, or alternative, porn is housed within the mainstream industry but modeled on a punk aesthetic.

17. I touch on these questions in Heather Berg, "Business as Usual," *Jacobin*, February 15, 2015, https://www.jacobinmag.com/2015/02/porn-industry-labor-adult-expo.

18. Mark Murphy, *Hiring for Attitude: A Revolutionary Approach to Recruiting Star Performers with Both Tremendous Skills and Superb Attitude* (New York: McGraw-Hill, 2012).

19. Sometimes feminist and queer productions understand themselves as discrete categories, but there is enough overlap here in terms of production norms and communities involved that I consider them together.

20. Dylan Ryan, "Fucking Feminism," in *The Feminist Porn Book: The Politics of Producing Pleasure*, ed. Tristan Taormino, Constance Penley, Celine Parreñas Shimizu, and Mireille Miller-Young (New York: Feminist Press, 2013), 125.

21. Gail Dines, "Porn: A Multibillion-Dollar Industry That Renders All Authentic Desire Plastic," *Guardian*, January 4, 2011, http://www.guardian.co.uk /commentisfree/2011/jan/04/pornography-big-business-influence-culture.

22. Melissa Farley, "Risks of Prostitution: When the Person Is the Product," *Journal of the Association for Consumer Research* 3, no. 1 (2018): 97.

23. Madison Young, "Authenticity and Its Role Within Feminist Pornography," *Porn Studies* 1, no. 1–2 (2014): 186–88.

24. Mikey Way, "Fuck Your Feminist Porn," *Tits and Sass* (blog), September 18, 2015, http://titsandsass.com/fuck-your-feminist-porn.

25. Levin Russo, "'The Real Thing.'"

26. Vex Ashley, "Porn—Artifice—Performance—and the Problem of Authenticity," *Porn Studies* 3, no. 2 (2016): 187.

27. Ashley, 188.

28. Way, "Fuck Your Feminist Porn."

29. Heather Berg, "Sex, Work, Queerly: Identity, Authenticity, and Labored Performance," in *Queer Sex Work*, ed. Mary Laing, Katy Pilcher, and Nicola Smith (London: Taylor and Francis, 2015), 23–32.

30. Constance Penley, "Crackers and Whackers: The White Trashing of Porn," in *Porn Studies*, ed. Linda Williams (Durham, N.C.: Duke University Press, 2004).

31. Mike South, interview by author, Skype, October 18, 2013.

32. Zahra Zsuzsanna Stardust, "Alternative Pornographies, Regulatory Fantasies and Resistance Politics" (PhD diss., University of New South Wales, 2019), 133.

33. Laura María Agustín, *Sex at the Margins: Migration, Labour Markets and the Rescue Industry* (New York: Zed Books, 2007).

34. Feona Attwood, "'Younger, Paler, and Decidedly Less Straight': The New Porn Professionals," in *Porn.Com: Making Sense of Online Pornography*, ed. Feona Attwood, Digital Formations (New York: Peter Lang, 2010), 91.

35. Fareen Parvez, "The Labor of Pleasure: How Perceptions of Emotional Labor Impact Women's Enjoyment of Pornography," *Gender & Society* 20, no. 5 (2006): 605–31.

36. See Melissa Gira Grant, *Playing the Whore: The Work of Sex Work* (London: Verso, 2014).

37. Elizabeth Bernstein, *Temporarily Yours: Intimacy, Authenticity, and the Commerce of Sex* (Chicago: University of Chicago Press, 2007), 127.

38. Farrell Timlake, interview by author, by phone, January 23, 2014; my emphasis.

39. Courtney Trouble, interview by author, Emeryville, Calif., March 18, 2014.

40. Peter Fleming and Andrew Sturdy, "'Just Be Yourself!': Towards a Neo-normative Control in Organizations," *Employee Relations* 31, no. 6 (2009): 569–83.

41. Kathi Weeks, *The Problem with Work: Feminism, Marxism, Antiwork Politics, and Postwork Imaginaries* (Durham, N.C.: Duke University Press, 2011), 46.

42. Angela McRobbie, "Re-thinking Creative Economy as Radical Social Enterprise," *Variant* 2, no. 41 (2011): 32.

43. Tokumitsu, *Do What You Love*. See also Grant, "For the Love of Kink."

44. Brooke Meredith Beloso, "Sex, Work, and the Feminist Erasure of Class," *Signs* 38, no. 1 (2012): 49.

45. Angela Jones, "'I Get Paid to Have Orgasms': Adult Webcam Models' Negotiation of Pleasure and Danger," *Signs* 42, no. 1 (2016): 236.

46. Maggie McNeill, "Whorearchy," *Honest Courtesan* (blog), May 10, 2012, https://maggiemcneill.wordpress.com/2012/05/10/whorearchy. This is part of what I have elsewhere critiqued as the conservative attitude toward waged work that undergirds strands of the sex worker activist narrative. Heather Berg, "Working for Love, Loving for Work: Discourses of Labor in Feminist Sex-Work Activism," *Feminist Studies* 40, no. 3 (2014): 693–721.

47. Stoya, interview by author, Woodland Hills, Calif., May 7, 2014.

48. Siri, interview by author, Los Angeles, February 27, 2014.

49. Siri interview.

50. Nina Ha®tley, interview by author, Los Angeles, February 17, 2012.

51. Richie Calhoun, interview by author, Los Angeles, October 15, 2013.

52. Raylene, interview by author, Northridge, Calif., October 29, 2013.

53. Chelsea Poe, interview by author, Skype, June 17, 2014.

54. Zahra Stardust, "DIY Porn under Capitalism," *Overland*, May 18, 2017, https://overland.org.au/2017/05/diy-porn-under-capitalism.

55. Tristan Taormino, "Calling the Shots: Feminist Porn in Theory and Practice," in Taormino et al., *Feminist Porn Book*, 260.

56. Taormino, 259.

57. Taormino, 261.

58. See David Montgomery, *Workers' Control in America: Studies in the History of Work, Technology, and Labor Struggles* (New York: Cambridge University Press, 1979).

59. Joanna Angel, interview by author, by phone, January 23, 2014; my emphasis.

60. Bella Vendetta, interview by author, by phone, March 18, 2014.

61. Way, "Fuck Your Feminist Porn."

62. Way.

63. Alex Linko, interview by author, Los Angeles, November 9, 2013.

64. Kristoffer Smemo, "Black Flag and the Political Economy of Hardcore," *U.S. Intellectual History Blog*, June 24, 2014, https://s-usih.org/2014/06/guest-post-kristoffer-smemo-on-black-flag-and-the-political-economy-of-hardcore.

65. Lynn Comella, *Vibrator Nation: How Feminist Sex-Toy Stores Changed the Business of Pleasure* (Durham, N.C.: Duke University Press, 2017), 190.

66. Anonymous performer, interview by author, Los Angeles, May 7, 2014.

67. Lily Cade, interview by author, Pasadena, Calif., November 10, 2013. Melissa Gira Grant describes similar critiques in her interviews with feminist porn performers. Melissa Gira Grant, "Who Speaks for Women Who Work in the Adult Industry?," *Guardian*, March 12, 2013, http://www.guardian.co.uk/commentisfree/2013/mar/12/who-speaks-for-women-work-adult-industry.

68. Poe interview.

69. Siouxsie Q, interview by author, Oakland, Calif., March 19, 2014.

70. Siouxsie Q, "Authentically Yours: Feminist Porn Gets Political," *SF Weekly*, April 16, 2014, http://www.sfweekly.com/2014-04-16/culture/whore-next-door-feminist-porn-authenticity.'

71. Maxine Holloway, interview by author, San Francisco, March 19, 2014.

72. Trouble interview.

73. Stardust, "Alternative Pornographies," 172.

74. Gala Vanting, "Manufacturing Realness" (Feminist Porn Conference, Toronto, ON, April 5, 2014).

75. Danny Wylde, interview by author, Los Angeles, November 4, 2013.

76. Tracy Clark-Flory, "Is 'Feminist' Porn Getting Its #MeToo Moment?," *Jezebel*, September 20, 2018, https://jezebel.com/is-feminist-porn-getting-its-metoo-moment-1828173419.

77. Clark-Flory.

78. "Performer's Bill of Rights," Erika Lust (website), accessed January 1, 2019, https://erikalust.com/wp-content/uploads/2018/09/EL_Bill_Of_Rights.pdf.

79. Holloway interview.

80. See Franco Berardi, *The Soul at Work: From Alienation to Autonomy* (Los Angeles: Semiotext(e), 2009); and Weeks, *Problem with Work*.

81. See Bernstein, *Temporarily Yours*; Katherine Frank, "The Production of Identity and the Negotiation of Intimacy," *Sexualities* 1, no. 2 (1998): 175–201; and Teela Sanders, "'It's Just Acting': Sex Workers' Strategies for Capitalizing on Sexuality," *Gender, Work & Organization* 12, no. 4 (2005): 319–42.

82. Conner Habib, interview by author, Los Angeles, February 27, 2014.

83. Hochschild identifies three stances workers take in relation to what exactly they exchange in doing emotional labor: Some develop too sincere an identification with work, which makes them more vulnerable to burnout. Others make clear distinctions between their work and nonwork selves, thus being less vulnerable to burnout but more likely to feel guilty about being insincere. A third group makes clear distinctions between work and nonwork selves but feels no guilt about this, instead viewing performance as part of the job, and in her telling this worker is most at risk for estrangement and cynicism. Arlie Russell Hochschild, *The Managed Heart: Commercialization of Human Feeling* (Berkeley: University of California Press, 2003).

84. Ela Darling, interview by author, Los Angeles, May 7, 2014.

85. On the heterosexual script and the "orgasm gap," see Lisa Wade, "Are Women Bad at Orgasms? Understanding the Gender Gap," in *Gender, Sex, and Politics: In the Streets and Between the Sheets,* ed. Shira Tarrant (New York: Routledge, 2015), 227–37.

86. Kelly Shibari, interview by author, Northridge, Calif., November 1, 2013.

87. Lexington Steele, interview by author, by phone, January 20, 2014.

88. See Laura Kipnis, *Bound and Gagged: Pornography and the Politics of Fantasy in America* (Durham, N.C.: Duke University Press, 1999); Penley, "Crackers and Whackers"; Williams, *Hard Core*; and Chauntelle Tibbals, "Gonzo, Trannys, and Teens—Current Trends in US Adult Content Production, Distribution, and Consumption," *Porn Studies* 1, no. 1–2 (2014): 127–35.

89. Ana Foxxx, interview by author, Los Angeles, January 24, 2014.

90. Mireille Miller-Young, "Putting Hypersexuality to Work: Black Women and Illicit Eroticism in Pornography," *Sexualities* 13, no. 2 (April 7, 2010): 219–35.

91. Jennifer Nash, *The Black Body in Ecstasy: Reading Race, Reading Pornography,* Next Wave (Durham, N.C.: Duke University Press, 2014), 5.

92. Tara Holiday, interview by author, by phone, February 22, 2014.

93. Lorelei Lee, interview by author, San Francisco, June 5, 2014.

94. Dancers' mimesis in this context focuses on gendered performances of desire. Danielle Egan, *Dancing for Dollars and Paying for Love: The Relationships between Exotic Dancers and Their Regulars* (New York: Palgrave Macmillan, 2006), 195.

95. VJ, interview by author, by phone, November 18, 2013.

96. Sara Jay, interview by author, by phone, February 10, 2013.

97. Holloway interview.

98. Foxxx interview; emphasis mine.

99. Holiday interview.

100. Kathleen Barry, *The Prostitution of Sexuality* (New York: New York University Press, 1996).

101. Charlotte Shane, "'Getting Away' with Hating It: Consent in the Context of Sex Work," *Tits and Sass* (blog), March 21, 2013, http://titsandsass.com/getting-away-with-hating-it-consent-in-the-context-of-sex-work.

102. See, e.g., Michel Foucault, *History of Sexuality*, vol. 1, trans. Robert Hurley (New York: Pantheon, 1978); and Theodor Adorno and Max Horkheimer, *Dialectic of Enlightenment*, trans. Gunzelin Noeri (Stanford, Calif.: Stanford University Press, 2002).

103. See Leopoldina Fortunati, *The Arcane of Reproduction: Housework, Prostitution, Labor and Capital*, trans. Hilary Creek (Brooklyn, N.Y.: Autonomedia, 1981).

104. Such scholars have found an indispensable resource in the theory of emotional labor that Arlie Hochschild developed in her study of flight attendants. Hochschild, *The Managed Heart*. My own perspective is indebted to this lineage and also critical of the ways the *labor* in some deployments of "emotional labor" can be detached from political economy and instead stand in for *effort*.

105. Bernstein, *Temporarily Yours*, 103.

106. Sanders, "'It's Just Acting,'" 322.

107. Susan Dewey, *Neon Wasteland: On Love, Motherhood, and Sex Work in a Rust Belt Town* (Berkeley: University of California Press, 2011), 72.

108. Herschel Savage, interview by author, Los Angeles, April 15, 2013.

109. Syre, "Porn Performer."

110. Syre.

111. Shira Tarrant, *The Pornography Industry: What Everyone Needs to Know* (New York: Oxford University Press, 2016), 60.

112. Juana María Rodríguez, "Pornographic Encounters and Interpretative Interventions: Vanessa Del Rio: Fifty Years of Slightly Slutty Behavior," *Women & Performance: A Journal of Feminist Theory* 25, no. 3 (2015): 7.

113. Rodríguez.

114. For an in-depth discussion of the discourse/materiality debates in feminist thought, see Clare Hemmings, *Why Stories Matter: The Political Grammar of Feminist Theory* (Durham, N.C.: Duke University Press, 2011).

115. Teresa L. Ebert, "Ludic Feminism, the Body, Performance, and Labor: Bringing 'Materialism' Back into Feminist Cultural Studies," *Cultural Critique*, no. 23 (1992): 9.

116. Ebert, 9.

117. Nash, *Black Body in Ecstasy*, 21.

118. Bernstein, *Temporarily Yours*, 81, 104.

119. Michael Hardt and Antonio Negri, *Assembly* (New York: Oxford University Press, 2017), 78.

120. Carole Vance, ed., *Pleasure and Danger: Exploring Female Sexuality* (London: Pandora, 1992), 24.

121. L. H. Horton-Stallings, *Funk the Erotic: Transaesthetics and Black Sexual Cultures* (Urbana: University of Illinois Press, 2015), 19.

122. Horton-Stallings, 19.

123. See Silvia Federici, *Revolution at Point Zero: Housework, Reproduction, and Feminist Struggle* (Oakland, Calif.: PM Press, 1975).

124. Camille Barbagallo, introduction to *Women and The Subversion of the Community: A Mariarosa Dalla Costa Reader*, by Mariarosa Dalla Costa, ed. Camille Barbagallo (Oakland, Calif.: PM Press, 2019), 11.

CHAPTER 3

1. Sara Jay, interview by author, by phone, December 10, 2013.

2. Dominic Ace, interview by author, Reseda, Calif., November 8, 2013.

3. Kelly Shibari, interview by author, Northridge, Calif., November 1, 2013.

4. Martha King, "Protecting and Representing Workers in the New Gig Economy: The Case of the Freelancers Union," in *New Labor in New York: Precarious Workers and the Future of the Labor Movement*, ed. Ruth Milkman and Ed Ott (Ithaca, N.Y.: ILR Press and Cornell University Press, 2014), 154.

5. See Louis Hyman, *Temp: How American Work, American Business, and the American Dream Became Temporary* (New York: Viking, 2018).

6. See Isabell Lorey, *State of Insecurity: Government of the Precarious*, trans. Allen Derieg (London: Verso, 2015).

7. Robin D. G. Kelley, *Race Rebels: Culture, Politics, and the Black Working Class* (New York: Free Press, 1996), 176.

8. See Daniel J. Clark, *Disruption in Detroit: Autoworkers and the Elusive Postwar Boom* (Urbana: University of Illinois Press, 2018).

9. Jeffrey Escoffier, *Bigger Than Life: The History of Gay Porn Cinema from Beefcake to Hardcore* (Philadelphia: Running Press, 2009), 319.

10. See Nelson Lichtenstein, *State of the Union: A Century of American Labor* (Princeton, N.J.: Princeton University Press, 2002), 27. Other workers, though, have long preferred independence to security; porn's class formations recall those of historic craft labor (work that relies more heavily on skill than capital investment). Historian Andrew Wender Cohen, for example, describes Chicago's early to mid-twentieth-century craft economy as one in which "some workers started their own businesses while many failed entrepreneurs returned to wage labor." Andrew Wender Cohen, *The Racketeer's Progress: Chicago and the Struggle for the Modern American Economy, 1900–1940*, Cambridge Historical Studies in American Law and Society (Cambridge: Cambridge University Press, 2009), 3.

11. In Andrew Ross, *Nice Work If You Can Get It: Life and Labor in Precarious Times* (New York: New York University Press, 2009), 34.

12. VJ, interview by author, by phone, November 18, 2013.

13. Charity Bangs, interview by author, by phone, November 7, 2013.

14. Camera operators report rates of $150–$500 per day depending on experience, production budgets, and the number of scenes shot in a given day. Production assistants make an average of $100–$150 per day.

15. Venus Lux, interview by author, by phone, June 30, 2014. "MILF" stands for "mother I'd like to fuck," a popular genre that markets actresses older than thirty. There is money to be made as a MILF performer in the business, but the transition to the MILF market can bring both a pay cut and a drop in casting opportunities. As Lux suggests, it can also mean a decrease in status and self-esteem.

16. Raylene, interview by author, Northridge, Calif., October 29, 2013.

17. Anonymous performer, interview by author, by phone, November 28, 2013.

18. Christopher Daniels, interview by author, Los Angeles, April 9, 2014. I anonymize other performers' quotes regarding escorting in order to protect them from legal repercussions. Daniels has published a book about his escorting work and was as such willing to go on the record.

19. See Heather Berg and Constance Penley, "Creative Precarity in the Adult Film Industry," in *Precarious Creativity: Global Media, Local Labor*, ed. Michael Curtin and Kevin Sanson (Oakland: University of California Press, 2016), 162.

20. David Schieber, "My Body of Work: Promotional Labor and the Bundling of Complementary Work," *Socius* 4 (2018).

21. Anonymous performer, interview by author, Los Angeles, June 29, 2014.

22. Samantha Grace, interview by author, Los Angeles, November 3, 2013.

23. Performers also draw incomes from a number of more tertiary sources. These include affiliate networks, which provide referral commissions for new website signups and scene downloads, self-branded toys and other merchandise, and product endorsements.

24. Georgina Voss, *Stigma and the Shaping of the Pornography Industry* (London: Routledge, 2015).

25. On termination due to off-duty conduct, see Marisa Anne Pagnattaro, "What Do You Do When You Are Not at Work? Limiting the Use of Off-Duty Conduct as the Basis for Adverse Employment Decisions," *University of Pennsylvania Journal of Business Law* 6, no. 3 (2004).

26. Lily Cade, interview by author, Pasadena, Calif., November 11, 2013.

27. On workers' negotiations of the risks associated with different types of sex work, see Melissa Gira Grant, *Playing the Whore: The Work of Sex Work* (London: Verso, 2014).

28. Felicia Fox, interview by author, by phone, November 4, 2013.

29. On labor practices in the erotic dance industry, see Kim Price-Glynn, *Strip Club: Gender, Power, and Sex Work*, Intersections (New York: New York University Press, 2010); and Susan Dewey, *Neon Wasteland: On Love, Motherhood, and Sex Work in a Rust Belt Town* (Berkeley: University of California Press, 2011).

30. Jay interview.

31. Tara Holiday, interview by author, by phone, February 22, 2014.

32. VJ interview.

33. Chanel Preston, interview by author, Los Angeles, November 13, 2013.

34. Niels van Doorn and Olav Velthuis, "A Good Hustle: The Moral Economy of Market Competition in Adult Webcam Modeling," *Journal of Cultural Economy* 11, no. 3 (2018): 181.

35. Van Doorn and Velthuis, 188.

36. Angela Jones, *Camming: Money, Power, and Pleasure in the Sex Work Industry* (New York: New York University Press, 2019).

37. Paul Bleakley, "'500 Tokens to Go Private': Camgirls, Cybersex and Feminist Entrepreneurship," *Sexuality & Culture* 18, no. 4 (December 2014): 892–910.

38. "Exclusive" refers to private videochats for which customers pay extra. Anonymous webcam model, Streamate session, February 12, 2015.

39. On "the myth of the free exhibitionist," see Theresa Senft, *Camgirls: Celebrity and Community in the Age of Social Networks*, Digital Formations (New York: Peter Lang, 2008), 80.

40. Anonymous performer interview, June 29, 2014.

41. Van Doorn and Velthuis, "Good Hustle," 178.

42. Anonymous performer, interview by author, by phone, February 1, 2014.

43. Anonymous performer, interview by author, Northridge, Calif., November 29, 2013.

44. Anonymous performer interview, February 1, 2014.

45. Chris Caine, interview by author, Canoga Park, Calif., November 6, 2013.

46. On the whole, the gay, trans, and queer porn production communities do not share this approach to performer escorting. Their distinct health protocols, different cultural norms surrounding serostatus, and removed location from discourses of feminine sexual vulnerability allow for a unique approach. In interviews, these workers and managers overwhelmingly voiced exasperation at the straight community's conservative approach and explained that escorting is both common and unremarkable in their communities.

47. Mark Schechter, interview by author, Woodland Hills, Calif., October 24, 2013.

48. Dan Przygoda, "Porn Actresses Accuse Powerful Industry Agent of Fraud, Sex Abuse," *NBC Los Angeles*, March 14, 2019, https://www.nbclosangeles.com/news/local/Porn-Actresses-Accuse-Top-Agent-of-Fraud-Sex-Abuse-506831051.html.

49. Siri, "The Official TeamBJ DVD!," *Official Blog of Siri*, accessed January 18, 2015, http://blog.siripornstar.com/shop/product/teambj-dvd.

50. Siri interview.

51. Kurt Vogner, interview by author, by phone, November 13, 2013.

52. Bud Lee, interview by author, West Hills, Calif., November 6, 2013.

53. Shibari interview.

54. Maxine Holloway, interview by author, San Francisco, March 19, 2014.

55. Tanya Tate, interview by author, by phone, February 4, 2014.

56. Courtney Trouble, "Love the One You're With" (Adult Entertainment Expo, Las Vegas, Nev., 2015).

57. Holloway interview.

58. jessica drake, interview by author, by phone, February 25, 2014.

59. Lexington Steele, interview by author, by phone, January 20, 2014.

60. Steele interview.

61. Cade interview.

62. Jacky St. James, interview by author, Northridge, Calif., November 4, 2013.

63. Dave Pounder, interview by author, by phone, April 8, 2014.

64. drake interview.

65. Sinnamon Love, interview by author, by phone, January 13, 2014.

66. On Black women porn performers' experiences in other sex industries, see Mireille Miller-Young, *A Taste for Brown Sugar: Black Women in Porn* (Durham, N.C.: Duke University Press, 2014), 254. On racialized hierarchy and "erotic capital" in the stripping industry, see Siobhan Brooks, *Unequal Desires: Race and Erotic Capital in the Stripping Industry* (Albany, N.Y.: SUNY Press, 2010). On racialized hierarchy in cam work, see Jones, *Camming*. On hierarchies according to weight, breast size, and appearance in the stripping industry, see Bernadette Barton, *Stripped: Inside the Lives of Exotic Dancers* (New York: New York University Press, 2006), 19. On middle-class escorting as dominated by class-privileged white women, see Elizabeth Bernstein, *Temporarily Yours: Intimacy, Authenticity, and the Commerce of Sex* (Chicago: University of Chicago Press, 2007), 75.

67. Love interview.

68. Sara Horowitz and Toni Sciarra Poynter, *The Freelancer's Bible: Everything You Need to Know to Have the Career of Your Dreams on Your Terms* (New York: Workman, 2012), 469.

69. Lucy Neville, *Girls Who Like Boys Who Like Boys: Women and Gay Male Pornography and Erotica* (Cham, Switzerland: Palgrave Macmillan, 2018), 300.

70. See Feona Attwood, "'Younger, Paler, and Decidedly Less Straight': The New Porn Professionals," in *Porn.Com: Making Sense of Online Pornography*, ed. Feona Attwood, Digital Formations (New York: Peter Lang, 2010), 88–104.

71. Jennifer Moorman, "'The Hardest of Hardcore': Locating Feminist Possibilities in Women's Extreme Pornography," *Signs* 42, no. 3 (2017): 693–716.

72. Ariane Cruz, *The Color of Kink: Black Women, BDSM, and Pornography* (New York: New York University Press, 2016), 133.

73. In addition to Cruz, see Miller-Young, *Taste for Brown Sugar*; and Jennifer Nash, *The Black Body in Ecstasy: Reading Race, Reading Pornography*, Next Wave (Durham, N.C.: Duke University Press, 2014).

74. Prince Yahshua, interview by author, Canoga Park, Calif., February 28, 2014.

75. Heather Berg, "An Honest Day's Wage for a Dishonest Day's Work: (Re) Productivism and Refusal," *Women's Studies Quarterly* 42, no. 1/2 (2014): 161–77.

76. Herschel Savage, interview by author, Los Angeles, April 5, 2013.

77. Karl Marx and Friedrich Engels, *The Marx-Engels Reader*, 2nd ed., ed. Robert C. Tucker (New York: Norton, 1978), 473.

78. Marx and Engels, 473.

79. J. K. Gibson-Graham, *The End of Capitalism (As We Knew It): A Feminist Critique of Political Economy* (Minneapolis: University of Minnesota Press, 2006), 170.

80. Jiz Lee, "Tricks of the Trade: Porn's 'Best Practices' for Content Trades and Shares," *XBIZ Magazine*, September 2014.

81. Marx's footnoted treatment of sex work assumes employment by others: "one who prostitutes." Karl Marx, *Economic and Philosophic Manuscripts of 1844*, trans. Martin Milligan (Amherst, N.Y.: Prometheus Books, 1988), 100.

82. Gibson-Graham, *End of Capitalism*.

83. Mireille Miller-Young, "Sexy and Smart: Black Women and the Politics of Self-Authorship in Netporn," in *C'lickme: A Netporn Studies Reader*, ed. Katrien Jacobs, Marije Janssen, and Matteo Pasquinelli (Amsterdam, Netherlands: Institute of Network Cultures, 2007), 207.

84. Stephen Resnick and Richard Wolff, *Knowledge and Class: A Marxian Critique of Political Economy* (Chicago: University of Chicago Press, 1989), 159.

85. Steele interview.

86. Conner Habib, interview by author, Los Angeles, February 27, 2014.

87. Mike Quasar (@mikequasar), Twitter, May 16, 2018, 12:25 A.M., https://twitter.com/mikequasar/status/996969902316503040.

88. Mike Quasar (@mikequasar), Twitter, May 17, 2018, 1:16 A.M., https://twitter.com/mikequasar/status/996982868684324864.

89. Porn is not unique in this dynamic. In his study of labor relations in the music recording industry, media studies scholar Matt Stahl notes "record companies' dependence on the musicians' independence." Alternative income streams augmented musicians' incomes but also "limited the companies' capacity to control the musicians' labor and products." Matt Stahl, *Unfree Masters: Recording Artists and the Politics of Work* (Durham, N.C.: Duke University Press, 2013), 9.

90. Stop Enabling Online Sex Traffickers Act of 2017, S. 1639, 115th Cong. (2017). So as not to overwhelm the reader with acronyms, I will refer to the joint bill simply as SESTA, as many sex worker activists do. See also Allow States and Victims to Fight Online Sex Trafficking Act of 2017, H.R. 1865, 115th Cong. (2017).

91. Elizabeth Nolan Brown, "Secret Memos Show the Government Has Been Lying about Backpage All Along," *Reason*, August 26, 2019, https://reason.com/2019/08/26/secret-memos-show-the-government-has-been-lying-about-backpage.

92. Melissa Gira Grant, "Anti–Online Trafficking Bills Advance in Congress, Despite Opposition from Survivors Themselves," *In Justice Today*, accessed March 14, 2018, https://injusticetoday.com/anti-online-trafficking-bills-advance-in-congress-despite-opposition-from-survivors-themselves-e741ea300307.

93. It is also true that "many survivors are sex workers," and "many sex workers are survivors," as campaigners against the proposed EARN IT Act made clear. "Survive EARN IT," accessed August 18, 2020, https://surviveearnit.com/?fbclid=IwAR1aePBVglaLvL2EnX94JZbIeu2pvbCyR9xCWWyzm8HowboGJF DQGcDjpb8.

94. Access to online advertising and screening platforms helps in-person sex workers work safely; a 2017 study found that Craigslist's now-shuttered erotic services advertising section reduced the female homicide rate by 17.4 percent. Scott Cunningham, Gregory DeAngelo, and John Tripp, "Craigslist's Effect on Violence against Women" (unpublished manuscript, 2017), PDF, http://scunning.com/craigslist70.pdf.

95. "Incomplete List of Legal Discrimination against Sex Workers," Liara's List, accessed April 11, 2018, https://liaraslist.org.

96. Samantha Cole, "Sex Workers Say Porn on Google Drive Is Suddenly Disappearing," *Motherboard*, March 21, 2018, https://motherboard.vice.com/en_us/article/9kgwnp/porn-on-google-drive-error.

97. Gustavo Turner, "Facebook, Instagram Target Sex Workers with Updated 'Community Standards,'" *XBIZ*, October 23, 2019, https://www.xbiz.com/news/247831/facebook-instagram-target-sex-workers-with-updated-community-standards.

98. Turner.

99. Anne McClintock, "Sex Workers and Sex Work: Introduction," *Social Text*, no. 37 (1993): 4.

100. Silvia Federici, *Caliban and the Witch: Women, the Body and Primitive Accumulation* (New York: Autonomedia, 2003), 49.

101. Silvia Federici, *Re-enchanting the World: Feminism and the Politics of the Commons* (Oakland, Calif.: PM Press, 2018), 16.

102. Tamara MacLeod, "Cyberwhores of Late Capitalism," *3:AM Magazine*, November 19, 2019, https://www.3ammagazine.com/3am/cyberwhores-of-late -capitalism/#.XcqoHMQfcsg.twitter.

CHAPTER 4

1. Stoya, interview by author, Woodland Hills, Calif., May 7, 2014.

2. Cristina Morini and Andrea Fumagalli, "Life Put to Work: Towards a Life Theory of Value," *Ephemera: Theory & Politics in Organization* 10, no. 3 (2010).

3. Ana Foxxx, interview by author, Los Angeles, January 24, 2014.

4. Mariarosa Dalla Costa, *Women and The Subversion of the Community: A Mariarosa Dalla Costa Reader*, ed. Camille Barbagallo (Oakland, Calif.: PM Press, 2019), 24.

5. Morini and Fumagalli, "Life Put to Work." Often, this gets narrated as the transition from productive to immaterial labor, a temporal argument Federici cautions against. Working-class people of color, especially in the global South, still do work that produces goods, she reminds us. Silvia Federici, "Precarious Labor: A Feminist Perspective," October 28, 2004, https://inthemiddleofthewhirlwind. wordpress.com/precarious-labor-a-feminist-viewpoint.

6. Sarah Sharma, *In the Meantime: Temporality and Cultural Politics* (Durham, N.C.: Duke University Press, 2014), 105.

7. Tara Holiday, interview by author, by phone, February 22, 2014.

8. Foxxx interview.

9. Danny Wylde, interview by author, Los Angeles, November 4, 2014.

10. Sinnamon Love, interview by author, by phone, January 13, 2014.

11. Lorelei Lee, interview by author, San Francisco, June 5, 2014.

12. Lexington Steele, interview by author, by phone, January 20, 2014.

13. Chanel Preston, interview by author, Los Angeles, November 13, 2013.

14. Tyler Knight, *Burn My Shadow: A Selective Memory of an X-Rated Life* (Los Angeles: Rare Bird, 2016) 172.

15. Lee interview.

16. Richie Calhoun, interview by author, Los Angeles, October 15, 2013.

17. See Brooke Erin Duffy, *(Not) Getting Paid to Do What You Love: Gender, Social Media, and Aspirational Work* (New Haven, Conn.: Yale University Press, 2017); and Alexandrea Ravenelle, *Hustle and Gig: Struggling and Surviving in the Sharing Economy* (Oakland: University of California Press, 2019).

18. Nicholas Ridout and Rebecca Schneider, "Precarity and Performance: An Introduction," *TDR* 56, no. 4 (2012): 7.

19. Lee interview.

20. Christopher Daniels, interview by author, Los Angeles, April 9, 2014.

21. Calhoun interview.

22. See Silvia Federici, *Revolution at Point Zero: Housework, Reproduction, and Feminist Struggle* (Oakland, Calif.: PM Press, 2012); and Leopoldina Fortunati, *The Arcane of Reproduction: Housework, Prostitution, Labor and Capital*, trans. Hilary Creek (Brooklyn, N.Y.: Autonomedia, 1981). Feminist labor scholars have long suggested that what comes to be understood as "private" is historically contingent. See Evelyn Nakano Glenn, "From Servitude to Service Work: Historical Continuities in the Racial Division of Paid Reproductive Labor," *Signs* 18, no. 1 (1992); and Eileen Boris, "Working in the Home: Continuing the Discussion of Women's Labors," *Journal of Women's History* 16, no. 2 (2004).

23. Silvia Federici, *Wages against Housework* (Bristol, UK: Power of Women Collective and Falling Wall Press, 1975), 2.

24. On the feminization of labor, see Cristina Morini, "The Feminization of Labour in Cognitive Capitalism," *Feminist Review* 87, no. 1 (2007): 40–59.

25. Paolo Virno, *Grammar of the Multitude: For an Analysis of Contemporary Forms of Life* (Los Angeles: Semiotext(e), 2004), 103.

26. Eva-Maria Swidler, "Marxism beyond the Economy and Exploitation beyond the Wage," *Capitalism Nature Socialism* 29, no. 2 (2018): 50.

27. Swidler, 50.

28. Venus Lux, interview by author, by phone, June 30, 2014.

29. Nina Power, *One-Dimensional Woman* (Winchester, UK: Zero Books, 2009), 23.

30. Vex Ashley (@vextape), Twitter, October 7, 2018, https://twitter.com/vextape/status/1048995367663099904.

31. Ela Darling (@ElaDarling), Twitter, January 17, 2015, https://twitter.com/ElaDarling/status/556505924701933568; Brian Street Team (@ brianstreetteam), Twitter, January 18, 2015, https://twitter.com/brianstreetteam/status/556860367788576768; Asa Akira (@AsaAkira), January 18, 2015 (tweet no longer available), Twitter. See also #realpornawards, Twitter, January 17, 2015, https://twitter.com/search?q=%23realpornawards&src=typd.

32. Tanya Tate (@tanyatate), (tweet no longer available), Twitter, June 24, 2014.

33. "How It Works," Verified Call, accessed May 6, 2014, https://verifiedcall.com/how-it-works.

34. Streamate Models, accessed January 19, 2015, https://www.streamatemodels.com.

35. Kelly Shibari, interview by author, Northridge, Calif., November 1, 2013.

36. See Christian Fuchs, *Digital Labour and Karl Marx* (New York: Routledge, Taylor and Francis, 2014), 246.

37. On employer scrutiny of workers' social media presence across mainstream industries, see Patricia Sanchez Abril, Avner Levin, and Alissa Del Riego, "Blurred Boundaries: Social Privacy and the Twenty-First-Century Employee," *American Business Law Journal* 49, no. 1 (2012): 63–124.

38. "A Primer on Scene Direction & Production" (Adult Entertainment Expo, Las Vegas, Nev., January 24, 2015).

39. Daniel Laurin, "Subscription Intimacy: Amateurism, Authenticity and Emotional Labour in Direct-to-Consumer Gay Pornography," *About Gender* 8, no. 16 (2019): 64.

40. Stoya interview.

41. Theresa Sneft, "Microcelebrity and the Branded Self," in *A Companion to New Media Dynamics*, ed. John Hartley, Jean Burgess, and Axel Bruns (Oxford, UK: Wiley-Blackwell, 2013), 349.

42. Tate interview.

43. See Ross Perlin, *Intern Nation: Earning Nothing and Learning Little in the Brave New Economy* (London: Verso, 2012), 129.

44. Jennifer Alsever, "How to Get a Job: Work for Free," *Fortune*, March 14, 2012, http://fortune.com/2012/03/14/how-to-get-a-job-work-for-free.

45. Andrew Ross, "In Search of the Lost Paycheck," in *Digital Labor: The Internet as Playground and Factory*, ed. Trebor Scholz (New York: Routledge, 2013), 14. Patronage apps such as Patreon offer one possibility of an exception.

46. Devlyn Red, interview by author, Granada Hills, Calif., February 21, 2014.

47. Exclusive services agreement, 2012, in author's possession.

48. Lux interview.

49. Sophie Pezzutto, "From Porn Performer to Porntrepreneur: Online Entrepreneurship, Social Media Branding, and Selfhood in Contemporary Trans Pornography," *About Gender* 8, no. 16 (2019): 40.

50. Mireille Miller-Young, *A Taste for Brown Sugar: Black Women in Porn* (Durham, N.C.: Duke University Press, 2014), 230.

51. Kimora Klein, interview by author, by phone, January 17, 2014.

52. Dominic Ace, interview by author, Reseda, Calif., November 8, 2013.

53. Daniels interview.

54. Asa Akira, "Project MILF," Indiegogo, April 10, 2016, https://www.indiegogo.com/projects/project-milf. "MILF" means "mother I'd like to fuck," a popular genre that markets actresses older than thirty.

55. Foxxx interview.

56. Charity Bangs, interview by author, by phone, November 7, 2013.

57. Chanel Preston (@ChanelPreston), Twitter, May 24, 2014, 5:48 P.M., https://twitter.com/ChanelPreston/status/470320533054033921.

58. See Paul Du Gay, *Consumption and Identity at Work* (London: SAGE, 1996).

59. Carter Stevens, interview by author, Skype, November 1, 2013.

60. Daniels interview.

61. Sharma, *In the Meantime*, 84.

62. Jason Newell and Gordon MacNeil, "Professional Burnout, Vicarious Trauma, Secondary Traumatic Stress, and Compassion Fatigue," *Best Practices in Mental Health* 6, no. 2 (2013): 57–69.

63. Kristoffer Smemo, Samir Sonti, and Gabriel Winant, "Conflict and Consensus: The Steel Strike of 1959 and the Anatomy of the New Deal Order," *Critical Historical Studies* 4, no. 1 (2017): 61.

64. Conner Habib, interview by author, Los Angeles, February 27, 2014.

65. Anonymous performer, interview by author, by phone, January 7, 2014.

66. In its time, Kink.com's workers' compensation policy stood out as a major exception. Several workers had filed workers' compensation with the company and received the appropriate care.

67. Prince Yahshua, interview by author, Canoga Park, Calif., February 28, 2014. My emphasis.

68. "Lara" is a pseudonym.

69. Lara, interview by author, Los Angeles, February 27, 2014.

70. Priapism is a painful condition that requires that excess blood in the penis be drained by a medical professional.

71. Jeffrey Escoffier, *Bigger Than Life: The History of Gay Porn Cinema from Beefcake to Hardcore* (Philadelphia: Running, 2009), 67.

72. Robert McRuer, ed., *Crip Theory: Cultural Signs of Queerness and Disability* (New York: New York University Press, 2006), 8.

73. Arlie Russell Hochschild, *The Managed Heart: Commercialization of Human Feeling* (Berkeley: University of California, 2003), 54.

74. Preston interview.

75. Daniels interview.

76. Gayle Rubin, "Thinking Sex: Notes for a Radical Theory of the Politics of Sexuality," in *Culture, Society and Sexuality: A Reader*, 2nd ed., ed. Richard G. Parker and Peter Aggleton, Sexuality, Culture and Health (London: Routledge, 1984), 151.

77. On the health consequences of straight work, see Nate Holdren, *Injury Impoverished: Workplace Accidents, Capitalism, and Law in the Progressive Era.* (New York: Cambridge University Press, 2020). Jeffrey Pfeffer, *Dying for a Paycheck: How Modern Management Harms Employee Health and Company Performance—and What We Can Do about It* (New York: Harper Collins, 2018).

78. Jeffreys, for example, offers dramatically that "live girls and women do have their orifices penetrated to produce pornography. They take drugs to survive the pain and humiliation, and they bleed." Sheila Jeffreys, *The Industrial Vagina: The Political Economy of the Global Sex Trade* (London: Routledge, 2009), 76.

79. McRuer, *Crip Theory*, 71.

80. Jasbir Puar, "Prognosis Time: Towards a Geopolitics of Affect, Debility, and Capacity," *Women & Performance* 19, no. 2 (2009): 168.

81. Calhoun interview.

82. Georgina Voss, *Stigma and the Shaping of the Pornography Industry* (London: Routledge, 2015).

83. Voss.

84. Whitney Strub, *Obscenity Rules: Roth v. United States and the Long Struggle Over Sexual Expression* (Lawrence: University Press of Kansas, 2013).

85. Survivors Against SESTA, accessed April 11, 2018, https://survivorsagainstsesta.org; Hacking//Hustling, accessed March 1, 2019, http://melissagiragrant.com/hackinghustling.

86. "Incomplete List of Legal Discrimination against Sex Workers," Liara's List, accessed April 11, 2018, https://liaraslist.org.

87. Danielle Blunt, "Health Equity in the Age of Shadowbanning and FOSTA-SESTA" (MPH thesis, CUNY School of Public Health, 2019), 15.

88. Mark Kernes, "JP Morgan Chase Closes Porn Star Accounts, Citing 'Ethics'!?!," *AVN*, April 22, 2014, http://business.avn.com/articles/legal/JPMorgan-Chase-Closes-Porn-Star-Accounts-Citing-Ethics-557577.html.

89. End Banking for Human Traffickers Act of 2018, H.B. 2219, 115th Cong. (2018).

90. VJ, interview by author, by phone, November 18, 2013.

91. Camille Barbagallo, introduction to *Women and The Subversion of the Community: A Mariarosa Dalla Costa Reader*, by Mariarosa Dalla Costa, ed. Camille Barbagallo (Oakland, Calif.: PM Press, 2019), 5.

92. Fortunati, *Arcane of Reproduction*; Zillah Eisenstein, ed., *Capitalist Patriarchy and the Case for Socialist Feminism* (New York: Monthly Review Press, 1978), 30.

93. Michael Hardt and Antonio Negri, *Commonwealth* (Cambridge, Mass.: Belknap Press of Harvard University Press, 2011), 142.

94. Steele interview.

95. Noah Zatz and Eileen Boris, "Seeing Work, Envisioning Citizenship," *Employee Rights and Employee Policy Journal* 95 (2014): 96.

96. Federici, *Wages against Housework*. See also Kathi Weeks, *The Problem with Work: Feminism, Marxism, Antiwork Politics, and Postwork Imaginaries* (Durham, N.C.: Duke University Press, 2011).

CHAPTER 5

1. Nina Ha®tley, interview by author, Los Angeles, February 17, 2012.

2. See Katherine Stone, *From Widgets to Digits: Employment Regulation for the Changing Workplace* (New York: Cambridge University Press, 2004).

3. Isabell Lorey, *State of Insecurity: Government of the Precarious*, trans. Allen Derieg (London: Verso, 2015), 88.

4. Model release agreement, November 1, 2013, in author's possession.

5. Employment policy varies somewhat state to state. Because most studio-produced porn is filmed in California, I will focus my analysis there. California Labor Code, §§ 3200–3219 (1937),https://leginfo.legislature.ca.gov/faces/codes_displaySection.xhtml?lawCode=LAB&sectionNum=3200 ; "Insurance Requirements for Filming on State Property," California Film Commission, accessed October 13, 2014, http://www.film.ca.gov/Permits_Insurance.htm.

6. See State of California Occupational Safety and Health Appeals Board, "In the Matter of the Appeal of Treasure Island Media, Inc.," Dockets 11-R6D1-1093–1095 (2014).

7. Jon Rodgers, interview by author, by phone, November 1, 2013.

8. Christian Mann, interview by author, Van Nuys, Calif., October 8, 2013.

9. On non-enforcement in the broader context, see Hendrik Hartog, "Pigs and Positivism," *University of Wisconsin Law Review*, no. 4 (1985): 899–935.

10. Annette Bernhardt, Heather Boushey, Laura Dresser, and Chris Tilley, introduction to *The Gloves-off Economy: Workplace Standards at the Bottom of America's Labor Market*, ed. Annette Bernhardt, Heather Boushey, Laura Dresser, and Chris Tilly (Champaign, Ill.: Labor and Employment Relations Association, 2008), 1.

11. Nate Holdren, *Injury Impoverished: Workplace Accidents, Capitalism, and Law in the Progressive Era* (New York: Cambridge University Press, 2020). See also Michael Grabell and Howard Berkes, "The Demolition of Workers' Comp," *ProPublica*, March 4, 2015, http://www.propublica.org/article/the-demolition-of-workers-compensation.

12. Alex Lindsey, Eden King, Tracy McCausland, and Kristen Jones, "What We Know and Don't: Eradicating Employment Discrimination 50 Years after the Civil

Rights Act," *Industrial and Organizational Psychology* 6, no. 4 (December 2013): 391–413.

13. Marianne Levine, "Behind the Minimum Wage Fight, a Sweeping Failure to Enforce the Law," *Politico*, February 18, 2018, https://www.politico.com/story/2018/02/18/minimum-wage-not-enforced-investigation-409644.

14. "Legal Panel: Perspectives on a Changing World" (Adult Entertainment Expo, Las Vegas, Nev., 2015).

15. Government agencies and individual states have slightly different rules for determining independent contractor status. The IRS, for example, has one set of standards, while OSHA has another. Individual states, too, have slightly different standards. Until 2018, California used the *Borello* test to determine status; S. G. Borello & Sons, Inc. v. Department of Industrial Relations, 48 Cal. 3d 341 (1989). After 2018, the simplified "ABC" test became the legal standard to determine wage and hour claims. *Borello* still holds for other matters. Dynamex Operations West, Inc. v. Superior Court, 4 Cal. 5th 903 (2018). In September 2019, the California State Assembly passed Assembly Bill 5, which standardizes employment status in the state, especially in app-based work. California Assembly Bill 5 (2019). The new law, like its predecessor, has not been enforced in porn production.

16. See State of California Occupational Safety and Health Appeals Board, "In the Matter of the Appeal"; and *Dynamex* 4 Cal. 5th at 903.

17. Similar contestations around intellectual property have played out in the music recording industry, where media studies scholar Matt Stahl finds that recording companies strain to fit musicians into "the form of labor that gives them the most freedom in the market." Whereas most employers prefer to classify employees as contractors, recording companies locked in legal battles over ownership claim artists as employees in order to maintain intellectual property rights. Matt Stahl, *Unfree Masters: Recording Artists and the Politics of Work* (Durham, N.C.: Duke University Press, 2013), 113.

18. "Independent Contractor versus Employee," State of California Department of Industrial Relations, accessed October 13, 2014, http://www.dir.ca.gov/dlse/faq_independentcontractor.htm.

19. Alex Linko, interview by author, Los Angeles, November 9, 2013.

20. Stoya, interview by author, Woodland Hills, Calif., May 7, 2014.

21. Charity Bangs, interview by author, by phone, November 7, 2013.

22. This, too, is largely unenforced. In his study on such hiring practices in Hollywood, legal scholar Russell Robinson found no published case in which a court deliberated an actor's Title VII claim. Russell Robinson, "Casting and Casteing: Reconciling Artistic Freedom and Antidiscrimination Norms," *California Law Review* 95, no. 1 (2007): 2.

23. Carter Stevens, interview by author, Skype, November 1, 2013.

24. Christopher Daniels, interview by author, Los Angeles, April 9, 2014.

25. Anonymous performer, interview by author, Los Angeles, February 27, 2014.

26. Juba Kalamka, interview by author, Las Vegas, Nev., July 17, 2013.

27. See Ann Stewart, "Legal Constructions of Body Work," in *Body/Sex/Work: Intimate, Embodied and Sexualized Labour*, ed. Carol Wolkowitz, Rachel Lara Cohen, Teela Sanders, and Kate Hardy (Hampshire, UK: Palgrave Macmillan, 2013), 62.

28. Stewart. See also Eileen Boris and Jennifer Klein, *Caring for America: Home Health Workers in the Shadow of the Welfare State* (New York: Oxford University Press, 2012).

29. *Contingent Workforce*, 3.

30. John T. Dunlop, *Fact Finding Report: Commission on the Future of Worker-Management Relations* (Washington, D.C.: U.S. Department of Commerce/U.S. Department of Labor, 1994), pt. 4, "Contingent Work."

31. See David Weil, "Mending the Fissured Workplace," in *What Works for Workers? Public Policies and Innovative Strategies for Low-Wage Workers*, ed. Stephanie Luce, Jennifer Luff, Joseph A. McCartin, and Ruth Milkman (New York: Russell Sage Foundation, 2013).

32. Linko interview.

33. Kimora Klein, interview by author, phone, January 17, 2014.

34. See Eileen Boris and Jennifer Klein on the costs of ill-fitting definitions of "employer" in the case of home healthcare workers, who for decades have struggled to identify a responsible employer legible to the law. Boris and Klein, *Caring for America*, 16. See also Chris Howell, "Regulating Class in the Neoliberal Era: The Role of the State in the Restructuring of Work and Employment Relations," *Work, Employment & Society* 30, no. 4 (August 1, 2016): 573–89.

35. Weil, "Mending the Fissured Workplace."

36. While OSHA standards include provisions for work done at home, the burden of showing that this is paid work sets up yet another circular arrangement in which an employer's choice to treat an activity as nonwork places it outside the purview of employment protections. Occupational Safety and Health Administration Regulations (Standards), § 1904.5, "Determination of Work-Relatedness."

37. Quoted in Allen Smithberg, "Weinstein: Performers 'Subject to the Same Laws as Anybody,'" *AVN*, September 14, 2015, http://business.avn.com/articles /legal/Weinstein-Performers-Subject-to-the-Same-Laws-as-Anybody-606483.html.

38. Lorelei Lee, interview by author, San Francisco, June 5, 2014.

39. Noah Zatz and Eileen Boris, "Seeing Work, Envisioning Citizenship," *Employee Rights and Employee Policy Journal* 95 (2014): 96. See also Jennifer Klein, *For All These Rights: Business, Labor, and the Shaping of America's Public-Private Welfare State*, Politics and Society in Twentieth-Century America (Princeton, N.J.: Princeton University Press, 2006).

40. On proletarianization and early antiprostitution policy, see Silvia Federici, *Caliban and the Witch: Women, the Body and Primitive Accumulation* (New York: Autonomedia, 2003).

41. On the "strategic terrain" of the state as a social relation, see Nicos Poulantzas, *State, Power, Socialism* (London: Verso, 2014).

42. She is referring to the National Labor Relations Act and the choice to protect the right to organize only for formal employees. National Labor Relations Act, 29 U.S.C. §§ 151–69, 1935.

43. Chelsea Poe, interview by author, Skype, June 17, 2014.

44. See also Chauntelle Tibbals, "'Anything that Forces Itself into My Vagina Is by Definition Raping Me . . .': Adult Performers and Occupational Safety and Health," *Stanford Law and Policy Review* 23, no. 1 (2012): 231–52.

45. Prince Yahshua, interview by author, Canoga Park, Calif., February 28, 2014.

46. "Industry Code of Ethics," Free Speech Coalition, accessed February 3, 2016, http://freespeechcoalition.com/fsc-code-of-ethics.

47. See Eileen Boris and Heather Berg, "Protecting Virtue, Erasing Labor: Historical Responses to Trafficking," in *Human Trafficking Reconsidered: Rethinking the Problem, Envisioning New Solutions*, ed. Kimberly Kay Hoang and Rhacel Salazar Parreñas (New York: International Debate Education Association, 2014).

48. See Jo Doezema, *Sex Slaves and Discourse Masters: The Construction of Trafficking* (London: Zed Books, 2010).

49. See Susan Dewey and Patty Kelly, introduction to *Policing Pleasure: Sex Work, Policy, and the State in Global Perspective*, ed. Susan Dewey and Patty Kelly (New York: New York University Press, 2011), 1–15; and Melinda Chateauvert, *Sex Workers Unite: A History of the Movement from Stonewall to Slutwalk* (Boston: Beacon, 2013).

50. See Dewey and Kelly, introduction to *Policing Pleasure*, 5.

51. Yasmina Katsulis, *Sex Work and the City: The Social Geography of Health and Safety in Tijuana, Mexico* (Austin: University of Texas Press, 2010), 83. For an analysis of the distinctions between these models, see Molly Smith and Juno Mac, *Revolting Prostitutes: The Fight for Sex Workers' Rights* (London: Verso, 2018).

52. City of Los Angeles Safer Sex in the Adult Film Industry Act § 3 (2012).

53. Kalamka interview.

54. On the politics of public health and performer privacy, see Valerie Webber, "Public Health versus Performer Privates: Measure B's Failure to Fix Subjects," *Porn Studies* 2, no. 4 (2015): 299–313.

55. Stoya interview.

56. See Whitney Strub, *Obscenity Rules: Roth v. United States and the Long Struggle Over Sexual Expression* (Lawrence: University Press of Kansas, 2013); and Finley Freibert, "Obscenity Regulation and Film Exhibition: Policing Gay and Feminist Media Industries in Southern California, 1960 to 1979" (PhD diss., University of California, Irvine, 2019).

57. See Lisa Duggan and Nan D. Hunter, *Sex Wars: Sexual Dissent and Political Culture* (New York: Routledge, 2006).

58. Raylene, interview by author, Northridge, Calif., October 29, 2013.

59. Webber, "Public Health," 11.

60. Adrienne Davis, "Regulating Sex Work: Erotic Assimilationism, Erotic Exceptionalism, and the Challenge of Intimate Labor," *California Law Review* 5 (2015): 1195–276.

61. Heather Berg, "Working for Love, Loving for Work: Discourses of Labor in Feminist Sex-Work Activism," *Feminist Studies* 40, no. 3 (2014): 693–721.

62. Adrienne Davis, "Regulating Sex Work," 1275.

63. Julia O'Connell Davidson, "Will the Real Sex Slave Please Stand Up?," *Feminist Review* 83 (2006): 19.

64. See Michele Estrin Gilman, "Welfare, Privacy, and Feminism," *University of Baltimore Law Forum* 39, no. 1 (2008): 1–25; and Gwendolyn Mink, "The Lady and the Tramp (II): Feminist Welfare Politics, Poor Single Mothers, and the Challenge of Welfare Justice," *Feminist Studies* 24, no. 1 (1998).

65. See Angela Davis, "Racism, Birth Control, and Reproductive Rights," in *Women, Race and Class* (New York: Vintage Books, 1983), 202–21; and Andrea

Smith, *Conquest: Sexual Violence and American Indian Genocide* (Cambridge, Mass.: South End, 2005).

66. Lauren Berlant and Michael Warner, "Sex in Public," *Critical Inquiry* 24, no. 2 (1998): 547.

67. Chateauvert, *Sex Workers Unite*, 13.

68. See Eileen Boris and Rhacel Salazar Parreñas, *Intimate Labors: Cultures, Technologies, and the Politics of Care* (Stanford, Calif.: Stanford Social Sciences, 2010).

69. Boris and Parreñas.

70. Leopoldina Fortunati, *The Arcane of Reproduction: Housework, Prostitution, Labor and Capital*, trans. Hilary Creek (Brooklyn, N.Y.: Autonomedia, 1981), 21.

71. For a critical assessment of decriminalization as the best of limited policy options, see Smith and Mac, *Revolting Prostitutes*, 190–207.

72. Adrienne Davis, "Regulating Sex Work," 1195.

73. Davis, 1254.

74. Zahra Stardust, "'Fisting Is Not Permitted': Criminal Intimacies, Queer Sexualities, and Feminist Porn in the Australian Legal Context," *Porn Studies* 1, no. 3 (2014): 242–59.

75. Quoted in Tibbals, "'Anything that Forces Itself.'"

76. Quoted in Rhett Parton, "Adult Performers Rally for Thursday's Cal/OSHA Hearing in San Diego," *XBIZ*, May 15, 2015, http://www.xbiz.com/news/194672.

77. These include Los Angeles County's Measure B (which passed in 2012); the proposal to the state assembly AB1576 (which failed to pass in 2014); and Proposition 60, a proposed statewide ballot measure (which failed to pass in 2016). In addition, AHF has pushed Cal/OSHA to enforce existing regulations governing blood-borne pathogens and to develop porn-specific regulations.

78. California Safer Sex in the Adult Film Industry Act § 3 (2015), 2, http://oag.ca.gov/system/files/initiatives/pdfs/15-0004%20%28Safer%20Sex%29_8.pdf?

79. Richie Calhoun, interview by author, Los Angeles, October 15, 2013.

80. Lee interview.

81. Linko interview.

82. Kalamka interview.

83. Conner Habib, interview by author, Los Angeles, February 27, 2014.

84. Tiffany Fox, interview by author, Skype, May 3, 2014.

85. Herschel Savage, interview by author, Los Angeles, April 5, 2013.

86. Jacky St. James, interview by author, Northridge, Calif., November 4, 2013.

87. Daniels interview.

88. Ela Darling, public comment, Cal/OSHA Standards Board Meeting," (Walnut Creek, Calif.),2015.

89. Lee interview.

90. Lorelei Lee, "Cash/Consent: The War on Sex Work," *n+1*, Fall 2019, https://nplusonemag.com/issue-35/essays/cashconsent.

91. Lee.

92. Fox interview.

93. "Adult Performers and Public Health Experts Join to Oppose Cal/OSHA Regulations at San Diego Hearing," press release, Free Speech Coalition, May 21,

2015, http://freespeechcoalition.com/adult-performers-and-public-health-experts
-join-to-oppose-calosha-regulations-at-san-diego-hearing.

94. Mark Schechter, interview by author, Woodland Hills, Calif., October 24, 2013.

95. Conner Habib, "Why the LGBTQ Community Should Oppose AB1576," *Slate*, June 24, 2014, http://www.slate.com/blogs/outward/2014/06/24/_ab1576_why _california_s_condoms_and_hiv_testing_in_porn_bill_is_a_bad_idea.html.

96. Yahshua interview.

97. Diane Duke, interview by author, Canoga Park, Calif., November 5, 2013.

98. Fox interview.

99. Linko interview.

100. Notable exceptions are queer and feminist productions and productions managed by a small number of mainstream, gay, and kink performer-directors who, depending on the production company they work with at a given time, sometimes take performer choice more seriously. But here too, making the "right" choice, and getting it on camera, might be part of the product.

101. Duke interview.

102. Schechter interview.

103. Lexington Steele, interview by author, by phone, January 20, 2014.

104. Lee interview.

105. Savage interview.

106. Stoya interview.

107. Lee interview.

108. Anonymous performer-producer, public comment, "Cal/OSHA Standards Board Meeting" (Walnut Creek, Calif., 2016).

109. Savage interview.

110. Gregor Gall, *An Agency of Their Own: Sex Worker Union Organizing* (Winchester, UK: Zero Books, 2012), 28.

111. Mr. Marcus, interview by author, Balboa Park, Calif., October 29, 2013.

112. Kelly Shibari, interview by author, Northridge, Calif., November 1, 2013.

113. jessica drake, interview by author, by phone, February 25, 2014.

114. Gall, *Agency of Their Own*, 28.

115. Steele interview.

116. Lee interview.

117. drake interview.

118. Lee interview.

119. Maxine Holloway, interview by author, San Francisco, March 19, 2014.

120. Jiz Lee, "Tricks of the Trade: Porn's 'Best Practices' for Content Trades and Shares," *XBIZ Magazine*, September 2014.

121. "Porn 101," APAC, accessed November 12, 2014, 101, http://apac-usa.com /education.

122. drake interview.

123. Chanel Preston, interview by author, Los Angeles, November 13, 2013.

124. Anonymous performer, interview by author, Los Angeles, May 7, 2014.

125. Anonymous performer, interview by author, Los Angeles, November 1, 2013.

126. Duke interview.

127. The BIPOC Adult Industry Collective, accessed June 15, 2020, https://www.bipoc-collective.org.

128. "BIPOC Adult Industry Collective Announces Objectives in Ending Systemic Racism," *Free Speech Coalition*, accessed June 29, 2020, https://www.freespeechcoalition.com/blog/2020/06/29/bipoc-adult-industry-collective-announces-objectives-in-ending-systemic-racism-xbiz.

129. And also ones from pro-worker academics—at the time of this writing I sit on the board that governs PASS, the FSC's testing system.

130. Stoya interview.

131. Anonymous performer interview, May 7, 2014.

132. Aimée Lutkin, "Adult Entertainer Nikki Benz Is Being Sued By the Men She Accused of Assaulting Her on Set," *Jezebel*, January 13, 2017, https://jezebel.com/adult-entertainer-nikki-benz-is-being-sued-by-the-men-s-1791166147.

133. Lorey, *State of Insecurity*, 9.

134. Lorey, 9.

135. Daniels interview.

136. Danny Wylde, interview by author, Los Angeles, November 4, 2013.

137. Mitchell coined this term in feedback on this writing.

138. On the discourse of "public good," see Zatz and Boris, "Seeing Work, Envisioning Citizenship," 105. On arguments against it, see Heather Berg, "An Honest Day's Wage for a Dishonest Day's Work: (Re)Productivism and Refusal," *Women's Studies Quarterly* 42, no. 1/2 (2014): 161–77.

139. Kathi Weeks, *The Problem with Work: Feminism, Marxism, Antiwork Politics, and Postwork Imaginaries* (Durham, N.C.: Duke University Press, 2011), 13.

140. See *Dynamex* 4 Cal. 5th at 903.

141. Anonymous performer-director, interview by author, Reseda, Calif., January 31, 2014. Interviewees did not report having benefited significantly from the Affordable Care Act (2010).

142. Tara Holiday, interview by author, by phone, February 22, 2014.

143. Cristina Morini and Andrea Fumagalli, "Life Put to Work: Towards a Life Theory of Value," *Ephemera: Theory & Politics in Organization* 10, no. 3 (2010).

144. Paolo Virno, *Grammar of the Multitude: For an Analysis of Contemporary Forms of Life* (Los Angeles: Semiotext(e), 2004), 40.

145. Holiday interview.

EPILOGUE

1. Conner Habib, interview by author, Los Angeles, February 27, 2014.

2. Kathi Weeks, *The Problem with Work: Feminism, Marxism, Antiwork Politics, and Postwork Imaginaries* (Durham, N.C.: Duke University Press, 2011); Kathi Weeks, "Life within and against Work: Affective Labor, Feminist Critique, and Post-Fordist Politics," *Ephemera* 7, no. 1 (2007): 233–49.

3. See Melinda Chateauvert, *Sex Workers Unite: A History of the Movement from Stonewall to Slutwalk* (Boston: Beacon, 2014). Juno Mac and Molly Smith, *Revolting Prostitutes: The Fight for Sex Workers' Rights* (London: Verso, 2018).

4. Dominic Ace, interview by author, Reseda, Calif., November 8, 2013.

5. Habib interview.

1. James D. Griffith, Lea T. Adams, Christian L. Hart, Sharon Mitchell, Alex Kruger, Bekah Phares, Rand Forbes, and Ashley Finkenbinder, "Pornography Actors: A Qualitative Analysis of Motivations and Dislikes," *North American Journal of Psychology* 14, no. 2 (2012): 245.

2. Juba Kalamka, interview by author, Las Vegas, Nev., July 17, 2013.

3. jessica drake, interview by author, by phone, February 25, 2014.

4. Yasmin Nair, "Scabs: Academic and Others Who Write for Free," *Yasmin Nair* (blog), March 11, 2014, http://yasminnair.net/content /scabs-academics-and-others-who-write-free.

5. Kalamka interview.

6. Stoya, interview by author, Woodland Hills, Calif., May 7, 2014.

7. Conner Habib, interview by author, Los Angeles, February 27, 2014.

8. Feona Attwood, *Porn.Com: Making Sense of Online Pornography*, Digital Formations (New York: Peter Lang, 2010), 91.

9. Being heard in this way is particularly important for subjects who are elsewhere presented in one-dimensional ways. Verta Taylor and Leila Rupp describe drag queens' investments in participating in research they hope will "tell the truth about us." Verta Taylor and Leila J. Rupp, "When the Girls Are Men: Negotiating Gender and Sexual Dynamics in a Study of Drag Queens," *Signs* 30, no. 4 (2005): 2120.

10. Zak Smith, *We Did Porn: Memoir and Drawings* (Portland, Ore.: Tin House Books, 2009), 12.

Index

Gorfinkel, Elena, 202n94

Grace, Samantha, 8, 101

Grant, Melissa Gira, 19, 22, 66–67

Great Britain, 89

Habib, Conner, 2–3, 29–30, 56–57, 81, 120, 145, 169, 171, 183–85, 191, 194

Hacking//Hustling, 8, 149

hair and makeup, 15, 39, 76, 141, 208n3. *See also* beauty work

Hall, Stuart, 24

Hardt, Michael, 8, 93

Hardy, Kate, 23

Ha®tley, Nina, 19, 27, 29, 37, 40, 73, 154, 177

health, of performers, 2, 28, 33–34, 144–48, 151, 154, 158–61, 167, 169, 177; burnout, 4, 86, 96, 145; occupational health regulations, 25, 33, 167–74, 178, 180–81; resting, 28, 127, 132–33, 144–48, 152; yeast infections, 145, 167. *See also* condom use; sexually transmitted infections; yeast infections

Hemmings, Clare, 23

Hennessy, Rosemary, 53

hepatitis C, 51, 208n33

herpes, 51

Hester, Helen, 20, 66

HIV/AIDS, 13, 39, 51, 98, 167, 169, 171, 173–74, 208nn33–34

Hochschild, Arlie, 81, 214n83, 215n104

Holdren, Nate, 156

Holiday, Tara, 1, 26, 85, 87–88, 104, 128, 181

Holloway, John, 7, 198n11

Holloway, Maxine, 59–61, 78, 80, 87, 110–11, 176

Hollywood, 12, 97

Homegrown Video, 72

homophobia, 169, 171, 175; and biphobia, 171

Horowitz, Sara, 96, 116

Houston, Shine Louise, 68

Hudson, Wolf, 33

human papilloma virus (HPV), 51

Hunter, Nan, 19

hustle. *See* gig economy

infrapolitics, 6–7

Instagram, 124, 135, 150

internet: censorship on, 4, 18, 123–24, 149–50; distribution of products/ services on, 108–10; and porn, 4, 11, 14, 16–17, 123; and satellite work, 95, 109–10, 122. *See also* social media; webcam work

interracial scenes, 32–33, 54–55, 57–58, 117, 136. *See also* Black performers

intimate labor, 16, 44, 46, 166

James, Kendra, 124

Jay, Sara, 87, 95, 104, 108

Jeffreys, Sheila, 224n78

Jensen, Robert, 201n77

Jones, Angela, 73, 105

Kalamka, Juba, 159, 164, 169, 193–94

Katsulis, Yasmina, 164

Kelley, Robin, 97

kink. *See* BDSM porn

Kink.com, 54, 66, 105, 130, 162, 207n25, 223n6

Kipnis, Laura, 19–20

Klein, Kimora, 142, 160

Knight, Tyler, 130

Raven, Leigh, 38
Ray, Audacia, 23–24
Raylene, 26, 32, 44, 47, 73, 99–100, 164–65
Red, Devlyn, 29, 39, 49–50, 141
reification, 18–20
representation (visual), 17–18, 20, 26, 33, 195, 197n5, 202n88; and class, 112; and race, 85, 111, 114, 117. *See also* reification
reproductive labor, 93–94, 133–34, 142, 146, 148, 150, 152–53, 166
resistance. *See* class: struggle
respectability, 8–9, 12, 20, 26, 46, 70, 102–3, 107, 164, 184
Resnick, David, 120
resting, 28, 127, 132–33, 144–48, 152. *See also* burnout
Ridout, Nicholas, 65, 131
Rio, Vanessa del, 91
Robinson, Cedric, 54
Rodgers, Jon, 155–56
Rodríguez, Juana María, 91
Roux, Liara, 150
Rubin, Gayle, 19, 22, 148
Rupp, Leila J., 232n9
Russo, Julie Levin, 69
Ryan, Dylan, 68

Safer Sex in the Adult Film Industry Act, 161
Sanders, Teela, 89
San Fernando Valley, 18, 29, 39, 136, 164, 192
San Francisco, 38, 89, 132, 174
satellite industries. *See* erotic dancing; escorting; webcam work
Savage, Herschel, 1, 10, 35, 89–93, 118, 169, 173–74

scene work: and consent, 34–39; and genre, 30–34; and gig economy, 96, 102, 121; as marketing tool, 15, 27, 95, 97, 99, 100–101, 106, 121, 123, 138–39; preparation for, 39–41, 143–44; on set, 41–51; and wages, 15, 52–60, 96–97, 111, 116; and worker safety, 106, 147
Schechter, Mark, 107, 171–72
Schieber, David, 100
Schneider, Rebecca, 65, 131
Scott, James, 6, 198n22
Screen Actors Guild, 175
self-care. *See* burnout; resting
self-employment. *See* gig economy; self-production
self-marketing. *See* marketing
self-presentation. *See* beauty work
self-production, 5, 13, 15, 17, 30, 32–33, 99, 109–12, 116–22, 136, 139–41, 149, 155. *See also* producers
sex: anal, 36–37, 55, 59–60, 63, 87, 109, 143, 168; oral, 37, 108, 168; and performance, 69, 79, 81–82; positions, 26, 42, 48–49, 61, 79, 83; rough, 37–38, 61; vaginal, 36, 59, 87, 168
sex positivity, 23–24, 73, 171
sex toys, 54, 76, 100, 126
sexuality studies, 18, 26–27
sexually transmitted infections (STIs): chlamydia, 51, 136, 147, 208n33; gonorrhea, 51, 208n33; hepatitis C, 51, 208n33; herpes, 51; HIV/AIDS, 13, 39, 51, 98, 167, 169, 171, 173–74, 208nn33–34; human papilloma virus (HPV), 51; risk of exposure to, 49–51, 55, 98, 107, 136, 144–45, 148, 167–71; syphilis, 51, 208n33; testing, mandatory, 39, 160, 162,

.

www.ingramcontent.com/pod-product-compliance
Lightning Source LLC
Chambersburg PA
CBHW020853270326
41928CB00006B/688